Fred Murray is a descendant of pioneer stock. His great-grandfather Murray, along with his two good wives and 17 children, were among a group of pioneers that Brigham Young sent to settle Northeastern Utah. His mother's family were among the first settlers in Northwest Colorado when the government opened the area to homesteading. His grandfather was a deputy sheriff at Vernal, Utah while the likes of Butch Cassidy roamed the country. His father ran away from home at the age of 12 and ran wild horses in the area that is now Dinosaur National Monument. Fred grew up working on ranches and listening to stories of his family and other old-time cowboys and pioneers. He came to Nebraska to go to college, fell in love, got married and never left. Over the years, Fred has entertained thousands of children and adults with his frontier stories at church, school and civic functions. Fred is a businessman who operates a construction company. Fred continues his love for horses by blacksmithing and taking trail rides. Occasionally he still helps his son start a colt.

Joe Murray followed his frontier heritage by starting a horse training business when he was 14, with the guidance and knowledge of his father. Over the last 15 years, he has trained hundreds of horses while finding time to become a historian, teacher and graduate of the University of Nebraska College of Law. He is married and has 3-year-old twin boys. He currently writes a weekly column and is the political correspondent for Sodbuster Online and editor of Murray Publishing. You may read his work at http://www.sodbuster.com/

Also by the Authors:

God Loves Even Cowboys

Author: D. Fred Murray
With: Jody L. Murray

CAUGHT IN A BLIZZARD
Grandmother and I

Library of Congress Cataloging-in-publication Number

ISBN: 0-9642685-5-8

CAUGHT IN A BLIZZARD
Grandmother and I

Table of Contents

This book is dedicated to the memory of my father.

NELSON IVAN MURRAY

Introduction

Most everyone who has ever spent many winters on the great plains or in the Rocky Mountains has their own story to tell about some great blizzard that came sweeping out of the northwest. It entangles you in a roaring, blinding mess of ice and snow with a wind chill of more than 50 below zero. The bitter cold can kill man or beast in a manner of minutes. Two such storms stick out in my mind.

It was early in January of 1975 and my father was gone when the storm hit. He had taken a trip to Denver to visit with family members and watch my cousins perform at the National Western Stock Show. The entire storm lasted about two days, but the main brunt of the storm hit us from about the middle of a Friday afternoon until just before daylight the next morning.

During the storm, you could only see a few feet in front of your face. Our electricity went out, so the fan on our furnace didn't work. However, we were able to keep nice and warm from the propane heat of our cook stove, which didn't need electricity to operate. Also, my mother pulled out some extra blankets to keep my brother and I warm in our bed that night.

At daylight Saturday morning, everything became still. It was clear as a bell and the sun shown brightly. However, it was extremely cold. It was well below zero and we had received well over a foot of snow.

When my brother went to feed and water our cows, he discovered that the snow had drifted to the top of the corrals and the cows were trapped in a shed with no food or water. It took my brother, my mother and me all day to dig through the huge drift so that we could get the door of the barn open.

Also, we had to shovel a path to the stock tank and dig it out so we could get to the water. By that time, the electric company had got the electricity working. The electric heater in the tank thawed the ice and the cows could drink.

The other blizzard that is etched in my memory happened in December of 1983 when I was a freshman in college. My father had just had heart surgery, so I had to do all the chores. A quarter of a mile from my parents home is a big old barn where I kept the horses I trained and where we stored our hay.

Before the storm finished, I had to go take care of the horses in the old barn. I bundled up, went outside and started our four wheel drive truck to let it warm up. Then, I started down our rock road, plowing through one big drift after the other. With one more giant drift to get through, I stepped on the gas and started through, but the drift was to big even for the four wheel drive truck. I was stuck with a forty mile per hour wind blowing with a wind chill of at least 50 below.

Nothing I tried would get the truck out, so I walked on to my destination which was just a few hundred yards from the truck. I took care of the colts inside. The barn was warm inside, but I had to get back home to take care of the animals at the home place.

I thought of saddling one of the colts, but we had also had an ice storm before the blizzard, so it was difficult for anyone or anything to walk. Because of the ice, I decided it wouldn't be safe to ride a gentle horse, let a lone a bronc who might not take kindly to leaving the warm barn with me on his back.

I waited a while until the storm let up enough to sort of see where I was going and started for home on foot. It only took about 20 minutes even with the ice, snow and wind to make it home to a warm house. However, in that short time I had frost bite on my face, despite having a warm scarf wrapped over my face.

Fortunately, a few days before, my father and I had saw a program on television that explained what to do for frost bite. We took a cool cloth and applied it my face. In a shot time I was thawed out without any damage being done.

These two stories are etched in my memory, but they pale in comparison to my great-great grandmother Mary and my grandfather Ivan's stories of getting caught in a blizzard. This book tells their story along with the experiences of great-grandfather Hatch as a sheriff in the days of Butch Cassidy and the wild bunch.

I have had a great honor to have parents, grandparents and other relatives who practiced the dying art of story telling. They have passed their life experiences from their ancestors and themselves down to my generation and I am already passing them on to the next generation, my three-year-old twin sons, Ryan and Joseph.

This story transcends our family and offers a reflection on what the people of America were like during this 70 year period that started with handcarts and ends with trucks and airplanes. This is not a history book per se because we haven't went around checking to make sure that every story told us can be documented. If you will read the history books, you will find that the stories in the book are either consistent with the scholars account or have not been proved as false. Many of the stories can't be documented anywhere else because the events took place in the middle of nowhere and the only account is that of the participant as told to their family. If you want a historians account of the handcart pioneer's and Mormon migration, I would recommend the work of Wallace Stegner or the Hafen's. If you want to know more about the history of Northwestern Colorado in the outlaw and ranching era, John Burroughs, **Were the Old West Stayed Young** is the best and most comprehensive that I have read.

While not having the family connection that I have to the stories in this book, I think you will enjoy this story as much as I have all my life. It is the story of normal people overcoming great adversity with their faith in God, loyalty to family as well as an abundance of internal fortitude and ingenuity. Mix in some rough riding, gun play and neck tie justice and there is plenty of action to go around. Snuggle down in a comfortable chair, by a warm fire and come get caught in a blizzard.

Joe Murray

Preface

IVAN

My hope is that you the reader will be patient and bear with me as you read the first few chapters of this book. You see there are three separate stories, and one cannot be told without the others. The first one sets the background for the other two which takes one through the time of the west that is thought to be filled with excitment and romance. In the first part I felt it nessesary to include names so you could see who many of the great men of the church were in my family back ground, These early leaders and pioneers moved from place to place such as Kirkland Ohio, Jackson County Missiouri, Navauo Illinios, Kanesville Iowa, and Florence Nebraska and then to the Salt Lake Valley and the Great Basin. They only wanted a place to call home where they could live in peace. Upon reaching the west they turned a desert that was uninhabitable into a productive land where they built cities with a cultural decorum that would make many cities of Europe envious. They built a strong political nation of their own centered around the church and it's teachings. It has lasted for over a century and a half, ever increasing in wealth and strength. The dates are included so you can see when the events took place that these people sang, danced, suffered, died, traveled, worshiped and became martyrs. As you read, bear in mind this was a nation on the move with their old, sick, new born, weak and strong. After my great Grandmother, who was only a child traveling by handcart, reached the valley and was married into a polygamous family, I felt it no longer necessary to burden you with the calender . I found in my years of research that the stories told to me as a child fit very closely to what diaries and historians also portray.

In my research of the places in this book I felt it necessary to trace the Mormon Trail. starting in the state of Missiouri, Illinois, Iowa , Nebraska and across Wyoming. I visited places where people fleeing religious persecution were forced to leave their fine modern homes, prosperous economy to be destitute homeless wayfaring wanderers in search of a home land. After time and much suffering the Saints moved to the valley in the mountains which at the time was in Mexico. From eastern America and Europe the Saints came by the thousands to build an empire. After living in peace for ten years they were once more living in territory taken from Mexico, and now owned by the United States. Zion was a thousand miles from any other civilization, but this did not stop the Federal Government from sending an army to "CONQUER and ANNIHILATE THE HATED SECT". I descended from those great pioneers that were leaders in the church and were so greatly hated. My great great grandfather Merkley was one of the men that burned Fort Bridger in view of Col. Johnston and his army, which led to he and his mens utter and disgracful defeat.

The stories in this book are stories I heard as a child and which have always fascinated me. The tellers of these stories were men and women of my grandfathers and fathers generation. Their parents and grandparents knew those that lived them or experienced them. They knew too many intimate details to have not been part of that time in western history. I would never be so arrogant as to think I could write a historical account of the times and events that are covered in this book. That I will leave to the great historians like DeVoto and Stegner who lived in the time when there were those pioneers still alive that had lived the time when the gathering of Zion took place. Also to men like Roy Hafen a son of of Mary Ann Stucki Hafen who as a six year old child walked with the last hand carts from Omaha to Salt Lake City. And when grown married a man who had three other wives.

As a child I knew families of polygamy and their troubles to maintain the cohesion as a unit. One family of nine wives that was distant relation was scattered over five states to avoid the man's arrest. He was a Medical Doctor but for many years traveled to see his families supporting them and himself as a common salesman. The fact my father was a Jack Mormon let me see the workings and happening within the Mormon community. My mother being a Gentile or non-Mormon, I was permitted to know the going's on in her community. This gave me the privilege to know what went on in each community. My father was accepted in both communities, but mother felt the prejudice that most all the Gentiles felt. These prejudices only whetted my appetite for knowledge about the Mormon ancestor.

I am thankful for those who can write the history of my ancestors. This book contains the true stories that were handed down to me in folk style story telling. Coming from a pioneer back ground of such rich heritage I felt it a responsibility to tell the story of three generations that made and changed the west. From the early pioneers in my family came generations of civic minded people. There have been and are great leaders within the church and those that are now serving their nation in the halls of Congress. As I watched on television congressional hearings and saw the chairman of the commitee working out justice I was proud to have descended from the same family of pioneers he had. This book takes you from England to the great basin of the west, from pioneer times through the Butch Cassidy era, and into the modern development times after world war one. The leading characters in the stories are my great grandmother, her son and grandson.

Following the trail as near as the modern highways would allow I sped along the great Interstate 80 highway across Iowa in my airconditioned automobile, I was enthralled with the sight that met my eyes. Mile after mile rolled by and I could not help but wonder what this would have looked like one hundred and fifty years ago. The middle of July the corn was in it's silk and the combines were harvesting the golden wheat. I began to think as I traced the Mormon Road from Iowa City west toward Utah how different these great plains looked to young Mary Ashby and her family as they pushed and pulled their two wheel hand cart on their way to Zion. Diaries and historians tell of the miles of endless space filled with heat and dryness. I crossed the Iowa, Missouri and the Elkhorn rivers at such a high rate of speed that if I had not been looking for them I would have missed them. Thirteen year old Mary Ashby knew without a doubt when she faced the terrible dangerous crossings of these blockades that lay in her path.

I crossed the Missouri river on the Mormon bridge at the very site my great great grandfather Merkley built and ran the first ferry between Kanesville and Florence a century and a half before. Turning on the first interchange at the west end of the bridge I was looking at the old flour mill that was used in the time of the gathering to Zion. Aside from that there is nothing to remind us of the settlement of Florence with it's log and sod houses or the thousands of pioneers that outfitted for their trip across the plains and mountains. A few blocks south of the interstate there is a small sign pointing up the hill to the west telling of the Mormon Cemetery. The Mormon Church has a fine visitor center across the road from the peaceful cemetery which is bordered on the west by a convent. As I stood on this peaceful hill looking at the large bronze statue of a pioneer and his wife with a small child laid in an open grave, I noticed cast in the base many family names that were familar to me.

As I drove west on highway 31 I topped a bluff and at the bottom was the Elkhorn river, a dirty narrow stream. If I had not been looking for it I would have sped down the hill and across the fertile valley toward Fremont. The first road leading south after crossing the Elkhorn River I turned onto and traveled for a mile, ahead I could see the place where the Mormons had operated their ferry. I stood looking at the now putrid stream filled with trash and agricultural chemicals and wondered if man has really improved this world in the last century. It is now in the condition as I see it because of mans use and abuse. When the pioneers crossed it was a wide, wild, swift and deep stream where many lives were lost in attemping it's crossing. When I reached the Platte River it was a shallow stream with airboats speeding on its surface. I wished I could have seen it when Mary Ashby camped on its banks.

Following the Trail I drove in comfort as I went through modern towns with their great grain elevators and country sides filled with farms and their graineries bursting at the seams with abundant harvest, it was hard to invision people starving in this fertile valley. When reaching Genoa I looked for the place where the Trail crossed the Loup River. After a few minutes driving south across the divide I was back on highway 30 traveling west toward my next stop which was at a marker in the middle of a private school campus. Standing beside this Trail marker it was hard to imagine the lonely desolate country filled with buffalo and travelers suffering hunger, death and privation one hundred and fifty years earlier. The small marker was almost lost in the fine place with its garden like campus filled with Brick buildings built on each side and in the middle of the trail.

It was hard to imagine that two companies numbering over one thousand Souls traveled this way in their desperate search for religious freedom. It was near here the buffalo stampeded over the travelers reeking havoc and sweeping away the teams that were used to pull their supply wagon. Without the teams the wagon's burdens were placed on the Saints flimsy hand carts adding extra burden and hardship which slowed them to a snails pace. This incident was one of the major contributors to the disaster, which led to the greatest effort man had ever undertaken to save it's fellow man.

Staying in a modern motel in North Platte I was thankful for the comfort in which I had traveled six hundred miles that day. I sat wondering about those Handcart Pioneers traveling the long distants of sixteen miles in one day if there were no obstacles to impede their progress. The next morning found me rolling west toward Scotts Bluff . By the middle of the morning I could see Chimney Rock and was soon passed it with Scotts Bluff in view. Crossing to the south side of the river I stopped and visited awhile at the monuments visitor center where there was a Mormon Handcart and a replica of the roademeter that was made and placed into use with the first pioneers going to the valley. The man that whittled and installed the device on a wagon was a distant relative. Before leaving I drove to the top of the bluff to view the valley. From the top of the bluff the river valley seemed like an unending green and golden field. As I looked west the dark form of Laramie Peak was lifted above the surrounding country in the most magnificent manner.

Part of the day was spent at Fort Laramie Park. It is a fine well kept place reminding us of the struggle that made America the great nation it is. Making a stop at Registery Cliff, I walked a short distant where after these many years one can still see the ruts made in the sand stone by the many who traveled that way. While visiting this place I often wondered how the stones in the trail must have hurt the bare feet of thirteen year old Mary Ashby and the many others like her that were passing along. Driving west following the trail, the Medicine Bow mountains were in sight for many miles.In the pioneer's day they were called the black hills. Reaching Casper Wyoming, by nightfall I ate supper in a fine restaurant after which I slept in a modern motel. My great grandmother and her family were not as fortunate when they camped in this vicinity, they were cold, starving and dying. It was here that nature turned it's furious wrath upon those traveling Saints. As you will read of the tragic Platte River crossing.

The next morning after traveling a few miles west I left the paved highway and traveled for thirty odd mile across the prairie where fine Hereford cattle grazed contentedly on rich grass. Diaries tell of this strip of the trail lacking grass and safe water for their weary starving teams. The dead animals with their unbearable stench lined the road because the beast in their driven thirst could not be held from drinking the alkali and poison water. Of faithful fathers, mothers and even children dragging their handcarts along in the mud and snow with other family members who were dying or dead. I saw rifle pits and wagon ruts which made me appreciate the sacrifice those who traveled before me made. Visiting Martins Cove I realized the great sacrifice that has been paid for the freedom to worship as the conscience dictates, because here my great great grandfather and his two sons were buried. They being some of the unrecorded ones of the fifth handcart company, we only know of their death through the story told by those that suffered with them.

As I stood there trying to imagine the horrible suffering, my mind moved on with the rescue of the fourth and fifth handcart companies, and to the marriage of thirteen year old Mary to a man that was as old as her mother. He already had a wife who was sick, and it became Mary's job to nurse her to health. Most families of polygamy the women resented the other wives, but from all family stories of my great grandfathers wives they lived in acceptable harmony. With their children it was another story, they felt it was the only sin the church committed. The practice of polygamy was brought in so there would be more mortal bodies for the spirit children, and to increase the numbers within the church. Most men entered those unions only because it was urged on them by the church officials. There are records of men telling of the heartaches and tears they shed because of the problems that it created. With from two to a dozen wives these men could not support their families and that became the responsibilty of the women to care for their ever increasing broods. When the U. S. Marshals came to enforce the Edmond Tucker Act, instead of helping it created severe problems and divided families for ever. This being caused by the men's imprisonment, after which they were not allowed to even contact their wives openly, the Government gave them the liberty of only one wife.

Leaving Independence Rock I saw a small herd of horses at a distant. That made me stop and think about my father who captured wild horses in this area as well as drove some of the first motor trucks Texaco Oil Company used in the west. This thought distracted me from the search of the overland trail, but the trails I now followed were much more personal. Many miles to the south was Craig, Colorado where I was born and the hub of my fathers activities. This city had changed from a sleepy little western cowtown to a busy city filled with business and commerce since my last visit. An oil refinery was casting its smoke and smell out for all to breathe, and on the mountain side south of town could be seen gigantic machines stripping the mountain so the large deposit of low sulphfur coal could be mined. I was told that at least two dozen unit trains a day left Craig loaded with coal. David Moffats dreams were finaly fulfilled when a railroad was run west to make connection with Salt Lake City. There were train tracks running southwest into Tom Isles' Axial Basin to large pit mines where one hundred tons of coal was placed on each train car. The top of Mt. Streeter no longer was there, but I could see the booms of large machines moving back and forth. I was told the mountain was one huge crater now with a railroad running into it. As I watched those large machines rip and tear away the earth as a wild starving beast eats it's fresh kill, I tried to imagine what the old time cowboy's reaction would be if it were possible for them to view what I was seeing. Oil and natural gas fields are as much part of the landscape as the mountains and deserts.

You see the true working old time cowboy knew and understood the practices of good conservation and the balances in nature. The depredation of the range by over stocking and the annihilation of the predatory species by homesteaders and the large cattle companies caused my father and many other westerners much alarm. The boom of the 1920s brought disaster to western America, and the drought and depression of the 1930s brought almost total ruin to the western rangeland. With grass in short supply and the predatators removed, the wild horses and mule deer increased at an alarming rate adding to the now threatening problem of depleted range grass. By 1950 the west was finally awakened to the fact something had to be done. The Governments answer as always was the horses must go. They would pay five dollars for every pair of horse ears that were turned in at Goverment offices in the west, so the horses were killed. One Sunday saw "sportsmen" kill over twenty five thousand horses wild or otherwise. There are lawsuits still in courts over the ownership of a good number of those ole ponies killed that black day. By the 1970s Environmental and Conservation groups working with the Ranchers and Government began to reclaim the destroyed west. Grazing and seeding programs were enforced under the watchful eye of the Conservations and Environmentalist so by the mid 1990s the range looks as pictures showed it before the turn of the century, as well as the way old timers talked about it.

I spent some time visiting some of the camp sites that my father used when running wild horses. I was impressed how different the landscape looked than it did forty years ago when I last visited. If one was camping there today with a horse, the beast could find all the feed it needed on a picket rope the same as eighty years ago. Visiting one cave that he and his friends used, I was shocked at the destruction that had taken place in the last forty three years since I had last been there. Because of a new highway being cut right through the ridge a few hundred feet away, water had cut a deep ravine in front and also in part of the cave it's self. The most disturbing thing was the amount of garbage such as bed springs and beer cans and bottles along with human filth. As I stood looking at the trash I felt as if I and the cave were violated. Standing in the cave I tried to imagine what it was like eighty years ago to a young man returning to camp to be greeted by an old black horse with neither ears nor tail. You see that ole pony lost them saving the mustangers life.

As I traveled northwest I passed the K ranch where ole Doc Kiaser pulled his joke on Grand Dad, and his deputies as well as Butch Cassidy and his friends. Doc invited them all to the ranch not letting the others know who was to be a guest also. From a distance I could see the mountain where Butch Cassidy stole Grand Dads and the other deputies horses, saddles and boots while they slept. Grand Dad used to talk about the days before the country was civilized and many of his stories are told in this narrative.

Through this country I traveled on to the Uintah Mountains, where my father herded sheep and hunted bighorn sheep, elk and moose. Then on down the mountain to Flaming Gorge and Fort Bridger. There I stood in this fine park in all it's tranquility trying to imagine what it was like on that cold November day when great great Grandfather Merkely set the place on fire so the U. S. Army could not occupy it. Few of the Mormon buildings remain so one couldnot see what the fort looked like in it's prime.

As I passed through the modern towns of Green River and Rock Springs Wyoming, it was hard to see anything that looked like the frontier towns the old time cowboys spoke so affectionately about. Crossing the desert south towards Browns Hole I drove on a fine paved highway that covered the wagon trail of sixty years ago. When I entered Browns Hole {or Park} we drove down a 17 precent grade and at the bottom we visited John Jarvie Historical site where the beginning of the Willie Strang story started. My wife and I toured the full length of the hole from Jarvie to the Gates of Ladore,and on to Douglas Mountain to see the coke ovens. Stopping at the Browns Park store, Fred Blevins kindly let us go to the old Basset ranch where none of the buildings remain. From there it was 70 miles back to Maybell, Colorado and modern U.S.A.

I toured the country that this book is about, from the modern cities of Colorado and Utah as well as off beaten paths, the land of the Mormons, Butch Cassidy country and the land of my heritage I share with you the reader. My wife and I stood on a mountain top where one can see snow covered peaks one hundred and fifty miles away, and by turning around peaks with their snowy mantle can be seen the same distant the other way. From this high point we could view the Bookcliffs which is now a wild horse refuge. The remnant of wild horses left, are placed on this refuge and others throughout the west. They are owned and managed by the Government in a responsible manner.

There are still ranches with sheep, but the big flocks no longer exist because of the modern synthetic cloth which has replaced wool. The generation that lived during the Colorado-Utah sheep war are only a memory. The ranchers today live and work together as friends and neighbors. The old bitterness and hatred that separated even families over sheep and cattle no longer exist. The Raftopoulos run a large cow operation and 12,000 sheep as one ranch unit. [hard to imagine !] As you will see in this book my father was a man that had no problem working with horses, cattle and sheep.

He lived and worked on both sides of this bloody war standing for what he thought was right, but never shedding another man's blood over the issue.

The livestock raised in the area are cattle which are a different type and managed in a manner that would shock the old time cowboy. As I stood in the Spring Creek Cow camp thoughts flooded my memory of the first time I was there 50 plus years before. At the pasture gate we were met by 7 fine Quarter horses that had to be pushed out of the way to get to the cabin. [The old range horse had to be roped and tied just to be saddled.] Under the roof over hang was an ATV with a two-way radio and a cell phone. There was an electrical generator for modern lights. [oh my what next indoor plumbing?] The modern cowman manages and operates his ranch using modern scientific technology and machinery, such as computers, genetics, insemination and ATV. Four-wheel drive trucks pull large trailers in which to transport cattle. With modern machines one man can handle more hay than thirty men did in just a fraction of the time. Fences line the highways and gates with padlocks stop a visitor where the old trails once took you into the back country. These trails are now roads maintained by the ranchers with their large bulldozers and motor graders. Because the cattle are no longer driven in herds for long distances the horse is no longer the number one tool used by the rancher. The modern cowboy goes to the rodeo where he shows and uses his skill on a horse trained just for this purpose. That is where a "remnant" of the old trade stays alive.

The third part of this book tells of Mary Asby's grandson Ivan who left home at twelve years old and learned the trade of capturing and breaking wild horses by himself. You will see that the old time cowboy was not as the media portrays them. We travel in our story on a trip that would take him to eastern Montana, then back to his beloved Blue Mountain. We will travel throughout the west with him while he works as a cowboy and horse breaker for the mighty Two Bars Cattle Company with their one hundred and fifty thousand head of cattle on the western slope. We will ride the Uinath Railroad, the Galloping Goose, and ride with him over Rollins Pass on the Moffat Railroad before the tunnel was dug through the Continental Divide. He will take us through six states working as a powder monkey in mines deep in the heart of the mountains. He was a sheepbuyer and a gardener, also while capturing wild horses and cattle. He will introduce us to men both good and bad. Men like Bill Patton, Guy McNurlen, Lute and Harry Armstrong, John Baker, Dave Knight and cowboy artist and story teller Will James along with many more who tamed and modernized the west. A change which most of the old time cowboys could not comprehend, but to young Ivan it was a grand adventure which he lived to the fullest. As a small boy he would see hangings, meet the Price-Vernal stage pulled by six horses, and live through the change of time to view on television a man walking on the moon. Ivan was not a man to live or relive the past, he would say "thats the way it was and it cannot be changed, we are living today". Over my early life time he and many of his friends along with other early pioneers would from time to time tell of an incident or about people, and when they started talking of the past I kept very quiet so they would keep talking. If my father or they were interrupted they would say " it don't matter now" and that was the end of the story.

D. Fred Murray

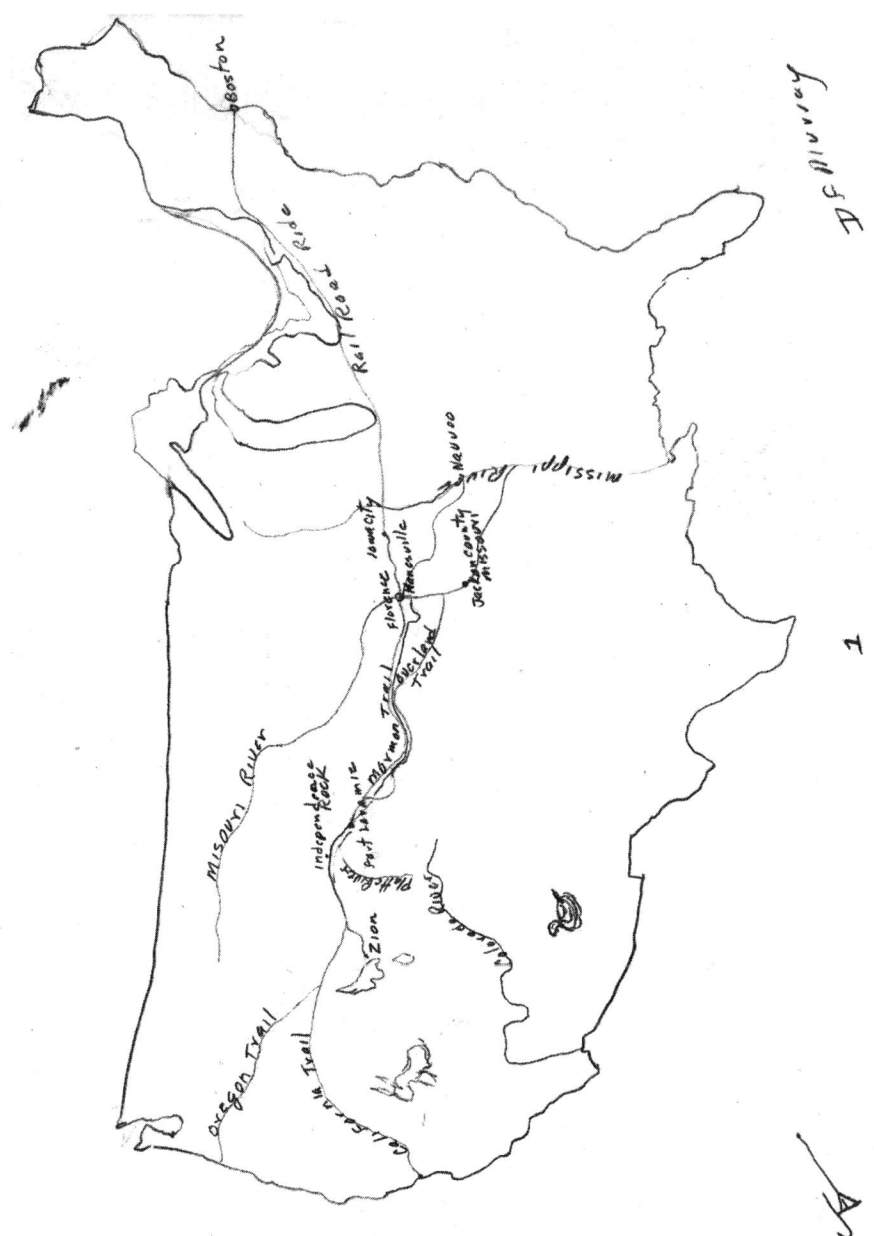

Washington

Montana

Oregon

Idaho

Wella Walla

Pendelton

Baker

Glendive

miles city

Bozeman

Sheridan

Boffelo

Wyoming

Casper

Independence Rock

Wamsutter

Winnemucca Elko

Rocksprings LaramiePlains

FlemingChrs. Baggs

Nevada

SaltLakeCity

Vernal

Craig steamboat springs

Denver

Utah

Grand Junction

Green River Aspen

Moab montrose

Colorado

Uravan

Telluride

Blanding Dolores

walsenberg

st.thomas Trinidad

st george

overton Raton Pass

Flagstaff

Taos

Arizona

New Mexico

Tucson

wildcattle

2

D F Murray

xiv

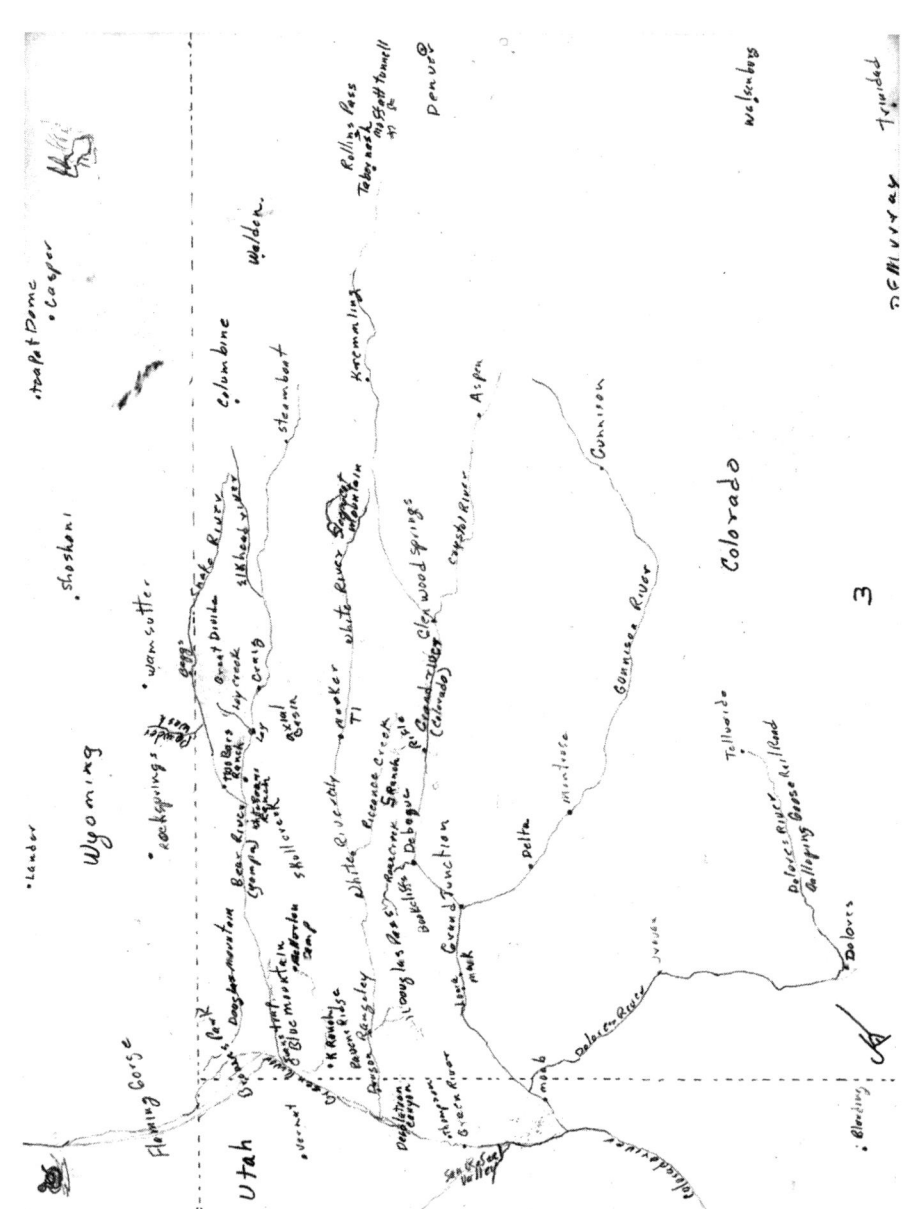

Flaming Gorge

Utah

Wyoming

Lander

Shoshoni

teapotDome

Casper

rock springs

Wamsutter

Baggs

Great Divide

Savery Creek

Cow Creek

Snake River

Elkhead valley

Steamboat

Columbine

Walden.

Colorado

Rolling Pass

Taby nesh

TabyStatt Tunnel

Denver

Walsenberg

Trinidad

DENVER

Kremmling

Yampa

White River

Meeker

Buford

Axial Basin

Bears River

Two Bars Ranch

Cross Mtn

Douglas mountain

Blue mountain

strawberry Camp

skull creek

Rangeley

Raven Ridge

K Ranch

vernal

Dragon

Bonanza

Wellington Canyon

Green River

strawberry Green River

Green Junction

Mack

Book cliffs

Debeque

Roan Creek

Plateau Creek

Presence Creek

Maverick S Ranch

White River

Grand River (Colorado)

Glenwood springs

Crystal River

Aspen

Gunnison

Gunnison River

Delta

Montrose

Telluride

Juves

Dolores River

Galloping Goose Railroad

Dolores

San Joaquin Valley

Uncompahgre

Dolores River

mack

Blanding

3

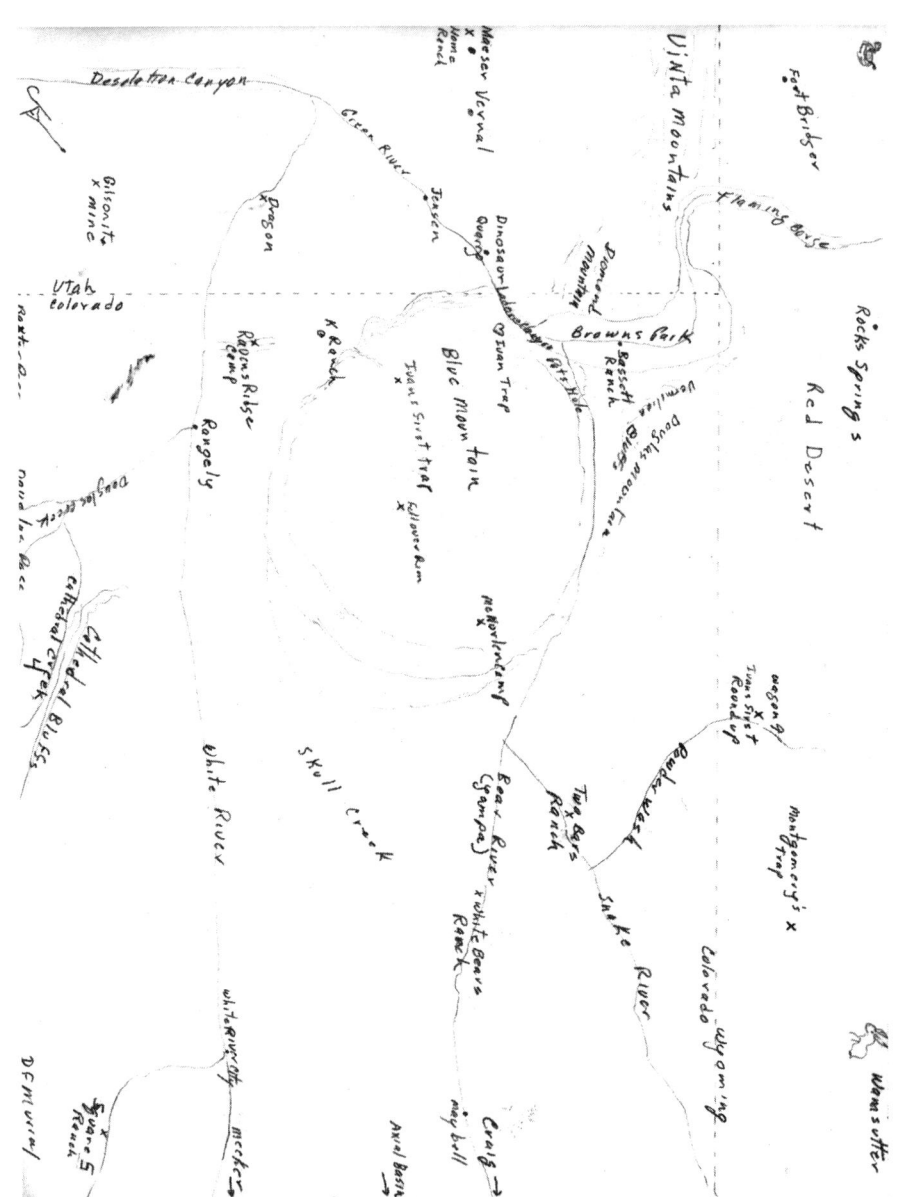

Called to Zion

Chapter 1

Little Mary Ashby trudged along the street behind her brother William. They were on their way to work at the box and glove factory. This morning did not seem different from any other. As they came to the factory entrance, an American man was asking everyone to come to a meeting in a nearby auditorium that evening. He spoke of God's plan for the human race. The man's message excited Mary, which made the morning seem as if it would never end. As William packed the gloves in boxes, Mary carried the full boxes to the storage shelves. By dinner time, she had the boxes all placed in their proper order.

William and Little Mary on their way to work

Finally, the noon whistle blew so she could hurry home to tell her mother about the American who was at the factory entrance. As mother fixed the meager meal, Mary chattered about what she heard the missionary say. That afternoon as Mary turned the fingers of the gloves inside out, she continued to talk about America and what the man had told them. Her mother sewed the gloves wrong side out to hide the stitches.

After father, Benjamin and William came home, the family talked a long while about the meeting planned for that evening. After brother Thomas came home, the family went to hear the message the missionary presented. The missionary convinced the family that it was from the Deity and invited the missionary to visit their home and tell them more.

Thomas with his Bundle of sticks

Life would go on the same, father working six days a week at the woolen mill, William, Mary and mother for the glove factory. Thomas had a job in the country working for a farmer. He was a very hard and dependable worker. The farmer noticed how well he did his jobs and in return gave him a bundle of sticks or straw for a bonus each day.

Thomas always brought the bundle home so the family had fuel for the fireplace. One night, the constable came to their home and told Father that someone claimed Thomas took the wood and straw. After talking with Mr. Ashby, the constable agreed to investigate the matter. He discovered that Thomas was innocent.

Sunday, the missionary came and spent the entire day teaching the words of Joseph Smith contained in the Book of Mormon. This was all new, but they accepted it as God's true message. As time passed, they learned of the Prophet's martyrdom and the church's persecution. They learned how the saints left Nauvoo in the middle of the winter. They also learned about the long road that leads to Zion the Valley in the mountains. As they continued to listen to Missionary Franklin Richards stories of the persecution of the Saints, the entire family accepted the teachings of the church to be true. The story of the church's persecution convinced the family to join the Mormon Church.

The day of June 27, 1844, is turning point in the history of the church. For twenty-one years, Joseph Smith and his followers faced hatred and persecution. The Mormons got driven out of town after town. Nonbelievers chased them from Kirkland, Jackson County, Missouri and then Nauvoo. At Nauvoo, they murdered the prophet Joseph Smith in the Carthage Illinois jail. They learned of the great leaders that had helped raise up the church. Difficulties or persecution could not dissuade these men.

The temple was complete enough by December of 1846 that they could conduct the sacred ceremonies of the church. This caused such an excitement among the gentiles that Governor Boggs of Illinois sent three thousand militia men against the saints. They agreed that Brigham Young and his followers would leave when the grass turned green to provide feed for their teams. However, the pressure was so strong that by February the first company of pioneers crossed the Mississippi River on the ice. Many more saints followed that cold, wet, Iowa winter. When the weather, the strength of the people and the draft animals could possibly endure, the Saints planned to travel toward Council Bluffs on the Missouri river. They left behind their wealth, modern luxurious homes, orchards, fields and business's to become homeless, hungry and destitute wanderers.

The wagons sank to the axles in the mud. It took several extra teams to extricate them. The rain never stopped and those dear folks could not get dry nor warm. Babies would be born with women holding tarps over the mother and the bed of birth. They buried many mothers and their babies along the trail. They were fleeing for their lives with barely enough clothes to cover them and not nearly enough to eat or keep them warm.

Suffering on the trail of tears was beyond all human comprehension. The church started settlements along the trail for those yet to come. Death had no respect for either age, strength, or health. They buried many saints along the trail. Upon reaching Council Bluffs, they chased them to the Indian territory of Nebraska. Again the United States Government drove them out as wild beasts back across the river. Eventually, they allowed them to resettle and establish Winter Quarters in what they called MISERY BOTTOM. Many died there where they rest till the resurrection as a memorial to stand for time and eternity. This place is now the town of Florence, Nebraska.

In June of 1847, Erastus Snow and Orson Pratt became the first saints to enter the Salt Lake valley in Mexican territory. A few days later, Wilford Woodruff arrived with the very ill leader and prophet Brigham Young, establishing the city of Zion to stand "forever."

The Ashby's learned of the new towns and of all the free land that was theirs by just taking and developing it. Mary and Thomas dreamed about the beautiful farm and their new life in America. Father, Thomas and William would all have a farm of their own. Mary would get married to a strong young man that would build a fine brick home on his own land where she could raise her sons to be good men.

The more the family heard of Zion, the more their hearts yearned for the life in the mountains. As the different missionaries visited their home, they soon became friends with men like Daniel McArthur, James Willie, Edward Martin and the head of the European Mission Franklin D. Richards. These kind and good men encouraged the family in their spiritual and financial matters. The brethren saw that these poor souls were in a hopeless trap. Their hearts yearned for the land that flowed with milk and honey. With the new Perpetual Emigrant Fund that the prophet set up, even the poorest could soon travel to Zion.

The news of the Perpetual Emigrant Fund renewed hope in the saints that had no way of ever raising the money for fare. Those that would come by this way would agree to travel straight through across the plains and mountains to the valley. After they arrived, they would work on church projects for script and would pay back the cost of the trip with interest. As the new year of 1856 began, it renewed hope in the Ashby family that this would be the year they would behold the Prophet's face. With much sacrifice and frugality, they would have the fare for passage. By April, they lost all hope of raising money for passage because the winter took too much money to feed and keep the family warm. Already the sailing ship, Enoch Train, had sailed from Liverpool, carrying 534 Saints. The group left on the twenty-third of March with the Ashby's good friend Edmund Ellsworth along. They longed to be with him.

The family knew that the ship, S. Curling, was to carry only those from the country of Wales. Captain Bunker was in charge of the 707 Saints that were aboard the ship. It left England on April 19. When the third ship, the SS Thornton sailed on May 4, taking with it James Willie as captain, the Ashby's felt too desperate to hope any longer. This ship sailed from Liverpool carrying 746 saints to America.

A few days after the Thornton sailed, Elder F. D. Richards came to visit the family. He explained that another ship would soon leave for America. He told the Ashby's that they could go if they wanted to sign a contract saying that they would pay with interest the remaining fare upon reaching the Salt Lake Valley. Being the eldest son, Benjamin agreed to stay in England for another year where he could work and save for his own trip. This gave the family more money to make the down payment on the fare. With sadness, they accepted his generous offer.

Little Mary was now thirteen and big enough to sew all of her own clothes. She made warm gloves, sweaters, coats and other things she needed for the trip to Zion. In addition, her father bought her a new pair of shoes. She placed her new clothes and shoes in a box for the trip to Zion.

Elder Richards called a prayer meeting the night before they were to leave. The Ashby's went to the meeting to receive instruction and counsel about the long trip ahead. With hearts filled with love and excitement, they went home.

Upon arriving, they found that someone had broken into their home and taken Mary's box that she had left on her bed. The police found the box the next morning in a pawn shop. Unfortunately, they had no money left to redeem it. They said their good-byes to Benjamin. Benjamin and Mary promised each other to reunite in the land of Zion.

Samuel Ashby, his wife Hanna, two sons and daughter Mary went to the docks at Liverpool and boarded the ship, SS Horizon, along with 856 other saints. The church chartered these ships that sailed to America carrying the Saints. President Richards came aboard the Horizon to organize the ship. He appointed a president and two counselors. Then he divided the ship into wards with bishops to head them. The elders worked out all the details of duty and time to the quarter hour. On May 25, it set sail for New York City, United States of America.

Edward Martin who had labored in England and had converted most of these Saints was to be the president, captain, leader, and counselor all the way to the valley. He was going home to be with his family that he had not seen for the two years he had been on his mission. He was very much aware of the lateness of which they departed England, but he believed that the Almighty would hold the snows until they could reach Zion. Elder Richards would stay long enough to close the church's business for that year and take another ship. Richards would catch up with them later in the trip.

The Mormon's organized all their ships in the same way. There was a president, two counselors, wards with bishops and elders that worked out and organized detail and routine. This sequence of duties

The SS Horizon
Carried 856 Saints from Liverpool
To Boston

was as follows, rise, clean quarters, dispose of waste over the ship's side, prayer and then to breakfast. They had three quarters of an hour to prepare their food, eat and leave the galley spotlessly clean. They spent the rest of the day in meetings of instruction, prayer meetings, often a wedding, sometimes a baptism and occasionally a funeral and burial. Then another orderly assault on the galley that would leave it so clean, it looked newly polished. The women spent their time cleaning, cooking and sewing tents. These tents would be their home as they traveled the plains and mountain road to Zion.

The travelers filled the evenings with music, singing and dancing. Mary loved the music that the fiddles made. The fiddlers played waltzes, jigs and squares dances. From the youngest to the oldest, all joined in the dance. Everyone was happy to be going to the valley in the mountains. They always ended by singing this hymn.

There is a land beyond the sea
Where I should like to be,
And dearer far than all the rest,
Is that bright land to me

These large ships were a whole community of people that included new born infants to the aged. The saints did not exclude anyone. They cared for the blind, crippled and the sick as they did the infants. The Saints by their deportment impressed the ship's crew and Captains. Upon reaching America, the whole crew would convert to the

6

church and its teaching. Passengers on the Horizon were no exception to the rule. Their deportment was very much in keeping with the principles kept by the church.

As the Horizon sailed on the high sea, the passengers soon adjusted to the routine of daily life. To the youth of the ship, it was a grand adventure. They made many new friends. Mary Ashby enjoyed each day to its fullness. She did her duties in the same manner as the grownups. Sometimes she felt that all people did was make a mess so someone else would have cleaning to do. However, Mary and her friends had a real holiday most of the time.

On days when the weather was warm and sunny, they got to stand at the rail and watch the ocean and the exciting creatures that were in it. There were always the dolphins, sharks and large whales. Large sharks followed the ship. When a burial at sea happened, they would not see the sharks for some time. Seeing who could spot the first spout of air the whales would make was fun.

When the ship was close to New Foundland, it was foggy for several days. One day, the sun shone brightly through the fog for just a few moments showing a huge iceberg. The ship narrowly missed hitting it.

On about July 1, 1856, Captain Edward Martin at evening prayer meeting told the emigrants that they would soon arrive in Boston instead of New York City. He gave instructions about leaving the ship and told them to follow instructions very closely. Elder John Taylor had the arrangements made so they could hurry to the plains, where the hand carts would be ready to load and their march would start. That night Mary along with many other Saints lay awake too excited to sleep as they thought about America. At last, sleep came to Mary. All too soon the bell rang to signal the start of a new day. The passengers talked all day about what America was like.

As evening prayers finished, a sailor who was way up in the sails shouted "LAND AHOY." Young and old alike hurried to get a glimpse of land, but the ocean looked the same as it had for the last thirty-eight days. As they were looking in the direction that the sailor pointed, they saw the skyline of Boston on the horizon.

Seeing the city filled the saints with many different emotions. Some like Mary stood and wept for joy as others shouted. Some knelt on their knees, thanking the Deity for safe passage. As the ship sailed into the harbor, the captain told the passengers they would spend another night aboard.

Early the next morning, the bell rang, signaling the start of a new day. Along with the other passengers, Mary set about the regular routine with an extra amount of energy. When the ship was spotlessly clean, they could disembark. The Mormons took to heart. "Cleanliness is next to Godliness."

The ship had been a boot camp for the pilgrims. As they passed through Boston's immigration with their little amount of luggage, the process bewildered them but they were never afraid or undisciplined. With good reason, they had total and complete faith in their Mormon leaders. Never in history was a more efficient system used to move an entire nation than the Mormon migration, except when Moses led the children of Israel from Egypt. They believed Brigham Young was the modern leader of Israel.

New Homeland

Chapter 2

After clearing the Boston harbor emigration office, the pilgrims went by conveyances to the train station. At the train station, they got on the train to head for Iowa. They rode in the cattle cars. This did not bother them because the people were thankful to be on the way to Zion. Mary loved the wide-open space of this new land. There were farms with houses, barns and fields full of crops and animals. Thomas and her spent many hours trying to imagine how wonderful it would be if Father owned one of those farms. Mother always assured them that one day soon they would have their own farm in the valley. When the train crossed the wide Mississippi River, Captain Martin told Mary that they would arrive in Iowa City in about three hours. She could not imagine the great speed of 25 miles an hour.

For some must Push
Some must Pull
To the Valley "Ho"

J S Murray

In Iowa City, supply superintendent Chauncey G. Webb's heart almost stopped when he saw the newly arrived saints. It was his job to outfit them for travel. Webb supplied the passengers from the Enoch Train, the SS Curling and was in the middle of out fitting the Thornton, a total of 1987 souls. Only by the might and power of the Mighty One could they accomplish the task. Five-hundred people shared five wagons, twenty-four oxen and forty-five head of beef and milk cows. Twenty persons shared one tent. They assigned five persons to each hand cart.

They made most of the hand carts the same way. The carts were flimsy little boxes set on wheels, with a track of five feet. They were an open affair sometimes with a cover. Two side pieces extended out with a cross bar that you could push against or pull. The carpenters covered the larger family carts with hoops for a cover. There were three different sizes of carts. The largest carts went to those with families. These sometimes had iron axles or skeins, also iron tires. Generally, they made the carts all from wood, ash for the box and shafts, Hickory for axles, Elm for hubs, White Oak for spokes and rim. Sometimes they used rawhide for tire and axle bushings. This was all to be first class dry and seasoned wood! As we will see, they could not always comply with these specifications.

Chauncey Webb was a very responsible person who took his job very seriously. By the time Edward Martin and the fifth company of emigrants arrived in Iowa City, he had outfitted more souls than seemed humanly possible. They bought hundreds of oxen and wagons, along with the material to make hundreds of hand carts. There was no longer any dry and seasoned lumber with which to make more vehicles.

When James Willie and the passengers from the Thornton arrived in Iowa City, they set to making hand carts from green wood. Day after day the preparations continued and soon the train consisted of 500 souls, 120 hand carts, five wagons, four mules, twenty-four oxen and forty-five cows for beef and milk. Also, the supplies consisted of flour, sugar and other food stuff.

On July 15, 1856, Willie's company started the 1367 mile trek to Salt Lake City. As they began, they sang, "For some must push and some must pull as we go marching up the hill, as merrily on the way we go until we reach the valley."

The prairie summer was cruel to the Saints. You could not see that little red chigger that made painful red spots on their legs. Also, some more frail people caught the American Fever and many died. The heat and humidity were an oppressive force that drained the strength from even the strong and powerful men.

Edward Martin and his elders set about building carts, wagons and tents. On July 28, 1856, they started their march to Zion. They had seven wagons, 146 hand carts, thirty oxen, fifty cows and 576 souls. How little did this brave leader know what would befall this multitude of people as the next three months unfolded. From the first night out and for the next 101 days, those hand carts made of green wood, would be like a rough galling and painful yoke on the pilgrims. The faithful men that were carpenters would work late into the night making repairs on those miserable contraptions.

One of the most noted and honored men that did this task was Archer Walters of Willie's company. This man's wife was too ill to walk, so he picked her up and put her in the cart. He hauled her along with the smallest of his children all the way to the valley. Along the way, he repaired carts, made coffins and buried the dead. He pulled his cart and its load all day. At night, he worked on carts or built coffins until most everyone else was in bed. Two weeks after arriving in the valley and beholding the Prophets face, he died of the exposure and work of the long hard trip.

On the morning that the fifth hand cart company left Iowa City, they were so happy they burst into singing,

How long in the world I have sigh'd,
From the days of my youth,
When, sick of its sin and its pride,
I sought and pray'd for the truth.

It came, and the Gospel I found,
To me it was life, joy, and peace;
Salvation was beaming around,
With hopes of a happy release.

And then I was longing to be
Where the will of my Father is done,
Where the noble, the pure, and the free
On the earth are united as one.

I go where no tyrants dare come,
Where oppressors would tremble to tread,
Where the honest in heart find a home,
Where the blessing of heaven are shed.

I go where fair virtue supplies
Rich fountains of blessing for all.
Where the Kingdom of Heaven will rise,
While the nations will crumble and fall.

Mary and her other girl friends often walked with Edward Martin. As they were traveling through the Iowa countryside, farmers came to the edge of the road, laughed and shouted insults as the Saints passed. "You are as low as the oxen or horses and mules. They should hang your leaders for using you as draft animals."

As the long line of people and carts went by, many of these critics changed their minds and offered acts of kindness. They always impressed them with the organization, but most of all, the happy cheerful and helpful spirit that the Saints reflected.

As they traveled day by day in the heat and dust, many of them were carrying a heavy bundle on their heads or backs. Some had objects tied to their waists that would reach the valley in that way. They allowed them only 17 pounds of personal belonging on the cart per individual. Joy filled their souls as they marched along. When they reached the Des Moines river, they walked across the bridge and soon beheld the fort. Before the day was over, they reached the Raccoon river and there made camp for the night. The next day, they crossed this stream twice.

The saints started on their way and so the leader began to teach them new songs of Zion. These pioneers spent many evenings singing and dancing. Mary loved to sing the song that gave so much hope to the travelers.

> *Cheer, Saints, cheer! we're bound for peaceful Zion;*
> *Cheer Saints, cheer! For that free and happy land!*
> *Cheer, Saints, cheer! we'll Israel's God rely on,*
> *We will be lead by the power of his right hand!*
>
> *Long, long in Bab'lon we have liv'd in sorrow,*
> *But God in his mercy hath open'd our way;*
> *Hope points before, and shows the bright tomorrow,*
> *Lets us forget the darkness of today.*

These songs made the path to Zion a cheerful way, as they marched along singing the songs of hope. Each night the travelers would learn these beautiful and loved hymns. Everyday the Saints broke into singing and for the three to seven miles that the train stretched, you heard the lovely voices raised in song and praise. They marked the Mormon road with mile markers to give the travelers the distance they had gone. Mary asked Captain Martin about these markers and this is the story he told her.

Elder William Clayton was the clerk for the pioneers of 1847. He took it upon himself to tie a rag on the wagon wheel of Heber Kimball's wagon. This wheel measured fourteen feet eight inches, which would be exactly 360 revolutions per mile. Day after day he trudged along, in the dust, counting the wheel turning. William Clayton figured out how

They Had only Greenwood

to make a roadometer that would fasten on the wagon hub. It was a crude affair consisting of cogs and screws. He had walked and counted more than 300 miles before Brother Brigham ordered Orson Pratt to start whittling the device. Orson Pratt took the credit for the invention. This was more than William Clayton could stand.

The feud between Pratt and Clayton started discontentment among the pioneers that lead to the famous "dressing down" they received from Brigham Young on the Platte river road, not far from the great land mark, Chimney Rock.

Travelers on the Mormon road always knew where the good camp sites were. Cholera was almost unheard of among the Saints. At the Mormon camp sites, they dug wells and latrines. When they arrived at camp, they always cleaned the wells. The next morning the pioneers covered the latrines with dirt before they left the camp, leaving their camp sites clean and ready for those that followed.

When the fifth hand cart company reached the Nishnabotna river, they met their first Indians. They were peaceful but the Saints soon learned that they were beggars the same as they would find the plain Indians to be. Mary had heard of the terrible crimes committed along the trail by the red man. Also, his begging, stealing and trading of every thing including women always made the white women very afraid.

As they were traveling through this part of Iowa, she found that many Saints lived there. They set up farms to provide food and supplies for the saints as they passed. Every evening since they left Iowa City many men would spend several hours repairing the carts. They had gotten used to that mournful screeching of the cart wheels. Some used bacon grease and precious soap to lubricate those noisy things.

At evening counsel and prayer meeting, Captain Martin told the Saints they were about to reach Kanesville and the Missouri River. Here they would rest and make final preparations for the trip across the plains. It took another three days to make the river because the carts were breaking down and they lost time repairing them.

As the Fifth Hand Cart Company passed through Kanesville, Mary took in the sights. The city had very modern homes made mostly of wood and a few of brick. The most interesting to Mary were the houses dug into a hillside covered with dirt. Someone told her they called these dugouts. She and Thomas talked a long time about those people that lived as animals in the ground. Thomas told of the little animals he had seen when he worked on the farm in England. These Americans sure had strange ways. Mary said she would marry a fine man that would build her a brick home on their farm. There she would raise her sons to be good farmers like their father.

The crossing of the Missouri River took several days because of the size of the company. As the Ashby family waited for their turn to board the ferry, Mary and Thomas spent many hours exploring the river banks. The river was a fearful thing. The water was just a thick mud rolling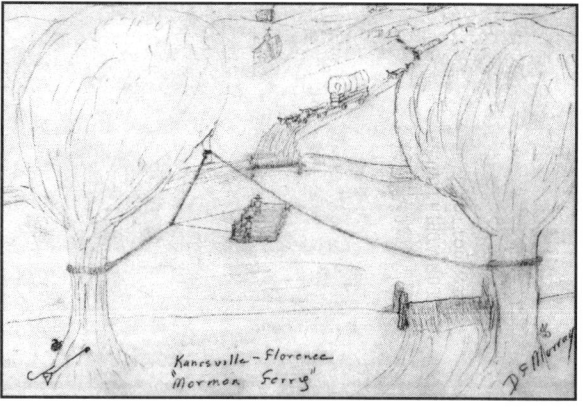

Kanesville – Florence
"Mormon Ferry"

by filled with trees and once they saw a large black dead animal that looked like a cow floating down the stream.

This ferry was a large flat platform with a fence around it to keep people and livestock from falling into the river. On each river bank, there was a platform attached to the bank on one end and the other was a large log so it would rise and lower with the water level. There was a heavy rope attached to a tree on the east shore and to two trees several hundred feet apart on the west side. This made a large V. With ropes tied to each end of the ferry and pulleys on the rope, the water pushed the ferry across. After the ferry men unloaded it on the west shore, they disconnected the ferry from the south rope and pulled it by oxen to the North rope and hooked on for the return trip. The river would push it back to the East bank. The Missouri river flowed south past Kanesville.

At last, it was time for the Ashby family to board the ferry that would take them across to the Nebraska Territory side of the river. Mary held tight to Thomas because the river was flowing very fast and the men running it had to work very hard to make it land at the right spot.

After they landed, one of their mother's friends realized she had left her shoes on the East bank. This lady always kept her shoes polished and cleaned. Not wanting to soil them, she took them off and laid them beside her family's cart. In getting her children safely on the ferry, she forgot them. When she appealed to the men that ran the ferry to help recover them, they only laughed and said, "It is a long way to the valley bare footed." They were sure right.

The family and the rest of the emigrants soon settled in a fine camp just to the west of Florence. Here they found Willie's company camped. They remained here until they repaired the hand carts and obtained provisions for the trip across the plains and mountains. The days were very hot and the air was wet and sticky. Even at night, it was hot and hard to sleep. They soon learned why this place got the name MISERY BOTTOMS. All worked hard. The women repaired tents, clothes and cooked hard little cakes to eat without having to stop very long at one time.

Mary thought the town of Florence would be an enjoyable place to live. It had a very modern grist mill about one fourth of a mile from the ferry, just on the north edge of town. There were fields of corn and other grain to the North that went clear to Fort Atkinson fifteen miles North. She watched as farmers brought their heavily loaded wagons to the mill where they made grain into flour for the fourth and fifth handcart companies to take with them. The town lay on a flat area near the rivers' edge and it laid out in a rectangle with the long way running North to South. The houses consisted of logs. They had dirt roofs on which grass grew. Also, the fire places consisted of sod and these had to be wet down from time to time. There were those houses made from the sod that were half buried in the ground, along the West street that was next to the bluff.

The men spent long hours finding wood from the forests along the river to repair carts. This was a disheartening task because the only wood to find was green wood obtained from trees still growing. With the green wood, they repaired their carts the best they could. These poor factory workers from England had no idea what lay ahead. If they did, they may have given up in despair. The only thought they had was to start the march to Zion. Flour and other provisions by the wagon loads daily arrived. As many as twenty oxen pulled these wagons. Mary and Thomas watched the supply train come to their camp and wondered if there were more oxen in America than people.

The evenings were a happy time filled with dancing, music, poetry and singing the familiar hymns and learning new ones.

Israel, Israel, God is calling--
Calling thee from lands of woe;
Babylon the Great is fallen;
God shall all her towers o'erthrow.
Come to Zion
'Ere His floods of anger flow.

Israel, Israel, God is speaking:
Hear your deliverer's voice!
Now a glorious morn is breaking
For the people of His choice.
Come to Zion
And within her walls rejoice.

After they finished repairing the carts, the people became restless and urged their leaders to start for the valley. As the murmuring continued, the leaders called a mass meeting. The Elders spoke, among them were those that had traveled this road and were eager to get home to their families. Those speaking at the meeting were Willie, Atwood, Savage, Woodward, Grant and Kimball and all but Savage supported starting for Utah.

Levi Savage told the gathering that he thought it was too late to take such a group across the plains and mountains this late in the season. He declared that they could not cross the mountains with a mixed company of aged people, little children and women this late in the season. If they tried, Savage predicted much suffering and death. After this, he advised going into winter quarters at Elkhorn, Loup or Wood rivers without delay. Every soul voted him down. Then this brave man told the company that if they must go he would go also. Then he added, "Brethren and sisters, what I have said is true this I know, but seeing you are to go forward, I will go with you, will help you all I can, will work with you, will rest with you, will suffer with you, and if necessary, I will die with you. May God in his great mercy bless and preserve you."

Across the Prairie

Chapter 3

August 18, 1856, the fourth hand cart company left Florence for Zion. They loaded the supply wagons to their capacity. In addition, they added 100 pounds of flour to each cart. A few people murmured but the majority bore the burden cheerfully. It was not long into the march that the songs of Zion and of the hand cart rang up and down the long line of marching Saints. As Mary watched the company leave, she longed to be going with these happy people. Father told her that they would soon start marching to their new home.

Trading for white Squaw

On August 21, Franklin Richards and the rest of the missionaries arrived at Florence on their way back to Utah. The Saints were very happy to see him and the Brethren. The missionaries encouraged the company by their help and assistance. Cyrus Wheelock testified to the truth of Brigham Young's prophecy that the people would increase in health and strength as they marched along. The saints carried the proof on their faces, in the summer sun.

The morning of August 25, 1856, the whole fifth hand cart company under the leadership of Edward Martin left Florence. Following were two wagon trains led by Captain W. B. Hodgett who had thirty-three wagons and 185 passengers. Captain John Hunt brought up the rear with fifty wagons and 200 emigrants. On the first day, they only made 2 miles and camped at Cutler's Park.

When the march started the second day, Mary grew sad to see her friends the Loaders left behind. Zilpha Loader gave birth to a son and one of her sisters was too sick to travel. The father appealed to Captain Martin to let the new mother, her baby and the sick girl ride in one of the supply wagons. Captain Martin refused, so they stayed where they were. Mary and Thomas helped push the cart because there were some very steep hills the first part of the day.

As they reached the top of a hill, they stopped and looked with wonder at how soon the country changed. Below them at the bottom of the hill, there was a wide and very swift river. Beyond the river, they saw a plain that seemed to run forever, with another river that was several miles away. This river was a long silver shimmering stream that ran till it met the sky. Captain Martin told Mary the river at the bottom of the hill was the Elkhorn and the one way to the West was the Platte. Up this valley road, they would travel for the next two and one half months.

After being ferried across the Elkhorn river, they traveled across a very flat plain. The road was dusty and the sand was soft, averaging two to four inches deep. The large company of Saints got so caught up in the excitement of at last getting a real start for the mountain valley that they hardly noticed the extra effort it took to push the carts. With great happiness and songs, the miles rolled by quickly. Off to the west and south, Mary could see brown hills that rose above the plain. As they marched on, the hills seemed to rise from the river's edge. When at last they reached the banks of the Platte river, it was getting late in the day, so they stopped to set up camp. Each person had a task to do. Father and the other men set about setting up the tents.

Elder Martin told the people to pick up buffalo chips to make camp fires when there was no wood. Mary and the other children picked up the buffalo chips. When wood was available, the men gathered it. At this camp site, they walked in the sandy river bottom and found a good supply of drift wood. Then, Mother cooked a good meal of beef and gruel, because the day before they left Florence the elders had issued a good portion of fresh killed beef.

Poor ole
Woman Trader

After supper, the elders called a meeting where they gave instructions and answered questions. Then the fiddlers tuned their fiddles and young and old enjoyed a lively time of dancing. The bugle sounded and all had time for devotions and prayers. Then all went to bed except those standing guard duty. The men of the Ashby family took their assigned turns at guard duty.

The next day started early with the same routine practiced since leaving Iowa City. A long way to the North, Mary could see low brown hills that looked as they were rising from a lake. As she looked in every direction, it seemed as if water surrounded them. Captain Martin told her the water she saw was not really a lake. The sun caused heat to rise from the ground making it look like water. The sand made pulling those carts very hard. Evening found them twenty miles closer to Zion.

After setting up camp and getting supper, they spent the rest of the evening in meetings and song. The weary pilgrims were thankful to lay in their beds and sleep. At the 2:00 A.M. changing of the guard, elder William Cluff rode into camp pulling the Loaders two hand carts with a rope tied to the saddle on his horse.

The night before the people in Florence saw a glow in the sky to the West all night. When morning came, Joseph A. Young and William Cluff rose early to find out what caused the glow. Upon arriving, they found the Loader family making ready to start. They explained that a boy baby had been born and one girl was sick and that is why they did not leave with the rest. Then, they appealed to the young men for help. Joseph Young laughed and said they would not help them. As a parting jester, he said they should name the baby boy Handcart.

William Cluff was a man with a gentle and compassionate spirit, and could not bear to see the sad plight of the Loaders. That is why he had pulled the carts and helped the family those many hard miles to catch up with the Saints. They fixed a meal of runny gruel and lay down for three hours sleep.

When the bugle blew at 5 A. M., the camp came to life following the daily routine of all Mormon pioneers. First they got up and had personal devotions. Next, they cooked and ate the meal. Then, they cleaned up camp and prepared to leave. Before leaving, they went to the general assembly for preaching, instruction and counsel.

The captains of the hundreds and tens assigned the daily order for marching and other tasks. When all were ready, the day's march began. The large number of supply wagons would take sometime to gather the oxen, yoke and hitch up. The men of the fifth hand cart company had no experience with oxen. Most of the men could not tell them apart. It took several days before their fear left them and to know which ones to yoke together.

On the second morning after reaching the Platte, the march started early. As the day wore on, the sand caused the carts to become a burden that took as many as three or four people pushing and pulling them to move forward. The river soon changed direction and the low bluffs to the South soon disappeared in the shimmering heat of the day. In every direction, only sand and shimmering heat looked like small lakes. They gained each mile with much effort because those heavily loaded cart wheels needed lubrication.

The days were much the same for the first week until they came to Genoa. Here once stood a Methodist mission to the Pawnee Indians. When the Methodist's abandoned the mission, the Mormons set up a supply farm. They left a settlement to raise crops to feed and supply other Saints on their way to the valley. Because of the scant rainfall and wild beasts destroying their crops, they too soon left. A day before they reached Genoa, they left the Platte and followed the Loup river. Here they met a band of Indians that tied ropes from their horses to the carts and pulled them across the river.

The country became one unending plain filled with sand. The brown dried grass and the unchanging landscape made Mary think there was not one thing that could live here. They camped by the Loup river that night. At the evening meeting, Captain Martin told the Saints to make sure they had plenty of water because the next day would be a long dry march to the South. Night would come before they reached the Platte.

One Indian, who helped in the river crossing, took such a liking to the sight of white women that he found one young woman and asked her husband if he would trade her for ten ponies. This was three times more than an Indian woman cost. When the man refused, the Indian brought more ponies. Again, the love struck Indian saw his offer turned down. The young Indian man could not understand. He hung around camp until all but the night guards went to bed.

While the trading took place, the men of the fifth hand cart company went about the business of preparing for the journey ahead. They butchered beef, repaired carts, filled water containers and organized the next day's march. The Ashby's were thankful for the generous portion of beef they received. At evening prayers, they thanked the Deities for the great blessing of the safe journey thus far.

While the camp was preparing to leave the next morning, the Indian came into camp with his ponies loaded with buffalo robes to trade them all for "white squaw." Most of the men laughed and teased the husband about the good deal he would be getting. Nevertheless, the women of the pioneers were very afraid that the Indians would attack, kill the men and take them captive.

At last, they were ready to start the day's march. The sand was still a problem to walk in and pull those heavily loaded carts. Many cut the tops from their boots as well as sacrificing tin from kettles and plates with which to make bearings for the axle and hubs on the carts. Then those poor souls used the precious bacon grease and soap to lubricate them. The more they greased those contraptions, the more sand collected in the hubs. They soon learned that if they did not grease the wheels dry, they worked better so there were fewer delays for repairs. Although without grease, the wheels made a terrible screeching sound.

It was not long till they reached the top of a divide that was several miles wide. This wide expanse was flat like the Platte river road. You did not hear songs as often now as during the crossing of Iowa. Mary and Thomas helped Mother push while Father and William pulled the heavy loaded cart. While the Saints were eating dinner, someone noticed a very strange looking cloud way off to the Southwest. It was very black and reached very high into the sky. At the top, it had large white billowy tops, but closer to the ground it looked greenish yellow. As they continued to march, it was if they and the cloud would soon meet head on.

About the middle of the afternoon, the road began to slope to the South and several miles ahead you could see the Platte river. When the travelers started going down that long hill, the cloud reached them. The

Lt Ware
Watching the Saints

wind blew with hurricane force upsetting wagons and carts alike. Dust and sand were so thick that those standing beside each other could not see each other. Then the rain came pouring down. This soon turned to hail with some large pieces of ice. In perhaps an hour, the storm passed and the sun shone as though nothing had happened.

The hail lay scattered about everywhere in drifts. It took a lot of hard work for all to get the wagons and carts upright and loaded again. Many had bruises from the hail, but no serious injuries. Much to the surprise of all, the carts did not sink into the wet sand. This gave them another reason to thank the Deity. The sun had set when they reached the river and made camp. There was no dancing that night because all were too tired to do anything but go to bed.

The next morning as Mary was gathering fuel for the morning meal, she noticed a group of horses with Indians riding them toward the camp. She sounded the alarm, causing the Captain and a group of men to hurry to see what was up. As the Indians drew near, it turned out to be the woman trader with his wares for the white woman. The men had a good laugh and the day's preparation went forward. Someone christened the Indian with the name Woman Trader. He and his party would be part of the company for several days.

When the march got under way, they soon noticed that the sand had dried and the carts were harder to move than before. The air seemed drier than before, which dried the wood on the carts. This caused them to become very loose, which led to axles and wheels breaking. One morning, it seemed that the country was alive with buffalo. They would be close enough that the young men could shoot and kill several to share with everyone. The Ashby's received a good portion that they enjoyed very much. It was very difficult to keep the beef and milk cows away from the wild beasts. Once the oxen got with the buffalo, they just disappeared.

When they reached the upper end of the Grand Island of the Platte river, the trail followed the Wood River. This river was about seven miles north and ran parallel with the Platte. There, the company met a group of young men from the Willie fourth handcart company.

The young men were looking for their oxen and told a story about a buffalo stampede that lasted the better part of one day. The stampede started about daylight with the emigrants caught in the main path. Carts, wagons and people got ran over alike. It was a miracle that nobody lost their life.

These brave, young men hunted for several days for the lost oxen without having any luck. Finally, they gave up and started back to catch Willie's company. On their way back, they happened to see the Martin company. When night came, they all made camp by the wagons, Willie Company left behind because of the lost oxen.

When it was over, the cattle were gone except for only a few heifers and milk cows. They could not find any oxen so they yoked the cows and heifers. However, those poor creatures could not budge those heavy wagons despite giving their best effort. The fourth company had just used up the extra flour carried on the carts. After the stampede, they abandoned the wagons and placed all the supplies from those wagons on the hand carts. Then, the march continued.

Break downs of those pesky carts and the constant threat of buffalo were slowing the company to a snail's pace. Many a morning found a dead ox or another that had disappeared. This caused a bigger burden for the surviving oxen in trying to pull the supply wagons. Eventually, necessity required them to abandon most of the supply wagons. They transferred the food supply to the better carts. The Elders asked strong young men to pull them. Dry weather, sand and the extra load caused more break downs and delays.

One morning Woman Trader made his demands for the trade in a very excited way and of course he got turned down the same as usual. When Mary and Thomas passed Woman Trader, he was sitting beside the road the most sad and dejected human they had ever seen. He was all alone because the rest of the Pawnee's had taken off early that morning. After a few miles of travel, they soon saw why those Pawnee's were in such hurry to leave. There was a war party of one thousand Sioux who were going to fight the Pawnee. The Sioux just sat on their ponies and watched the Saints tug their carts along. The Indians watched the carts with their human draft animals with pity and sympathy for them. Without horses and wagons, they had nothing the Indians wanted. They had seen the same kind of traveler often before.

At this time, they were over taken by the group of returning missionaries on their way to Salt Lake. This encouraged them and made the hard road seem easier. That night they butchered a fine fat beef so the missionaries would have fresh meat to take with them. The Franklin Richards' company had fine teams of four mules hitched to light carriages. He promised that there would be a large supply of food and provisions waiting for the traveling Saints when they reached Fort Laramie.

When they reached a point across the river from Fort Kearney, Captain Wharton crossed the river to talk to Elder Edward Martin. The army officer told him that the Southern Cheyenne were creating the most terrible atrocities to pioneers he had ever seen. Dog Soldiers led by Charles Bent whose father was William Bent, a white man who ran the great Bents Fort and Trading Company south on the Arkansas river. His mother was a Cheyenne Indian named Yellow Woman who was the daughter of the great medicine man Yellow Wolf, keeper of the sacred arrows.

The army officer told of Elder A.W. Babbitt's ox teams and wagons that were freighting for the Mormon church being attacked. Of the four teamsters, two got killed plus a woman and her small child. In retaliation, the troopers attacked a Cheyenne village and killed ten warriors as punishment. This set them into an uncontrollable rage that was now bringing many atrocities upon the white traveler. Also, he told of another train going East from California in which they killed a woman and took the small children captive. The Indians tortured these young children to death. He also said that the Willie company had crossed the river and traveled the south side from Fort Kearney West.

The brave Edward Martin believed that God would protect the camp of Israel as it moved toward the promised land. The weather was beginning to cool at nights and the days were not so hot. This helped them to make more miles each day. For several days, they could see Lt. Ware with a small detachment watching the Saints in their long line of march as they dragged their carts with bundles tied on their backs and heads. The only encounter they had with Indians was when several came along and tied their lariats on the carts. The Indians drug the carts for several miles with their ponies. Those poor weary Saints appreciated this gesture of kindness.

Summer Was Gone

Chapter 4

The long weary days went as usual. When they reached the forks of the Platte, they continued up the north fork and soon reached some very steep hills that were nothing but sand. It took all their strength to get through them. The loads were much lighter now but the people were beginning to wear out. It took a couple of days to get out onto the level road again. The country was changing every day and the weather was much colder. SUMMER WAS GONE! One night they camped across the river where the trail on the south side of the river came down a steep canyon. Elder Martin said they called this place Ash Hollow. Also, he told how they lowered wagons down windlass hill with ropes.

The road was no longer sand. Now, the dust rose in great clouds, which made breathing very hard. To the West, they could see what looked like a church spire on the horizon. This rock formation was the famous landmark known as Chimney Rock. The country contained many strange looking formations. One looked like a courthouse. They traveled several days before they passed Chimney Rock. For several days, they could still see Chimney rock when they looked back to the East. They passed a large bluff of rock on the South side of the Platte called Scottsbluff. Scottsbluff got its name from a fur trapper that died at the bluff. Scott's partner left him to die when he got sick. Scott traveled for many miles before dying at the bluff that bears his name.

The country was changing in looks every day. Up ahead, they could see the dark outline of Laramie Peak. This was the beginning of the Black Hills of the Laramie range. Excitement grew as they came to Fort Laramie where here they would get new supplies and warm clothes. The weather became very cold. They were about out of food so they cut rations in half. There had been no fresh meat for many days. This weakened the physical condition of those poor souls, which made it ever harder to drag the carts along.

On October 8, they reached the river crossing to the fort and made camp. They spent the next day crossing the river and trading for what

Chimney Rock

little they could. The Indians had caused so many problems and death to the freighters that they quit hauling from West Port Missouri for the season. The fort had few supplies to sell. What they did have went for very high prices. Many Saints traded watches, jewelry and even wedding rings for food and warm robes.

The fort commander offered to marry one young lady offering a life of ease and luxury. She politely turned him down because her faith required her to go on to Salt Lake and behold the Prophet. Elder F. D. Richards bought 100 buffalo robes when he passed on his way to the valley. The Elders distributed these to the most needy.

After a short but needed rest, they started the march again. That day they passed Registry Cliff where early travelers cut their names in the sandstone cliff. This is where the road became harder to travel. In many places, there were ruts in the sandstone made by the oxen's feet and wagon wheels. Beside the wagon ruts, there were ruts made by man as he walked beside his teams.

Not much changed except the landscape for the next ten days. Feed was very poor for the few oxen they had left and these were growing weaker every mile of the way. The colder weather made the forward progress much slower.

When they reached Deer Crossing, they reduced the loads carried on the cart to 10 pounds for an adult and 5 pounds for a child less than eight. This was due to their weakened condition caused by lack of food. To lighten their loads, they left blankets along with robes and coats behind.

When they reached Red Butte, it was time to cross the Platte River for the last time. The site of that river filled with floating clumps of slush ice was enough to stop the most brave souls among them. Many just gave in to despair and refused to move any farther. Starvation and cold were taking its toll on the once strong and confident people. The weather grew colder all that day, making the thought of crossing even harder. Nevertheless, those stronger in heart waded in and crossed the half mile wide river. The water was waist deep, which made pulling their carts almost impossible.

A brother Jackson made it half way through the river to a sand bar and could not move any farther. His wife's sister waded to help him, but she was too late to get any response from the depleted man. While she was trying to get him to move, a man placed the poor soul on the horse with him and carried brother Jackson to the north shore.

They placed the children on carts. With everyone helping each other, they got across the river. This dreadful crossing wrought more fatalities than the whole trip thus far. The young men who had the strength made the crossing many times that day. The brave young ladies marched into that river with the courage that would gain them a reward for time and eternity. The swift current swept the Loader's two daughters down the stream past the landing. With their mother screaming, men rescued them from their watery grave. The Ashby family bravely marched into the ice-filled river and crossed while giving aid to others. Martin's company moved on for a couple of miles where they made camp. This gave the Hodgett and Hunt trains space to make camp.

They were hardly out of the river when a terrifying storm broke upon them. Rain, lighting, hail and snow all mixed in a swirling wind, while the wind stirred up the sand along the river to make for miserable conditions. These horrible conditions combined with the Saint's weakened condition required them to muster every ounce of strength they had to set up their tents and prepare for that night. The only thing to make a fire with was scrubby sagebrush. This was not enough to cook a good meal on much less get warm and dry. The trauma of the crossing caused several people to go out of their minds. It took several months for many of them to recover their sanity.

At the time the guard changed, Sister Jackson awakened to find her husband dead. Thinking of others, she lay quietly beside the cold body until morning. The tragic death of her husband left sister Jackson a widow with five children four hundred miles from the city of Zion.

With the snow still falling when morning came, the Saints started gathering the dead for burial. They planned to bury them all in one grave. When those men started to dig, they found the ground frozen and could not make the grave. They stacked the dead together and covered the corpses with snow. Then they poured water over the snow on the bodies to make ice. This ensured that the wolves could not dig them out and eat them. In the spring, someone would return to bury these dear souls.

Upon Breaking their ice locked wheels loose, they resumed the march. The snow fell so hard they could hardly see from one cart to the next. With so many sick people riding on carts, the progress was very slow and difficult. One man sat beside the trail to rest. When the last cart passed, they did not see him. After they discovered the missing man, a few young men went back along the road in search of him. When they found him, they chased a pack of hungry wolves from the half-devoured corpse.

Upon stopping for the night, they began the normal routine of setting up the tent. However, with a foot of snow on the ground it was not an easy process. Everyone pitched in with whatever they could find to dig through the snow to set up the tents. They used plates, kettles and even their hands. They finally finished setting up the tents late in the night.

The next day was the same as the one before. Some men buried the dead while others kept the hungry wolves at bay. That day the sky cleared and the temperature dropped below zero. They hauled those that died during the day on the handcarts to the next camp site. Thomas and William were both ill from the cold river crossing. Father, Mother and Mary worked with all the strength they had to haul them along on the cart. With rations cut to less than half a pound of flour a day and the biting cold, they had no strength left to set up any tents. With very few blankets and the flimsy clothing they were wearing, they lay down on the snow with the vault of heaven's stars as their roof. Many widowed mothers sat holding their children close all that long terrible night. They were unable to move the next day because of their worn out and starving condition.

While they gathered the dead for burial, Elder Martin stood guard over the corpses with a shotgun firing at the crows and vultures. He told one person that he prayed to God to let him close his eyes in death so he could no longer witness the unforgettable scene before him. Many lost the will to live. They no longer knew or cared what was going on around them. The families of Ashby, Parker, Schofield, and Moss remained determined to reach the valley and behold the prophet's face. The will to live and press on was strong within them. These weary people shared the privations and death as only life long friends knew how. Unknown to them, they and following generations would always have close connections.

The Hodgett wagons moved up beside the fifth hand cart company and stalled because their teams were in the same condition of the handcart people. Deep snow and the shortage of feed for the last few days wore their teams out. Many oxen died. When they saw the terrible condition of those wore out handcart people, they set up tents and did all they could to relieve their suffering. Despite their help the weak and sick kept on dying. They stalled in that camp for several days. Sister Scott a very devout lady stood beside her covered wagon, praying just as the sun sat. When she finished, she looked to the west and saw three men mounted on horses riding toward them leading pack horses. She screamed, "The Angel of Deliverance has arrived!"

The beleaguered company gathered to meet Joseph A. Young, Dan W. Jones and Abel Garr who were scouting ahead for the relief wagons sent from the valley. The men told Edward Martin and W. B. Hodgett that wagons with supplies were a few days behind them on the road. These young men spent the night with the fifth handcart company. They gave the starving people their small supply of food and aid to all they could. Early the next morning after prayer and counseling them to move on, they started on east to find the Hunt wagon train.

Those within the company still strong enough to care, encouraged and rendered aid to the dejected ones. Though the weather was biting cold, the road churned into a muddy path that only added to the work and discomfort of all. The Saints strong enough to walk pulled the carts. Those sick and dying outnumbered  the ones that could walk. Hodgett's wagons were even struggling worse because most of their teams were dead or near death.

As father pulled the cart that William and Thomas rode, Mother and Mary pushed with all the will they had. Often, Mary thought of the box she laid on her bed to bring to the valley. Her bare feet covered with frozen mud and raw sores made her dream of those stolen shoes.

While they were struggling up a long, muddy hill, two of the young men that went in search of the Hunt train came up from the rear. When they reached the hand carts, they tied their riatas to the more weakened one's carts and helped pull them along. They helped the Ashby's by pulling their cart for several miles. These two brave men made many trips back and forth pulling carts that day.

Joseph Young stopped on his way back west to give a detailed report to Captain Grant about the plight of the three companies. That night the three men appealed to the people to struggle on and help would soon come. As they left early the next morning, the burial squad was busy collecting the dead. They beheld the orphans, the widow and the widower, and with breaking hearts went westward.

The pioneers started with a glimmer of hope that perhaps on this day help would arrive. Death and sickness were slowing them to a snail's pace, but only with faith did they keep struggling. As they crept along, the company strung out along the trail in its usual fashion for three to five miles. The three Ashbys' able to walk grew weaker each day from the lack of food and the extra effort that the two sick boys made. They bore this burden with cheerful acceptance and with acts of loving kindness to all their fellow travelers. Only one-third of the company could walk and these were hauling the rest. The sun shone for a couple of days turning the road into a muddy slop that made travel more difficult.

On the last day of October, the Grant rescue wagons met this near dead company camped on Greasewood Creek. They distributed all the provisions of flour, clothing and warm blankets to those suffering souls. That night the rescuers set about helping anywhere they could and encouraging them to fight to live.

That night was no different when it was time to set up the tents. These weakened men scraped the foot of snow with hands, plates, cups or whatever they had. However, that night they rested much better than they had for the last month, with a good meal and warm bed in which to sleep.

The next morning the rescuers placed all they had room for in the wagons with the sick and dying. The company then pressed forward. Progress slowed because those suffering from dysentery became worse after eating two good meals. By noon, the snow began to fall very thick and heavy. This slowed the forward movement even more. The supply wagons were too full for the Ashby boys so the parents and Mary hauled them on their cart. They camped that night at Independence Rock.

Sunday, November 2, they awakened to bury the dead and move forward. With fewer sick people on carts they made a little more progress. William and Thomas Ashby died that day and Father Ashby hauled the bodies to camp so the wolves would not eat them. With fatherly love, Samuel Ashby tugged the cart bearing his beloved sons through eighteen inches

angels of Mercy

of snow. When at last they reached camp, he sat beside the cart where it stopped and started to eat a little cake when he died. His life stopped as easily as a lamp that runs out of oil. Before Hanna or Mary could reach him, some starving soul took the little cake from his dead hand and ate it. Like so many others, he worked himself to death. His friend Samuel Pucell hauled his sick wife Margaret on the handcart until it weakened him so much he died. Margaret died five days later, leaving ten-year-old Ellen and fourteen years old Maggie orphans.

This camp was at Devils Gate. The camp was near a ridge of rock that afforded shelter from the biting wind. Two days later Brother Hunt's wagon train arrived along time after dark. The thermometer read eleven below zero. They did not move for a week because of the bitterly cold temperature. They left the church supplies from the Hodgett and Hunt wagons at the station nearby. This allowed them to fill their wagons with people. Some men stayed to guard the cache of supplies. There was now enough to eat but it took several days before the burial squad did not have any work to do. Soon they heard laughter in the camp of Israel again.

Sunday, November 9, the sun shone and the temperature was very mild. They tucked all they could under the wagon covers. Then the march to Zion started again. Elder Grant told them he would get them to Salt Lake City, even if he had to shovel snow all the way himself. The going was slow but they made a little progress each day. Mary and her mother Hanna were of the stronger ones that continued to pull their carts. It was easier with no sick or dying riding on them. Each day they struggled onto the best of their ability.

When they came to the first crossing of the Sweetwater, the river looked frozen. The first wagon crossed safely but the second wagon broke through the ice. Therefore for the rest of the group to cross, they would have to wade through the icy water in the stream. The people refused to wade into the icy water. C. Allen Huntington, David P. Kimball and George W. Grant spent the entire day wading the waist-deep river filled with broken  ice, carrying every soul and pulling every cart across. Again the weather turned its fury upon the children of Israel. Three days from Devils Gate, they met the Mormon's greatest scout Ephraim Hanks, and his two horses loaded down with fresh killed buffalo meat. This great man would later tell of the sight that met his eyes. The sight was so terrible that the memory of it never left him. At first, he tried to pass the meat out to those starving souls but he soon could not stand their pleas, telling them to help themselves. In a very short time his horses no longer had a burden to carry.

This man spent his time helping the saints by washing and dressing their frozen limbs. When he washed Maggie Pucell's feet and legs, most of the flesh washed away, but she refused to let them amputate her legs. Little Ellen's feet and legs were both beyond saving as all the flesh washed from the bone, so they amputated just below the knee with a meat saw. The rescuers spent their time helping the suffering ones, and appealing to the ones that had no will to live or even had any realization of their surroundings. They talked of the Prophet and begged them to live. They reminded them that Zion drew closer with every step. Brother Hanks would not leave the stalled company, so he sent a messenger to the supply wagon waiting at South Pass.

At five o'clock on the morning of November twelve, four heavily loaded wagons arrived at the Three Crossings on the Sweetwater where Martin, Hodgett and Hunt's companies camped. With beef, flour, and three days of improved weather, they started making good time toward the City. Death's Angel had passed without stopping.

On the sixteenth of November, they reached Rocky Ridge and cheered when they saw ten wagons of supplies waiting. Two days more of fine weather helped them to cover many miles. On November 18, the sky was over cast and had a foreboding look. When it started snowing, they met another company of rescuers going east from the valley. These included Captain William Kimball, James Ferguson J. Simmons, Hosea Stout and a large number of teamsters with teams and wagons.

When they crossed South Pass three days later, it was snowing very hard. Tucked under wagon covers, the pioneers suffered very little. Mary was thankful that she and her mother no longer had to pull the handcart. She wondered at those few determined Scotsmen that were too stubborn to leave their worldly possessions along the road and continued to drag their carts toward the valley. The most determined was seventy-two years old Margaret Dalglish who had lost her husband, two sons, their wives and children at the Platte river crossing. All she had left to show for her life's work was that handcart with the little bundle riding in it.

When the company reached the Dry Sandy, they made a very large camp with the men from the supply wagons. The next morning Brothers Grant and Kimball left for the City, leaving Robert T. Burton in charge. As they traveled West, the wagons carrying those weak souls from the ox trains and the fifth handcart company soon pulled away from the ox trains. The fine mules and horses walked twice as fast as the slow-moving cattle. At their camp on Big Sandy, more wagons passed going east with relief for the ox drawn trains.

Upon reaching the Green River, they met more wagons loaded to the bows with beef, flour, potatoes, onions, turnips and carrots packed in bedding and clothing. With warm fires, warm clothes, rest from walking and with the much needed food their condition as a whole was improving. Mary and her friend Patience along with many other young ladies again enjoyed travel, but she missed her faithful and loving Thomas.

Sunday, November twenty-three, they camped for the night at Fort Bridger and loaded on more supplies. Apostle Christopher Merkley spoke to the travelers and encouraged them in the Gospel. He spoke of his suffering for the gospel and the rewards to come. He spoke of how soon they would be in Zion where the land flowed with milk and honey. "Even now you're at the door." Mary was entering the land of Zion at last and was happy to learn the Mormon church owned and operated this fort.

As she looked south, she asked if they would be going over those snow clad peaks. They told her it would take about ten more days of travel to reach the City of Zion. The days were getting colder and even riding in the wagons caused much suffering for those with frozen and frost bitten limbs. Hanna and Mary only suffered from frost bite. Mary knew that the Almighty had spared them from a worse calamity.

As they traveled along one cold and snowy day, a baby was born in a wagon, which never stopped. The child's mother wrapped her in a Temple undergarment. Both baby and mother survived to live to old age. Being born in Echo Canyon, the mother named the child Echo at the suggestion of one teamster.

The brethren told them in a few days they would behold the Prophet's face, which was a great encouragement. The road was easy to travel because the supply wagons heading East packed the snow down. Also, brave young men lived beside the road and kept it passable by driving loose herds of horses back and forth to help pack the snow. This was done from South Pass to Salt Lake City.

That night they set up camp in Echo Canyon where plenty of wood existed to make a warm fire. Therefore, everyone went to sleep in a warm bed. Snow was falling when the bugle to rise blew. The snow stopped falling about mid morning. They pushed the teams to their limit for the teamsters knew snow could trap them within just miles of the City. That night found camp set up on the banks of the Weber River. Friday, November 29, they passed over Big Mountain where the road was so slick and steep at times it took expert driving it keep the wagons upright. Passing over Little Mountain, they camped in the head of Emigration Canyon. Here another train of wagons reached them with supplies.

With morning, came the realization that today the two remaining Ashby's would behold the City of Zion. The first person to start the day's march was the determined little "Scot" and her worn out handcart with its small bundle. As the starved gaunt figure of Margaret Dalglish led the wagons toward the city, she was the symbol of the character of those stuffed under the wagon covers. They were a death defiant and determined lot of people that started many generations of good loyal Americans.

When Margaret Dalglish reached the point of the valley's rim, she pushed her handcart over the edge of the road. With hands on hips, she watched as it rolled, tumbled and smashed to splinters at the bottom of Emigration Canyon. Margaret dusted her hands together and straightened her back with the pride of a conquering hero although rags covered her back. With head held high, she led the three hundred and fifty horses, mules and thirty-two oxen, pulling one hundred and four wagons loaded with cold, sick and hungry souls of the fifth handcart company into the City of Zion. Here she started her new and prosperous life alone.

Zion

Chapter 5

As they drew to a stop in Temple Square, church let out. The Prophet Brigham Young told the waiting congregation that, "A dish of pudding and milk with a baked potato and a little salt would do these weary souls more good than all the prayers of a life time could do." The sick, those with frozen hands, feet and limbs were soon all carried away to the homes of the Saints for nursing. They cared for them as if they were their own children. The Ashby's and those who survived the ordeal in much better shape were left to be taken in by whoever would. Being of the shy and timid nature, the Ashby's soon got lost in the excitement of the hour. Dressed in the clothing sent with the rescuers, they did not stand out in the crowd.

Two lonely, penniless and bewildered figures set out to find a place to call home in this strange barren and bleak land six thousand miles from any thing familiar. As they neared the south edge of the city, they met a Swedish man who excitedly waved his arms and shouted to them in his native tongue. They could not understand him so they hurried on as fast as possible. If they had only known, he was trying to get them to follow him to his house where he and his wives would have taken them in and cared for them.

That night they slept beside the road with no food nor shelter. Two days later found them at the church in Spanish Fork, where they asked the Ward Bishop for help. He said the church and its congregation was too poor to help anyone, except one young man who never turned away anyone in need.

After receiving directions to his home, they soon stood at his door. As they were knocking, a fine handsome looking man came and opened the door. The first thing Mary noticed were his eyes. They had such an intense look in them. Mother very timidly told him who they were and their problem of not having a place to call home. He received them into his home with great kindness and love. As he set about preparing them a fine meal, he told of his wife that had a few days before gave him another son, but was near death with milk fever.

While Mary and Hanna were eating the fine meal that set before them, Hanna and Jeremiah Hatch Murray busily discussed their future. He could not afford to hire them as money and winter supplies were short in the valley. He had contributed heavily to the rescue of the fourth and fifth handcart companies as well as the Hodgett and Hunt ox trains. Jeremiah had sent two good teams with wagons loaded with flour, potatoes, and clothing. Because of Hanna's physical condition and her age he would give her a home as long as she lived if she would let him marry Mary. Hanna soon agreed to this arrangement.

They spent the rest of the day getting acquainted with and caring for the wife Karen Maria Neilson Murray. They would soon grow to love and care for this poor soul as their own sister. Their evening prayers lasted longer than usual because they had many reasons to thank God. Mary and her mother could see the hand of the Deity leading them to this home and went to bed in a very fine feather bed with thankful hearts. It had been more than six months since they had slept in such comfortable surroundings.

The next morning while Hanna was preparing breakfast, Jeremiah took Mary to the stable where he taught her to milk the cows. This would be her job until she had sons old enough to take over. After breakfast, Jeremiah left with a team of oxen pulling a wagon. By noon, the yard filled with men and wagons loaded with material to start building two rooms on the house for Mary and Hanna. Mary took a little time to watch the men as they busily worked together in harmony building her own home.

Mary spent her days cleaning, milking and caring for sister Karen and her baby. The addition to the house did not take long with so many men helping. She had never seen such a lovely room and this was hers to share only with her husband. The day after they finished the room, Jeremiah took the Ashby women to the city for things to furnish their rooms and new clothes. She was happy with the new shoes that her husband bought her. He bought her shoes to wear around the house, shoes to do chores and shoes for Sunday services. Traveling home in the carriage, she looked at her new shoes and thought how good they felt. It was the first time in more than eight months she had shoes for her feet.

The next day Jeremiah's father, who was a bishop, came to marry them. Mary and Jeremiah stood beside Karen's sick bed so she could witness the ceremony.

It saddened Mary to hear the news from the annual council blaming Franklin Richards for the disaster of the newly arrived pioneers. Someone had to be blamed and made a scapegoat, and that fell his lot being head of the European Missions. The Lion of the Lord in his sermon lay down the principle they should have followed. Brigham Young was no one to cross or fail in his expectations of you. Erastus Snow, Franklin Richards and many others suffered under his insulting tirades. To the Gentile, he described exactly the plan brother Richards had followed. Those that had passed through the valley of death could never place blame on anyone. They all voted at Florence to start to the valley with Levi Savage's warning ringing in their ears.

"Strong men...
Stronger coffee"

War with the United States

Chapter 6

The Spring of 1857 brought news that the United States government was planning to send an army led by Col. Albert Johnston against the Latter Day Saint Church in Utah Territory. Their orders from President James Buchanan were to "conquer and annihilate the hated sect."

With this threat hanging over the Saints in Utah Territory, two more handcart companies left Iowa City. The sixth leaving May twenty-two with one hundred and fifty-four souls pushing thirty-one carts, they arrived in Salt Lake City on September eleven. Benjamin Ashby arrived with this company and reunited with his sister Mary and his mother Hanna. The seventh handcart company made up of 303 Danish immigrants pushing sixty-six carts with four supply wagons drawn by mules left Iowa City June 12 and arrived in the valley three days after the sixth company.

Excitement filled the summer as the news spread that the U.S. army was marching against the Saints. Great frontiersmen like Porter Rockwell, Ephraim Hanks, Hosea Stout, with platoons of men were riding the trail as far East as the Platte River Crossing. In the area between the crossing and South Pass, they intercepted the army's supply trains. They did not kill any of the freighters, but, disarmed them and sent them back East on foot with no shoes.

They took the army wagons filled with armaments and supplies to Fort Bridger and the City of Zion. The city made preparations for defense. In Echo Canyon, they built a crude stone wall across the canyon that served as battlements to use the army's own armaments against them. In the wall where the road went, they left a gate that wagons could pass through and they could close. This wall was more than a hundred feet high. It was in a narrow and deep place. This meant that the Mormon men placed on the wall and cliffs would have the army trapped when they came through the canyon. Once in the canyon, they could destroy the army with little loss to the defenders.

Young men like Nelson Merkley armed themselves and waited to do battle at the fortification in Echo Canyon. They were taking the women and children from the city and only the Mormon Legion that consisted of 49,000 men was to remain there. If the army reached the city, they were to leave it in a scorched earth manner, homes, churches, and fields. They piled straw so firing all structures and fields would be easy if the United States Army reached the valley. Those that suffered persecution in Kirkland, Jackson County Missouri, Nauvoo, on the trail of tears, across Iowa and at Florence were ready to fight to the death. They came to the mountains to escape the government's iron hand of death.

Just one year after the great rescue of the pioneers on the plains, the same men that brought them to Zion were setting up defenses to protect their homes and families. At Fort Bridger, the Mormon men led by Apostle Christopher Merkley emptied the Fort and filled it with hay. They were waiting for Col. Albert Johnston and his army to arrive there.

Christopher Merkley set up trading stations along the Overland trail where he traded and sold cattle, horses, wagons and other supplies. At this trading station, he traded fresh draft animals for worn out ones, one fresh for two depleted and food that the Saints grew in the valley. He would trade light wagons for the heavy ones the traveler's animals could no longer pull. This good man was always a blessing to others. He now turned on his fellow man for the protection of his four wives, families and church.

When the army was within five miles, Merkley ordered the brave Mormon men to set Fort Bridger a fire. When the army arrived, they found a smoldering ruin. Because the Mormon mercenaries had taken the army supply wagon train, there was no food, bedding or warm clothing for the soldiers. The army was in such desperate straights they ate their horses and mules for food while they were trying to rebuild the Fort. They made harnesses for the men to drag logs and other materials to rebuild the Fort. Winter was now fully upon them and they were starving.

They survived that long cold winter because the Shoshone Indians had mercy on them. They brought food and showed them how to kill wild game on which to survive. When Spring came in l858, the dejected and defeated army made their long march back to Leavenworth in time to go to the Civil War. The Mormons won the war without a shot being fired.

Moapas Valley

Chapter 7

Again in the valley, peace and prosperity returned. The church asked the Murray clan made up of Bishop John and his son to go on a mission. The church wanted them to settle the Muddy River south of Saint George in Southern Utah. These pioneers were not the claustrophobic or itchy footed frontiersmen as was the average early American settler. Often before, people forced them to move to protect their religious freedom. Most had lived and suffered in Kirkland, Jackson County Missouri, Nauvoo, Florence and lived through the Mormon war. They sold their farms, orchards, homes and business's and became wanderers in search of a new land. They loaded their wagons with plows, seeds, flour, ammunition, machinery and their families. These dear souls knew that there were not any gold fields and the land did not flow with milk and honey. The land was a barren wasteland in the middle of a desert where the chances of starvation were better than fifty-fifty. They would have preferred to stay in the comfort of a developed community, but obeying the command of the Prophet they prepared to leave.

When spring arrived, the Murray clan, along with many Saints under the leadership of Captain Benson, drove south from Salt Lake Valley to open a new country. Upon arriving on the Muddy, they chose a site in which to settle, this was the Moapas valley with the Rio Virgin river running through it. They established the settlements of Overton, Saint Joseph and Saint Thomas. They had ordained Patriarch John Murray to the Quorum of seventy, which made him a Bishop of the Stake church. Warren Foote was the Presiding Elder.

John, his wives' Sarah Bates, Ann Densten and Mary Gale and the multitude of their children were among the pioneers that laid out the towns. Jeremiah took his family and went with his father. Ten days after their arrival, water flowed down the new irrigation ditches. Then they went on to plant corn, sugar cane, cotton, melons and a large variety of garden produce. As the corn ripened, the Indians stole most of it by night. They managed to save a little corn and that along with molasses, melons and garden produce would carry them through to another harvest. The winters were mild and it was a pleasant place to live, but it was not Canaan.

Along the streams in this valley, grew large cottonwood and ash trees. The pioneers soon cut them down and made them into lumber. Building their homes, barns, churches, schools and places of businesses the trees that grew in abundance were soon all gone. In their place they planted the Salt Cedar that originally came from the Middle East. The pioneers soon found that this tree was of no value for making lumber, and it soon became a pest. With the large cottonwood and ash trees gone, the country became more lonely and barren adding to the discouragement of the settlers.

Jeremiah often told the story of when the sea gulls came to Salt Lake Valley. Mary enjoyed hearing it because it made her know that God would take care of them when times and conditions were very hard. In 1848, the crickets came to the valley in a moving massive horde. They ate every living plant. Not only did the crickets eat vegetation, they ate clothing, leather on saddles and harness. They were in the houses and fields. The hordes were like the Egyptian plagues in the Bible. When the plague of crickets was at its worse, great flocks of sea gulls arrived and started eating the pest. They soon had eaten them, saving the Saints from starvation and famine. When times of discouragement came in this new settlement, someone told the sea gull story to encourage the settlers to have faith in their Heavenly Father. Each spring when the gulls arrived, the Saints rejoiced because they knew the crickets would not destroy their crops.

Brigham Young planned to make Overton the river port where the Saints would have access to river boats that connected them with the Gulf of California. The plan was to ship new immigrants to the Isthmus of Panama. Then they and all supplies would travel over land to the Pacific Ocean. From there, ships would carry them to the mouth of the Colorado river. The church would own a fleet of river boats that would go up the stream to Overton on the Muddy Crossing. The plan also had envisioned a railroad connecting Salt Lake City with the Muddy. This port was just a few miles from Saint George, which was where they built the Prophets winter home and the Temple there.

News reached the pioneers that they would never develop the proposed landing at Muddy Crossing into the river port planned by Brigham Young. The railroad would never reach this place. The Union Pacific Railroad had reached Salt Lake City and the immigrants and supplies could come from the East on this rail line. They also learned that they were living in Nevada and the taxes they paid to Utah did not satisfy Nevada officials. It took four years to complete the survey and they were left owing four year's taxes. This did not dissuade the pioneers from developing this land into the Promised Land that would blossom as a rose. When Spring came, they planted crops. However, the Indian problems increased.

Jeremiah's threshing machine

Jeremiah took his family on a trip to Saint George for supplies. On their way back to the Moapas's Valley, they saw five Indians with war paint running toward them. Jeremiah hid the women and children in the wagon under supplies covering them with blankets. Then, he hid in some nearby rocks with his rifle loaded and ready. The Indians reached the wagon all excited looking at the oxen and the wagon. When the chief could not see any thing he wanted in the wagon, he and the others left without taking anything. When the Indians were out of sight, Jeremiah and his family went on their way.

Another time while they were traveling, some Indians came in the night and was going to kill one of their oxen for food. Shooting the oxen with an arrow only wounded the beast, which enraged it. Awakened by the noise, Jeremiah saw the wounded ox trying to gore the man. He raised his rifle and shot the oxen, saving the Red man's life. He soon had part of the dead animal cooking, which he fed to the hungry Indians. Whenever Indian problems occurred, Jeremiah would go to help protect the settlement. When the Indians found out he was there, they left doing no harm, because they remembered the kindness shown to them when he saved the Indian's life.

Because of drought, Indian problems, no waterway and taxes owed to the state of Nevada, the Mormons abandoned two of the settlements in the Moapas Valley. Thus, the Murray clan and the other pioneers returned to the Salt Lake valley. John returned to Spanish Fork and Jeremiah to what would become Murray, Utah. Here Jeremiah returned to his broom making business along with his farming and became a prosperous and wealthy man. With his families on the increase, with many sons and daughters being born to Karen and Mary, Jeremiah gained the respect and admiration of the community.

Thomas Robertson and a few more hardy souls stayed at Overton and started the United Order. This true communal society was after the plan laid out by Joseph Smith. It lasted eleven years.

Uintah Basin

Chapter 8

When Uintah Basin opened for settlements, Brigham Young asked Jeremiah to take his family to this valley. He loaded Mary, her children, their household and farming equipment into wagons and headed for Eastern Utah. He left Karen and her family in Spanish Forks. It broke their hearts to leave this dear wife and sister behind. However, it was necessary for the safety of Jeremiah and his families. They must divide or else he would go to prison and all he had taken from them. The United States Government sent troops and Marshals to the Great Basin to wipe out polygamy. The Edmond-Tucker act passed in Congress making polygamy illegal. It would be seven years before the family reunited.

At this time, the terrible Doctrine of Blood Atonement was reaching its highest proportion. Because of this, the terrible and tragic story of Mountain Meadow Massacre reached the outside world. They accused John Doyle Lee of masterminding this terrible massacre. They butchered one hundred and thirty-five Missourians in that lovely meadow that sad day. Children less than ten, they took and distributed among Mormon families. No one ever again heard of these children.

The only man that escaped the long siege was many miles south on the desert in Nevada. He came across what he presumed to be a squaw man's camp. This squaw man was married to an Indian woman named Rachel. As a tiny baby, One Indian tribe stole Rachel from another tribe. Then they sold her to a white settler by the name of John Allred who was a Bishop in the church. When she grew up, she married John Murray II, brother of Jeremiah. John spent many years with his wife as a missionary, teaching in Indian schools in Northern Arizona.

They received the Missourian with all courtesies. They fed him and gave him a bed roll in which to sleep. That night around the camp fire he told of the tragic siege of the Missouri Immigrant Train near Powran at Mountain Meadow. Also he bragged about being among those that killed the Mormon people in Jackson County, Missouri.

When John, his wife and his family left camp the next morning, the Missourian was left behind, still in bed without his head. They never connected John to Mountain Meadow and he continued his work teaching in Indian schools.

Upon reaching Uintah Basin, Jeremiah chose a farm that would become part of Mill Ward when the organization of the valley was completed. Here in Ashley Valley, he would prosper by the hand of the Almighty. He, Mary and the children started preparing the land for farming. They dug water ditches and cleared fields. Then, they plowed and planted. Also, Jeremiah set out a fine orchard with many different fruits.

Jeremiah set about building Mary a fine brick home in which to raise her sons. He had no place to buy bricks, so he built himself a kiln. He dug the clay and mixed it, placing the wet clay in molds to dry. After they were dry, they could stack them in the kiln to fire. As they took the bricks from the kiln, he would lay them in the walls of the new house. After he finished Mary's house, Jeremiah kept on making brick for the house he would build for Karen Maria.

When completed, it was the very house that Mary and her brother Thomas had dreamed about for so long. Poor Thomas who perished at Independence Rock was never to realize the dream that Mary now lived. Into this new home, she moved her six sons and three daughters. Their names were John Richard, Thomas Ward, Elizabeth (who died when only a few days old), Mary Lovina, Samuel Ashby, Margaret, Jeremiah Hatch, Joseph Smith and William Ashby.

Each fall and spring she and her husband traveled to Salt Lake for the Fall and Spring Church Council. Many of her old friends like Patience, Little Maggie Pucell and Ellen, her sister, would attend these meetings. These old friends would have a grand reunion. These young ladies had all married and were raising families the same as Mary. Little Ellen married and in her life time raised seventeen children on her stub legs that had been cut off below the knee so many years back on the Sweetwater River in Wyoming.

The army increased its persecution and arrest on the families of plural marriages. Friends hid men like Thomas Scofield, who owned woolen and cotton mills in Southern Utah. Maximillen and Robert Parker hid Scofield at their ranch for three years. They took care of this gentle man in safety while the government intimidated and persecuted his two wives.

After three years, Thomas secretly visited his wives' Betty and Mona. Months later word reached Thomas at the Parker Ranch near Circleville that his beloved wife Mona was ready to have another child. He then surrendered to the "demons," U. S. Marshall James Sergeant and Judge Bormon. The government convicted him under the Edmond-Tucker Act that condemned polygamy. He went to the Utah

State Prison for five years. When Marshall Sergeant, came to Betty's house, he walked in without knocking. She was changing her under- clothes. Being a large woman, she grabbed the Marshall by the nap of the neck and by the seat of his pants. She carried him to the door and threw him face down in the dirt in front of his deputies. To get even with Betty, he got a court order for her arrest. He charged her with assault- ing an officer of the law. The local jury ruled her not guilty.

While Thomas Scofield languished in prison, Mona survived with hard work and thrift. The government did not allow Mona or her chil- dren to visit Thomas in prison because the law did not recognize them as his family. After serving his prison time, Thomas came home to be with Betty and her children. He only visited Mona once to tell her he could never live with her again. He asked her to leave the area where they lived so no accusations of having contact with her or the children could be made. Loading her family in a wagon, she moved them to Uintah Basin where she staked a claim. This hard working lady cleared the sage brush, plowed the land and planted her crops and orchard. She also built her self a fine home. She alone raised her family and livestock, and remained in the basin the rest of her life.

After several trying years, the Church could stand the pressure no longer because they had no where else to move. Therefore, President Wilford Woodruff issued the Manifesto of Destiny that put a stop to the Churches official stand on plural marriages. The year was 1890 and they were making many changes all over Utah Territory. The citizens of the Territory were asking to become a State. With the question of polygamy no longer an issue, The U.S. accepted Utah as a State. Jeremiah staked a homestead at Jensen seventeen miles east of Mill Ward, which they now called Maeser Ward. On which, he built a fine brick home and developed the land into a fine farm with an orchard where Karen Maria and her sons and her daughters would live. Then Jeremiah traveled to Spanish Fork to bring his family to Jensen to live.

After returning from Spanish Fork with this family, they settled on the farm and life became prosperous for all. Jeremiah traveled east to Racine Wisconsin and bought a new threshing machine that he brought back to Ashley Valley. The first new threshing machine with the horse power drive that would power the machine arrived at Helper Utah on a train. It took several teams of horses to pull the new threshing ma- chine to the Uintah basin. In addition, it took several other wagons to haul the power machine and other supplies.

As he moved his new threshing machine toward Vernal, he had to repair and build new portions of the road. He paid for this out of his own pocket. Jeremiah built many new bridges and repaired the exist- ing ones. He cut the Juniper trees to use in the construction of the bridges. He did this because the bridges could not support the weight of the thresher. The road was in better condition a few years later when he drove his steam powered tractor, pulling a new and larger threshing machine to Ashley Valley.

The widows with their children could count on this good man to see that they thrashed their crops without a charge being made. The Deities blessed him because he and his family always treated widows, orphans and the homeless with tender care.

The one thing that made Mary the saddest was when her husband's first wife and her dear sister Karen Maria Neilson Murray passed to her rest. After Karen's death, Jeremiah spent his time living with Mary at her home in Maeser Ward. Before that, he spent much of his time traveling between the two families since the sons and daughters did the work to his pleasing. He always drove a fine team of driving mules hitched to a fine carriage. He would drive to Jensen one day, spend the night, a day and the night, then drive back to Maeser Ward spending the same amount of time.

Mary watched as her sons became men and good farmers and stockmen like their Father. She was pleased to see them marry good women, and their sisters marry good men. As her sons became men, they were like their father. They enjoyed digging sagebrush and developing that wasteland into productive farms and pastures. The years of hard work and privations that accompanied the pioneer's life had taken its toll on Jeremiah Hatch Murray. In September of 1909, they laid him to rest. He left a large successful family and the Ashley Valley was now a thriving community.

Mary's youngest son, William Ashby, married Beatrice M. Howarth and she blessed him with four children, Monille, Clarence, Bessie and Beatrice. This wife died leaving him with one son and three daughters under the age of seven. Mary moved to his home to care for the children, the youngest one being just a tiny baby. It was not many months until he married Emma Estella Woodruff, daughter of church President Wilford Woodruff. Two children were born to this union, Virginia and Clara.

When little Clara was eight months old, tragedy struck this family again by taking the mother in death. Again Mary moved to William's house where she could care for the children. When possible, William took one or all the children with him as he worked on his fine ranch. His children sat on the wagon seat beside him or holding to his belt seated behind the saddle on a fine horse. He later married Emma Elizabeth Hughes and they grew old together raising the family to be good citizens. All his life he was a kind and gentle man known as Uncle Bill.

48

Her son, Jeremiah Hatch married Rachel Ellen Merkley, the daughter of Apostle Nelson Merkley. Rachel was the granddaughter of Apostle Christopher Merkley who had preached the everlasting gospel and baptized hundreds to the church. Being an early convert, he lived through the years of terrible persecution with the Saints. He was at Kirkland Ohio, Jackson County Missouri and Nauvoo Illinois. At Kanesville, he built the first ferry, and for three years Christopher was head ferryman on the Missouri River between Kanesville Iowa and Florence Nebraska Territory. As he ferried the Gentile Gold Seekers rushing west to California across the river, he was thankful the Prophet had warned the Saints against the greed that came with the lust for gold.

His many missions took him to places like Canada, Ohio, New York, Illinois and Nevada to pioneer settlements on the Carson and Humboldt rivers. Then he went to California where he worked on the survey crew surveying the eastern border. He was on the mission that built Fort Supply eight miles south of Fort Bridger and hoodwinked Jim Bridger out of his fort. He took his son Nelson with him on mission trips through out the West. These missions would separate him from his family for a year or more.

To the marriage of Hatch and Rachel, were born four sons and two daughters. The eldest son, Ellen named Nelson Ivan. Ivan was very close to his Grandmother Mary. All of Mary's grandchildren loved to hear the stories she told of her home in England and sailing to America. She thrilled them with the story of her trip to Zion.

When Ivan was five years old, they baptized him and other children in the Green River. The only thing that he could ever remember was the men cutting a hole in the ice and how cold the water was. The cold water terrified him. Mary was always so proud of this boy. When he was just a very small boy, Rachel would send Ivan to the jail with dinner for the prisoners. He took the keys, unlocked the cells and gave the prisoners their food. While the prisoners ate, Ivan sat and talked to them. When they finished eating, he would leave locking the cell doors behind. Not one prisoner ever escaped because of the kindness shown by this kind and gentle women and her loving son.

When Rachel Ellen Merkley Murray gave birth to her last child, Deaths Angel took her away two days after the birth. Little Ivan, nine years old, stood by his mother's bedside when she died, after which he was left to be Mother to this small family. There were five little ones to care for: Merle, Milton (Milt), Glen (Penny), Nile, and Ellen. Rachel Ellen's brother Nelson and his wife Kate took the last baby girl born to raise as their own. Mary soon came to live with Hatch to care for the children that he treated so unkindly.

RAY PECK
"Quarter Bushel"

Lawman

Chapter 9

J. Hatch was always angry because he came from a family that practiced polygamy, he felt cheated by having to share his father with another family. His fathers' first family acted as if Mary and her children never existed. He blamed women for the plural marriages and had no respect for them. He said the only sin the Church ever committed was to command men to take more than one wife. As far as his own children, he had no interest in them, he was now Sheriff of Vernal, Utah. Everybody who knew Jeremiah Hatch Murray liked him. He took his civic duties very seriously. His fearless character in the face of danger made him one of the most feared and leading sheriffs in Utah.

Hatch worked many years as Sheriff Pope's Deputy. Over the years, he dealt with some of the most famous outlaws in the history of the West. He learned their ways and how to deal with them. During that time, he became acquainted with Butch Cassidy or better known to the Mormons as Robert Leroy Parker, grandson of Maximellen Parker. The Parker family traveled and suffered with the Ashby family in the fifth handcart company. Mary was interested in this young man and saddened when he chose a life of crime. Because of their feelings toward the United States Government, they would hide and protect him and his friends. People looked upon him as a modern day Robin Hood, because he stole from the rich and gave to the poor. He and his friends had no mercy on the rich Gentile companies.

The people in Eastern Utah and Western Colorado would not turn in Butch Cassidy, Elzey Lay, Matt Warner and the McCarteys. These young men were robbers, not murderers. They stole from banks, mine pay rolls, the Union Pacific Railroad and drove herds of cattle and horses for many miles to an area where no one recognized them. After they sold the herds, they generously shared their money with many a Mormon settler living in the great basin.

Because of their generosity, the settlers kept saddle horses in their corrals at night so if these young men hurriedly passed by, they would have fresh mounts to ride. When there was a jaded horse in their corral when daylight came, the settlers quickly hid the horse so if a Federal Marshal was close by they would not find it and intimidate or arrest the settler.

Young Hatch helped Sheriff Pope capture and take Elzey Lay to the Utah Penitentiary. To Sheriff Pope, it was more of a game than an official duty. Butch Cassidy and his friends made the brag that there was not a Sheriff alive that could take them to a State Penitentiary. One day Hatch and Sheriff Pope happened to find Elzey Lay in one of the little outlying outposts too drunk to move. He placed him in handcuffs, threw him in a wagon and hauled him back to Vernal.

Sheriff Pope and Deputy Hatch left for Ogden and the State Penitentiary in the night with Elzey Lay chained to a horse. They went straight north to the top of the Uintah Mountains where they followed the top of those mountains west to where they dropped off near Salt Lake City. Butch Cassidy, Matt Warner and the McCarteys found out about Elzey's capture and set out on the road toward Salt Lake to stop the Sheriff and the Deputy from reaching there. This time they vowed to kill anyone that dared place them in chains.

After leaving Elzey Lay at the Utah Penitentiary, the lawmen rode home on the main road, defying those outlaws trying to stop them. Lay spent three years in the Utah Penitentiary. After getting out, he went straight. He and his wife raised a large family. He never got in trouble again.

The local sheriffs were always trying to capture and take them to prison but this was a game on both sides. When a Pinkerton Detective or a Federal Marshal ordered any local lawmen to take them to Robbers Roost country, the local law always rode a white horse and wore a white hat and shirt. This was a warning sign that the law was coming. This is where we get the saying, "The good guys all wear white hats." This was the locals way of warning the outlaws that an outside lawman was approaching.

From the Roost, you could see anyone coming for many miles around. Many lawmen drank fresh warm coffee and ate a fresh cooked meal when they arrived at the Roost, but they never found anyone. Many Federal Marshals and Pinkerton Detectives started to the Roost but they and their horses would perish from the heat and lack of water. Also, getting lost in the maze of canyons was easy. Several died because they got lost and could not find their way out. The local law knew where the water was or how to find it.

Rimrocker Joe Biddlecome, his wife Millie and their daughters lived eight miles south of Robbers Roost at Crow Seep where there was a spring flowing to a pond giving water for man and beast. At Robbers

Checkin the Brand

Roost, Joe fenced the spring and built wooden troughs that held water where his cattle and horses could get a drink. The Biddlecomes knew the outlaws and their activities but never betrayed their trust. All men good or bad were welcome to their ranch and received with hospitality and friendship with no questions asked. Hatch became a good friend of Joe, when he made the long ride across the Green River desert he would rest a few days at Crow Seep Ranch.

Once a federal marshal ordered sheriff Pope and his deputies to go on a trip into Northeast Utah's Brown's Park country to help him capture the Cassidy bunch. Brown's Hole or Park is a valley that lays where Utah, Colorado and Wyoming all meet. This valley is almost equally divided among the three states, with the Green River running through the center of the valley. It is about sixty miles long and averages five to fifteen miles wide. The winters are very mild and they sometimes call it the banana belt. Because of its geographic location nearly sixty miles from any town, it made a perfect hang out for the most desperate of men. Lawmen never liked to go there because the outlaw would ride to another part of the valley and be out of his jurisdiction. Only a Federal Marshal could travel the whole valley. This Marshal had information of their location and was sure they would still be there because it was in the winter. The Marshal chose Hatch as guide because he knew the country very well. When night came, he persuaded the Marshal to set up camp in the mouth of a canyon where he knew the outlaws stayed. That way they had them as good as captured.

Butch and his friend's had been watching the mouth of that canyon and had seen the lawmen on their white horses. Coming from fun loving Mormon backgrounds, they decided to play a prank on the Marshal. Sometime during the night they slipped into the Marshal's camp, stole the lawmen's boots, saddles and horses. When morning came, they discovered the prank. While walking, they swore they would make a capture or die trying. After walking several miles to a ranch with their feet in their cut off coat sleeves, they lost all interest in the outlaws. The local rancher had a good laugh and that marshal never graced that country again.

Three men escaped from the Utah State Prison by the names of Harry Tracy, David Lant and Pat Johnson. They all came to Browns Hole to hide out. They threw in with "Judge" Jack Bennet who was a local cow thief but not a desperado. "Judge" Bennet would work for the local ranchers and from time to time butcher a fat steer and sell it to the local miners. William Strang was a prospector from Kentucky that had come west for his health and had enjoyed becoming a strong man again. Due to the location of his mine in the high elevation of Douglas Mountain, one winter his wife caught pneumonia and died leaving two teen age sons.

About this time, three young men from Browns Hole decided they could rob banks as well as the Cassidy Bunch. They rode seventy miles southeast to Meeker, Colorado where they would start their life of crime. They stole extra horses and left them tied to trees in several locations so after the great robbery they would have fresh mounts for the ride back home. The three rode into Meeker with a mighty big opinion of their ability as bank robbers. When they walked into the bank, they stuck their guns in the face of Banker Oland. He was the only one in the bank. This tough old rancher was not about to let kids that were not dry behind the ears get the best of him. He shot through the front of the teller's desk killing the one making the demands. The other two fled in terror with him right on their heels. He shot one as he mounted his horse. A man coming out of Oland's general store shot the other robber. This ended the crime career of those young men. Later they found their extra horses starved to death still tied to the tree.

Father Strang left Willie with Albert "Speck" Wellhouse who ran a ferry on Green River, when he went to Rocks Springs, Wyoming for supplies. Albert Speck had been born a slave. He gained his freedom as General Sherman marched to the sea. Being a child, he followed Sherman on that long march. After growing up, Speck came West with a wagon train hauling freight for the army. Willie's only dream was to be able to rope and ride like Ebb Basset whose ability to rope and handle wild cows and horses were famous in these parts. Willie soon tired of the old man's stories and his philosophy of "I'se to busy minden

54

my own business to get into other folk's." Tracy and his friend's rode by the ferry one day and let Willie ride one of their horses. This made him beg to go along with them when they left. One of them rode off and in a while returned leading a horse for Willie.

Willie went along with these men when they returned to the Valentine Hoy ranch where they were working. Things went quite well for a few days because the men liked the boy. One morning after a night of hard drinking, the men stayed in bed till the middle of the day. This made Willie angry because he wanted to be about his cowboy life. He took a dipper of cold water from the bucket on the table and threw it in Harry Tracy's face. Harry was instantly wide awake with a gun in hand. As Willie ran from the house, Harry shot him in the back. Willie did not die instantly. While the other men were saddling horses and loading one with a camp outfit, Pat Johnson made the kid comfortable until he died. The Hoy's had moved a few miles away to another ranch and left a Mr. and Mrs. Blair at the home ranch. After the three men left, Mr. Blair who was eighty years old walked five miles to the John Chew sheep ranch to summon help.

Someone went to the sheriffs at Hahn's Peak, Colorado, Rocks Springs, Wyoming and Vernal, Utah to get them and their deputies to come to the Hole and help capture these outlaws. Sheriff Charles Willis Neiman and Deputy Ethan Farnham from Colorado left Hahn's Peak in a sled drawn by a team of fast traveling horses. When they reached the town of Lay, they borrowed a spring wagon from the Post Mistress Wilingham. Although snow was covering the ground, the road turned too muddy for a sled. When Sheriff Neiman and his deputy were within a few miles of the Bassett ranch, they saw three men leading a pack horse but were never close enough to see who they were. When he arrived at the Bassett ranch, a large posse was there including Sheriff Pete Swanson and his deputies from Wyoming.

The sheriff at Vernal sent three deputies over Diamond Mountain. The three were (Jerry) Hatch Murray, Pete Dillman and a man named Thompson. After crossing Diamond Mountain and entering the valley, they met "Judge" Jack Bennett with three heavily loaded pack horses. Upon questioning Bennett, he told them he was leaving the country and knew nothing about the Strang boy's killing. They placed him under arrest and continued toward the Bassett ranch. When they came to a gate with a cross bar overhead, they placed a rope around the "Judges" neck and hanged him. They thought he was a part of the crime because he was a friend of Lant, Tracy and Johnson. They thought he was taking supplies to them, although he said he was leaving Brown's Hole forever. Upon reaching the Bassett ranch they found out that he had nothing to do with the crime and was really leaving the country.

Although it was winter most of the men had to stay outside by a large bonfire the first night they were in Brown's Hole. When morning came, the Bassetts fed the men breakfast. Then sheriff Nieman led the large posse to where he saw the three men and their pack horse. This portion of Brown's Hole was in Colorado making it in his jurisdiction. Nieman had spent several years working for the Two Bars cattle company in this very area. The trail was easy to find and follow. After a few miles, the posse came on the camp of the outlaws and surprised them. The outlaws tried to escape by climbing a steep hill where they could hide in a boulder field. The sheriff saw the men and told his posse they would set up a siege that would starve and freeze them into surrendering. The local ranchers said they would not wait but would rather fight it out now.

Valentine Hoy was a man of peace and told sheriff Nieman he would climb up to the outlaws and talk them into surrendering. Nieman knew whom he was dealing with and argued against any negotiations, but the locals out numbered him. Nieman, Valentine, Jim McKnight and deputy Farnham started climbing the steep hill to where the outlaws remained hidden. When they were within thirty feet of the rocks where the three were hiding, Valentine Hoy lay down his gun. With hands up, he started talking while he was walking the last few feet, while the others hid behind rocks. Sheriff Nieman's instincts had been right because when Valentine was fifteen feet away, all three outlaws shot, killing him instantly.

Nieman, McKnight and Farnham scrambled back to where the rest of the posse was waiting. Hatch Murray suggested they move back to a knoll that would give them a complete view of the mountain side and be out of rifle range. All day the posse watched that boulder field waiting for the outlaws to leave, but they stayed put. Valentine's body was in a kneeling position over a large rock where he had fallen. As night drew on, the posse rode back to the Bassett ranch taking the outlaws' horses and camp outfit with them. Nieman and Murray felt the outlaws would try to walk out of the valley and by morning be out in the open so there would be a fair fight.

Early the next morning, the posse was in the saddle riding back to the outlaws camp when they came across the trail made by three men on foot. The outlaws had walked to Ladore Canyon where they traveled twenty miles down the stream on the ice frozen along the river bank. When the canyon narrowed and the river became so rapid it would not freeze, they turned around and retraced their way out of the canyon. The lawmen found the back trail the three had made five miles out in the open. They had found a wild mare with a small colt. Killing the colt they ate their fill of raw meat. Lant and

Johnson made shoes from the green hide as their boots had worn out from the many miles they had traveled. The green hide soon froze and made walking almost impossible. When the posse found them, they eagerly surrendered.

With the capture made, a few men went to bring Valentine's body back to the home ranch. Later, they shipped his body to Fremont Nebraska where he came to rest in the family cemetery plot. Having no hand cuffs, they bound the men with pieces of rope. Tracy soon had his hands worked free. While no one was watching, he grabbed the bridle reins from the one that was leading him. Spurring his horse, he soon was out of sight. Nieman sent half the posse with Farnham and the two captured men, while he took the rest to recapture Tracy. Wyoming sheriff, Pete Swanson, had a warrant for David Lant so he and his deputies took charge of him. He rode onto a ranch in the Wyoming section of Brown's Hole where he would not lose his man.

At the Basset ranch, Ethan Farnham placed Pat Johnson tied on a chair fastened to the bunk house wall, where he stood guard himself. The Utah posse decided they would save the tax payer's money if they hanged Johnson. They cut the sleeves off their slickers and after making eye holes in them pulled these masks over their heads. They knocked on the door and told Ethan they had brought supper. When the door opened, the deputy looked down three gun barrels. Once inside they disarmed and tied Ethan to a chair. With hands tied behind his back, Pat Johnson cried, whimpered and begged for his life while they carried him to sheriff Nieman's spring wagon under the bar of the corral gate. They placed a rope around his neck, which they threw over the bar tying the other end to a post leaving a little slack.

These amateur Hangmen did not leave enough slack for the drop to break his neck. While they were eating supper in the house, Josie Bassett McKnight looked out the kitchen window and saw the hanged man still gyrating. Ebb Bassett found Ethan Farnham tied to the chair and cut him free. Then they cut Johnson down and dragged him a few yards up a draw and buried him in a shallow grave.

When sheriff Nieman returned to the ranch, they told him the story. To avoid another lynching, he set extra guards on Tracy, while he rode to the ranch where Wyoming Sheriff Swanson was. Upon arriving at the ranch, he talked Swanson out of his prisoner. He returned with David Lant to the Bassett ranch where early the next morning he tied the two outlaws in the spring wagon. After two days of travel they reached Hahn's Peak safely. It would have changed history if he had let the Utah Posse hang Tracy and Lant, it seems jails could not hold those two. A posse near Walla Walla, Washington, surrounded Harry Tracy in a wheat field. The field was set a fire, thus ending his life.

David Lant was recaptured and sent to prison. Upon release, he took the name David Stillwell and returned to Northwestern Colorado. He spent his life herding sheep or any other ranch work he could find. He lived in a sheep wagon pulled by four matched black horses. He never stayed in the same place for more than a few days. When he got old he took a gun and blew his brains out. Hatch always cussed and said, "We should have hung him when we had the chance."

When sheriff Charles Willis Nieman and deputy Ethan Farnham left with Harry Tracy and David Lant hogtied in their spring wagon that morning, law and peace at last arrived to Brown's Hole. For one hundred years the lawless white man had ruled supreme. This valley had been the wintering place for the peaceful White River Ute Indians from the beginning of their time on the western slope until their removal to the White Rocks Indian reservation in Uintah Basin. The fur traders had used this valley for the greatest rendezvous ever attended. The worst outlaws the West produced followed the trappers. The good white men settled here to make it their home. Mountain men like Jim Bridger, William H. Ashley, Babtiste Brown, Phil Thompson, William Craig and poor crippled Bibleback Brown to name a few, most of whom were connected with either the American Fur Company or Hudson Bay Fur Company.

A few years before this, Doc Kaiser came to the country just east of the Colorado border, a days ride from Vernal. He lead one old blind steer and with him started the K Ranch. In a few years, he had "acquired" a very large herd of cattle by using a long rope tied to his saddle on a fast horse. Doc was very hospitable to whoever rode by. They were always welcome to a meal and bed. He never questioned his guest about their past, present or future.

One cold January morning when the sheriff and his deputies arrived at the office, there was a very excited man waiting. He told them the Cassidy bunch was holed up at the K ranch. The lawmen were soon on the trail East to make the much coveted capture. The snow was belly deep on the horses, making travel difficult. They arrived at ten o'clock in the evening at the K Ranch hungry, cold and tired. They unsaddled their horses and turned them into a pen with a hay stack so the horses would have feed and shelter.

When they went in the house, they found the outlaws seated along one wall with Doc holding a gun on them. He had their guns all piled on a table behind him. When the lawmen had taken their coats and chaps off, Doc turned the captured outlaws over to the sheriff. While Doc set about fixing a meal, he brought out a bottle of his famous Barley Wine just as an appetizer. With an empty stomach, they soon forgot they were hungry and turned very sociable as if they were the host. Doc supplied more Barley and he passed drinks all around. As the barley began to make them feel better, the more they forgot why they had ridden so far on a cold day. They had a fine party. They talked a lot and played cards until all lost conscientiousness. Ole Doc never partook of the treats and so early the next morning he awoke the whole bunch to start them on their separate ways. After saddling their horses, they all shook hands at Doc's request and left in opposite directions. Only after a good many miles riding in the cold toward home did the lawmen realize the trick Doc and Butch had pulled on them.

A few months later they stole a large herd of horses from Ashley Valley. The rancher reported to the sheriff of his loss. As the lawmen picked up the trail, the tracks showed there were only two shod horses. This lead Sheriff Pope to believe that just two men were driving the stolen animals. The local rancher's horses were not shod. The trail led south past Desolation Canyon on toward the Robbers Roost country. The sheriff and his two deputies took spare horses so that when one played out there would be fresh ones to ride. In three days, they were beginning to see fresh droppings on the trail indicating they were very close behind the horses. When they reached Crescent Junction, a man was leaving to the South in a big hurry. When they made inquiries about the rider, they were told he was the mail carrier going to Moab.

At the store in Crescent Junction, the owner did all he could to delay the posse from leaving. This made them wonder about the rider leaving in such a hurry as they rode into town. The posse rented fresh horses and left on the trail as fast as their horses could stand the travel. Upon reaching Moab, they met Matt Warner and a man that gave his name as Joe Wall. Deputy Hatch Murray noticed the brands on the horses Warner and Wall were riding. They were two of the stolen horses. Hatch pulled his gun and arrested the two men. They left the two thieves in the custody of the local sheriff. They then searched the country for the rest of the horses. The horse herd seemed to have vanished from the earth so after three days of searching they took the prisoners and rode back to Vernal.

When they reached Vernal, they jailed the outlaws in the courthouse. A warrant was waiting the sheriff for Warner's arrest on charges he killed a man on Diamond Mountain. They posted extra guards at the courthouse because word had reached town saying that a group of Warner's friends was coming to set him free. When the friend's arrived, the deputies let them in the courthouse hallway. Then they shut the doors on each end, locking them in the building. At the same time, the sheriff and deputy Murray took the prisoners out the back door and started to Ogden. They arrived safely at the prison. Matt spent five years there. They could not prove the murder charges.

A few months after Warners arrest, a cowboy found the stolen horses starved to death on what they now call Dead Horse Point near Moab. This high bluff had only one trail leading to the top. The two thieves had made a pole fence across the trail, shutting the horses on the bluff when word had reached them the law was near. The "Mail Carrier" that had sped away from Crescent Junction had given the warning. Warner and Wall planned to return in a few hours to feed and water the horses. At the bottom of the bluff, they found a few horses who jumped to their death trying to reach water in the river. The rest died on the bluff.

End of an Era

Chapter 10

The increase of new settlements in Northwestern Colorado, Eastern Utah and the Red Desert of Southwestern Wyoming brought an end to the free open range pastures that the large English cattle companies had long used. As they looked for pastures elsewhere, they soon moved their operations and horse herds to South America. The new settlements had the same effect on the outlaws of the area. Butch Cassidy and Harvey Longbaugh decided they wanted to stop running so they followed the large cattle companies to the South. For a while they were content to work as cowboys, but this proved too dull a life for them. They robbed a Tin Mines payroll and stopped at a hacienda to enjoy their newly acquired wealth.

The Federalies soon were on their trail in hot pursuit, seeing the posse coming they fled. As they were leaving, two American Cowboys were riding into the hacienda, so Butch told them to flee with him. Having done nothing wrong, they refused and rode into the ambush. The lawmen thinking they had killed Butch and Harvey closed the case of the wild bunch. Butch and Harvey came back to Oregon and lived out their lives as peaceful citizens.

Matt Warner, as he grew older, became tired of the life on the run and wanted to spend time with his wife and family. He went back to Circleville and started a saloon in which he prospered. People in Circleville wanted Matt to run for Sheriff and he finally agreed to do so. Being afraid to use the name Matt Warner thinking no one would vote for an ex-outlaw, he used his given name Willard Christensen. Not knowing who this Christensen was, the people voted for the other man and Matt lost the election. When asked why his name was not on the ballot, he told them it was. He explained that he had used his given name Willard Christensen. The people of the county were so angry his business was slow for many months but eventually they forgave him. He never ran for a political office again. He died in 1924, a tired old man.

Wiskey Runnin

"They Killed the only good one of the outfit"

D E Murray

Growing Up and Criminal Justice

Chapter 11

When Ivan was seven years old, Hatch brought a herd of three and four-year-old wild horses to the ranch. As Ivan looked in the corral at these fine horses, a big buckskin took his fancy and he pleaded with Father to let him have it. "Well kid if you think you are man enough to have a horse, then you have to earn it like any other man. You have to break him to ride." Hatch roped and snubbed the bronc colt up to another horse and saddled it. When Ivan got on, Hatch turned that bronc loose. The horse exploded, jumping, turning, and twisting in every direction at once. It was too much horse for a seven-year-old boy. The bronc sent Ivan flying. Hatch laughed and started calling him Sky because that bronc had thrown him "sky high." Ivan resented it, but the name stuck with the family.

Ivan kept on trying until he could finally ride that bronc. When he did, Hatch told him he was a man now and he could now start smoking, which he did. He smoked the cowhand's tobacco called Bull Durham that came in small sacks with a package of papers in which they made the cigarettes. He smoked this kind of "makens" for fifty years.

With the excitement of the outlaws in the past, life in Eastern Utah became slow and routine. Hatch was elected sheriff and prospered on his ranch. Little Ivan was being the mother to his brothers and sister as well as carrying the responsibility of running the ranch. He would take the sheep to pasture in the mountains where he or Milt would herd them. He also irrigated the hay and crop fields and checked on the range cattle.

Early every spring, Hatch went to Winnemuca, Nevada, and bought a herd of steers with the roundup wagon and saddle horse herd. He would take his two small sons Ivan and Milt along to help drive these large herds back to Uintah Basin in Eastern Utah. Some years he would hire men in Nevada but usually he would take a crew from Uintah Basin to drive the cattle home. These drives would take over a month because it was five hundred miles of herding the beasts home.

They expected Ivan and Milt to take their turn on night herd with the grown men.

School was one thing Ivan enjoyed because he had a keen mind and learned very fast. He enjoyed arithmetic the most. He could soon add large numbers, multiply and divide. School was easy and when he had his lessons learned he would think of ways to tease the teacher. The thing he most enjoyed teasing the teacher with was saying the alphabet backwards from Z to A. When Ivan finished the third grade of Mormon primer, he never had time to attend school again. With Mother dead and the small children to care for along with the work father assigned, he never had time for school.

The one thing Ivan enjoyed was to watch the Price Vernal Stage arrive in town. The driver would blow a bugle when they were a mile from town. Ivan loved to watch those fine coach horses run into town.

One cold winter morning, Ivan and Father butchered a large steer so the family would have fresh meat to eat. When they finished butchering, they hung the carcass on the derrick that they used to stack hay. They had cut the carcass in half length wise. This left the two pieces to freeze solidly over night so it would keep and not spoil.

The next morning when Ivan and Milt started to the barn to milk the dairy cows, they noticed that half the beef was gone. Leaving their buckets, they ran to the house to tell Father. Hatch told Ivan to saddle his horse, while he was putting on his chaps and coat.

The boys went about their morning chores as their sheriff father rode away following wagon tracks in the snow. The tracks led to the desert southeast of town. After several miles, he came to a homesteader's cabin were the wagon tracks led to the front porch. He never stopped but turned his horse around and headed home. Upon reaching home, he and Ivan hitched a team of horses to the bobsled and put the other half of the beef in the sled. Hatch started back down the trail he had just come hauling the second half of the beef to the homesteader. When he arrived, he drove his team as close to the porch as possible and rolled the half of beef onto the porch.

As he was driving away, the man came to the door and shouted, "What are you doing?" Hatch hollered back, "Well, if I had known you and your family was starving, I would have driven the live steer over here and you could have helped me butcher it. This would have saved us both a trip."

Known for his laziness, the Homesteader borrowed things at night never to return them. He had a very large family that was always hungry and bordered on near nakedness. Hatch looked out the sheriff's office window that afternoon and saw the homesteader going from store to store. Hatch became interested in what was happening so he went to one of the stores and asked what the homesteader was doing.

The store keeper told the sheriff that he was looking for a job. The homesteader found a job and in a few months moved his family to a pleasant home in town. After several years, he owned a business and became a liked and trusted citizen. Many years later he told Hatch that getting caught stealing the half of beef and Hatch bringing him the other half to his door was what made him change his life from thievery to productivity.

That winter Ivan caught a cold that settled in his lungs. Grandmother Mary took him to the Doctor who said, "The boy has pneumonia, take him home and put him to bed. If he survives, he will never amount to much." After several weeks of near death, the lad did survive, which made Mary very happy.

A farmer that lived in Ashley Valley was notorious for his ability to get drunk. He drank a lot and was very cruel to his family. The family had to do the work on his farm. If it did not suit him, he gave the offending child a cruel beating. The neighbors had talked to Sheriff Murray many times about the abuse. Hatch had warned him that it must stop. The farmer always promised to treat his family better but in a short time he reverted to his old ways. The sheriff locked him in jail on several occasions until the farmer was sober. The farmers always promised to quit drinking. When in his drunken rages, the wife always bore the brunt of his extreme cruelty. Often he beat her until she was unconscious.

One evening, he came home drunker and meaner than usual. He beat his poor wife to death and left the children in very bad condition. Then he rode to a neighbor's farm where he told them he had killed his worthless wife. He then galloped his horse out of their yard down the road to the west.

The word of this tragedy soon spread through the neighborhood. Then, someone rode to tell the sheriff who was at home eating supper. Sheriff Murray sent those who came to him with the news to summon his deputies to meet at the courthouse. By the time all had reached the courthouse, there was a crowd of people gathered where they told many different stories of what happened and where the farmer went. The sheriff went to the farm where the dead lady was. He found that the farmer beat the children as well. Kind neighbors brought the doctor who cared for the children. He dressed their wounds. The neighbors helped comfort the children.

The gathering crowd talked about using their lariat to teach the farmer a lesson and set an example for anyone else who treated women and children that way. When the sheriff asked if any knew which way he had gone, there was much confusion to which way he had ridden. After a while, they decided that he rode east toward Blue Mountain. The sheriff and his deputies knew that many hours had passed since the crime occurred so the farmer would be many miles away. It might take several days of hard riding to catch up with him. When they started on the search, they stopped by their homes and loaded a pack horse with a camp outfit and bed rolls. By daylight, the posse was at the Green River ready to swim their horses across.

They pushed their horses hard for most of the day, stopping at ranches making inquiries about the criminal. They searched for several days but could not even find any tracks that showed a horse and rider going in that direction. They gave up the search and rode for two days back to Vernal. As they neared the courthouse, they smelled something that made them sick to their stomachs and the horses refused to go near. The smell they found was the farmer hanging from a cottonwood tree in front of the courthouse. The hot July sun had caused him to bloat and swell to three times his normal size.

Sheriff Murray sent one deputy to find a grave digger and the other deputy to his ranch to have Ivan bring a team of horses and wagon. When Ivan was within two blocks of the courthouse, the horses refused to go any farther toward the hanging man. Ivan, the sheriff and his deputies had to pull the wagon by hand to the tree so they could cut the dead man down. They then pulled the wagon by hand to the cemetery. The smell in the wagon from the body was so bad that it you couldn't get rid of it. Finally they gave up and burned the wagon. Upon investigation, the sheriff found out that while he was at the farm where the wife lay dead a group of men had already caught the farmer and was only waiting for the posse to go East. The vigilantes hanged the murderer just before day light so no one would know who they were. Young Ivan never forgot that horrifying sight and smell.

The Mormon communities in Ashley Valley were peaceful at the beginning of the pioneer days, but as the valley grew there were those that moved in that were not of the Mormon Faith. Many arriving in the valley, brought their loathsome habits with them as we have seen. They started a saloon on main street a long with all its vice. A mule skinner that hauled freight for the Denver and Rio Grande railroad from Helper to Vernal was an example of the type that was coming to the valley. This man thought he could do as he pleased by drinking and abusing women.

One hot August day as he was entering the valley with his twenty mule team and two wagons, he met a young lady on the road. He stopped her, then proceeded to give her a beating and raped her in a very violent manner. After which, he drove onto town as if nothing had happened. He left her beside the road. Someone soon came by and found the body.

The Freighter was unloading his wagons when one of his friends told him they were men looking for him because of what he had done to the young lady. He quickly saddled his horse and left town with the lady's family in hot pursuit. A short time later someone told Sheriff Murray about the terrible deed. The sheriff and his deputies along with other good men started after the criminal. The day was very hot. This made them travel much slower so their horse would not over heat and die. The trail led south toward the Green River Desert where this country was very hot and rugged. When the posse reached the area near Desolation Canyon, they found the freighters worn out horse, but could not find the man. The posse decided the man must have gotten lost or was trying to walk over the desert to Thompson. Either way he would die of heat and thirst, so they went back home.

The next spring a sheep herder came to the sheriff's office with a corpse dried to a mummy. The sheepherder said he found it hidden in a canyon where it was sitting naked with his private parts nailed to a tree stump. After several weeks, the county coroner and the sheriff decided that it was the freighter's body. Vigilantes caught him and stripped his cloths off, nailing him to the stump. It was very noticeable how the bad element soon left the country bringing peace to Ashley Valley. No one ever admitted to knowing who hanged the farmer on the courthouse tree or nailed the freighter to that stump, but all were thankful to whomever they were.

Sheriff Hatch Murray received a visit from an Indian agent and a federal marshal wanting him to help investigate who was selling whiskey to the Indians. For Several months the Indians on the White Rock Reservation were drinking whiskey in an alarming amount. The Indians acted as if they never understood what the agent or marshal was talking about when they questioned them concerning the source of the contraband. They asked sheriff Murray not to say any thing about the whiskey to the local population. They wanted him to be an under cover agent for the federal government, which he agreed to do.

In a few days after the visit about the Indian whiskey, Hatch received a letter from the Governor of Utah. The Governor asked him to come to Salt Lake as soon as possible. Upon arriving at the Governors Office, the Governor talked to him about the Indian whiskey. He presented Hatch with a new nickel barreled 30-40 repeating Winchester Rifle. They made this gun for the Colorado Cavalry. It had a short barrel that made it easy to carry and fire from a horse. They also asked him to serve on the Utah State Firing Squad for the execution of criminals. Before he left the Salt Lake Valley, he did this duty along with two other sheriffs.

Checking on a complaint one day, Hatch rode by the out post of Dragon Utah. This place consisting of several low dirt roofed log cabins that housed a store, hotel and bar. A man named Bill Calthorpe owned all the buildings. Also, there was a bunkhouse, icehouse, saddle and harness storage, as well as a warehouse for supplies to be kept for the store, hotel and bar. There were many people living at this trading post, most of whom worked for Bill. Miners from the Gilsonite mine ten miles to the south, Indians from the nearby White Rock Reservation, cowboys, sheep herders, homesteaders and those traveling through the area patronized the convenience of this oasis in the desert.

Bill's two brothers and two sisters helped him run the operation. His sister Mary kept house for Bill and never took part in the activities of this place. Although she hated what went on around her, she stayed, thinking she had no choice in the matter. She could drive a six horse hitch on a freight wagon better than most men. Mary always drove a team and wagon when they went to Rangley, Colorado, forty miles to the east for supplies. This trip broke the monotony of her existence. Her only enjoyment of living at this place was the green fields and the Green River. Dragon was situated on the East bank of this river where life giving water was available for man, beast and irrigation for the fields.

Bill's bar and hotel were famous for their whiskey and young beautiful whores. Bill purchased these young women from the poor homesteaders in the surrounding country, paying from five hundred to one thousand dollars for them. He always took them to Denver, Colorado, where he purchased fine clothes and married them. Back at Dragon when he tired of them or found a new one that suited his fancy better, he would set the one he tired of on the bar where they would be on display for anyone to buy for a few minutes of pleasure. There was always a mystery about their disappearance when they became infected with a venereal disease or grew old before their time and were no longer profitable.

Bill was one of Hatch's cousins. The sheriff talked to him hoping he would have some information about the case he was checking on, as well as seeing if he could secretly learn anything about the Indian whiskey. He stayed a couple of days enjoying the hospitality, thinking he could get some information from one of the young ladies. There was gambling to fill the time not spent in other activities. The sheriff could not receive any information on either case so he rode back home, suspecting Bill of being the whiskey runner.

Caught in a Blizzard

Chapter 12

The Mormons started raising sheep with financial backing from the Church. The Church officials hoped by using the sheep to ruin the range they could gain more territory to settle in nearby Western Colorado. There were clashes of violence between the Mormon sheep men and the Colorado cattle men. Colorado cattleman Tom Berry and his hired men killed a fifteen-year-old boy. Then, they clubbed his three hundred sheep to death because the boy had strayed one fourth of a mile inside Colorado. At DeBeque, Colorado, a group of masked men tied two sheep herders to a tree and drove their flock of three thousand sheep over a five hundred-foot cliff. The herders escaped to the nearby town of Parachute where they sent Federal Marshals a telegram telling of the crime.

The Marshals knowing they would not get any help from the local Colorado sheriffs because they were either cattlemen or owned by the Cattleman Association. So they came to Vernal Utah asking sheriff Murray if he would ride to DeBeque helping them to solve the crime and arrest the guilty ones. The sheriff had been looking east to the area near Aspen and Crested Butte to pasture his sheep in the high mountains for the summer. He felt if a few of these cattlemen received a necktie party, they would leave the Mormon sheep men alone. Then he could safely take his sheep to Colorado.

The lawmen rode east to Rangley where they spent the night. Before daylight the next morning, they were riding south on the road that led to Douglas Pass. Reaching the summit of the Pass, they turned East for a few miles to the head of Roan Creek, which they followed to the town of DeBeque that was on the bank of the Grand River. (Later named the Colorado River.) Reaching there after two hard days ride, they made inquiries about shipping and receiving cattle. Also, they asked if there was available range on which to turn a herd loose. This did not let the local people know what their real mission was. With the pretense of looking for pasture for a soon arriving herd of cattle, they could learn about the feeling toward the encroaching sheep men.

Two young men whose names were Preston (Pres) and Peter (Pete) Stoner agreed to show the new cattlemen the range north of town on the high Shale Oil plateau. For several days, they looked over the range and saw evidence that sheep had grazed there. When they asked Pres about the sheep, he told them a group of cattlemen drove the herd of sheep over a rim. After hearing the news, the rest of the sheep men left this area. When asked if he knew where the place where the sheep were, he said, "yes, it is the local tourist site." He took them to the pile of dead stinking sheep and vowed with an oath he nor anyone else in the DeBeque area had any knowledge of that terrible crime.

The lawmen figured that everyone in the DeBeque area knew who had committed the crime but the law would never find a clue. The Marshals boarded a train and left for the East leaving Hatch to return their rented horses to Vernal one hundred and thirty miles away. (Pres told the author when he was a child about him and his brother organizing that sheep raid and how he took the lawmen to show them his handy work.) The town's people knew they were law-men when they arrived in town. They decided Pres would be the best guide on their investigation trip. (I never told Pres my grandfather was one of the lawmen.)

Each year Hatch gave Ivan more work and responsibility. This made life very hard. In the summers, he would take Milt and the sheep to the high Uintah Mountains where the pastures were very lush. He would often make trips to the sheep camp to make sure little brother was all right. He stayed with Milt as long as possible.

At home, Ivan plowed, planted and irrigated the fields. When haying time came, Father hired a crew to help Ivan get the crop put in stacks. One summer while Ivan was running a bullrake, the teeth caught in the ground, bringing the team and rake to a sudden stop. It threw him forward into a lever that cut through his lip and knocked out three teeth. When he arrived at the stack, the men noticed blood coming from his mouth and asked what happened. He made no reply. However when he shut his mouth, his tongue was sticking through a hole just under his nose. They took Ivan to the Doctor where he sewed the lip shut. Arriving home, he climbed on the bullrake and helped stack the hay.

When fall came, Ivan brought the sheep and Milt back to the ranch for the winter so Milt could go to school. Then he helped Hatch and some hired hands round up the cattle and horses. He put them in the fenced field so they could feed them hay during the winter. After they sorted the sheep, horses and cattle, they drove those they wished to sell to market. Life settled into a regular routine.

"ole Dick"

Hatch went to the office during the day and played poker in town till late into the night. The mornings after he lost at the game tables he would be in a very bad mood and the children would bear the brunt of his anger. Those mornings as he rode his horse to town he would ride by the field gates, opening them so the livestock could leave the fields. Ivan would have to gather them and put them back in the fields or when Hatch came home he would get a terrible beating. Feeding the animals took most of Ivan's time as it would take four horses to pull the loaded bobsled. He would have to hand pitch the hay on and off the rack.

After Rachel Ellen's death, Mary would spend as much time as her son would allow caring for the small children Rachel had left behind. When Hatch was in a good mood she could stay for several months, but if he were not she would stay only a short time. Ivan was always happy to have his grandmother come to stay. Mary would tell him of her home in England, of Thomas, William and of her father, mother and the long hard trip to Zion. She told of the terrible blizzard along the road near Independence Rock in Wyoming. The rescue was the part about which Ivan never tired of hearing. She often told him of her marriage and how the early pioneer life really was. This small boy loved this dear lady very much. She made his life more bearable.

When Ivan was looking after the livestock near Jensen, he always went and watched the great Paleontologist Earl Douglass and his three helpers chisel, blast and scrape the rocks from the mighty bones of the dinosaur. Pearl Douglass always fed this boy if he were there at meal time. Ivan spent many days checking the cattle on Split Mountain. Being just a boy, he wasted many hours at the quarry. When Earl Douglass unearthed a giant camel, he spent time showing it to young Ivan. (When Ivan was an old man, I took him to the University of Nebraska's Morrill Hall where he could see that very camel again. With much excitement, he told the story of seeing it as a boy as Douglass chiseled it from rock.) Ivan knew many things about the prehistoric plants and animals. Eastern Utah and Western Colorado contained many petrified species that showed evidence of the flood spoken of in the Bible.

While checking on his father's cattle and horses, he would travel forty or more miles in a day on his horse Dick. Uncle Jerry who was Hatch's half-brother gave this old black horse to him. When Jerry gave this old horse to Ivan, he told Hatch the ole pony belonged to the boy. Although the ole Pony had a few years on him, he was one of the top cow horses in Uintah Basin and still would give Ivan a honest days work. When he rode other horses, they never quite measured up to Ole Dick. Ole Dick taught this boy the art of handling cattle and horses. The ole pony could out think those other dumb brutes.

Ivan was just a very small child when his grandmother Mary took him to Uncle Jake Workman's general store and bought him a high crowned Stetson Hat with a wide brim. Mary said, "A man's head should be protected when he is working out doors." The high crowned, wide brimmed hat would always be worn by Ivan and his brothers, thanks to Grandmother. For winter wear, Mary saw that Ivan had a warm sheep skin coat and a silk scarf that would cover his head still letting the Stetson be worn.

When Ivan started to school, Hatch took him to the Newton Saddle shop in Vernal where he had a new saddle made for him. The saddle maker, Newton, was blind. When a man needed a new saddle, Mister Newton felt the man from head to toe. From this, he decided the length of time for him to finish the saddle. The saddle maker carved the tree from hard maple. Then he went to the butcher shop for a fresh raw hide.

Back at his shop, he would scrape both sides clean. He would cover the tree, stretching the hide very tight and sewing it with the same raw hide. After a few days in the desert sun, the hide would shrink, leaving a solid saddle tree that no one could break. He would place a full horse hide on his work table and from memory cut the pieces that he used for the saddle. His saddles always fit like an English glove. Other saddle makers envied Newton's beautiful, practical and useful saddles. They tried without success to copy them. Cowhands rode many miles from all over the West to have a saddle made by the Blind Saddle Maker.

One Sunday, Hatch brought a fine lady home to meet his children. A short while later Hatch married Olive Reeder. Ivan resented the fact someone else was in his kitchen. He and Merle had done a fine job with the household chores. They kept the house as clean as any woman could and scrubbed the family's cloths on the wash board. They had always kept the beds made and helped Grandmother raise a garden that they canned. If they needed anyone, there was always Grandmother.

Ivan had run the house too long to share it with this woman. The work Father expected him to complete, along with having this old lady bossing everyone around, made him very angry. He quickly grew tired of hearing, "Did you wash your hands, did you say your prayers, do not eat like that, sit up straight at the table, say please and thank you, clean your feet before entering the house and take a bath tonight." Ivan began to plan how he could run away and start a life without Olive. Although, he knew she was trying to be a good mother. The other children loved her.

As he figured on the subject, there were more obstacles than he thought could be over come: When to leave, where to go, what to do after he got there, what about the sister and brothers, how would he leave without the dog barking? If he left during the day, someone would tell Hatch.

After a few weeks, he had a plan put together that he was sure would work. Uncle Jerry had said that Ole Dick was his horse, so when he pulled out he would ride him. He would saddle Ole Dick when he did his evening chores and tie a gunny sack around his waist under his shirt to carry his few belongings. He left his hat and coat in the barn. If at supper time for several days he could slip some food like bread or biscuits in his shirt from the table, He could feed the dog from the bedroom window. The dog feeding plan worked better than he had hoped. When the window opened, the dog came running to be fed after a couple of nights.

With the demands his father placed on him, as well as the hard beatings he received when he could not measure up, it made him decide tonight was the NIGHT. When he tucked the children in bed, he wanted to cry. Merle asked what was wrong. After kissing her, he said, "Oh nothing." He went to bed fully clothed with his heart pounding so hard he was afraid it would keep his father awake. Ivan waited until he heard the grandfather clock in the hall strike eleven. Then he quietly opened the window and slipped to the ground. After closing the window, he fed the dog who stayed busy eating as he left.

At the barn, Ole Dick was waiting. After they were through the gate, Ivan walked, leading Dick for a half of mile before mounting. He was afraid someone might hear him if he were riding. After a couple of miles walking his horse, he reached the edge of the farm land where he put Ole Dick in a slow mile eating lope.

When he reached the Green River, It was bank full from the spring melt with chunks of ice floating by. Ole Dick swam the river without any problems. On the East bank, Ivan stopped and built a fire in a draw to dry his clothes where no one could see him.

After he was dry and warm, he again let his horse lope in that mile eating pace, as he tried to plan where he was going. The half April moon shed enough light to make travel easy. Ivan was so busy with his own thoughts, he never noticed the wind beginning to blow from the northwest. He decided he would stop by the K Ranch and try to get a job working on Blue Mountain.

Finally, he noticed the wind was blowing. He looked to the north and could no longer see the outline of the Uintah peaks. Within a few miles, the moon disappeared and it started snowing. The wind blew so hard Ivan could not see where he was going. Soon, Ole Dick stopped, turned his tail to the wind and refused to move.

Ivan had been in many blizzards before, but had never experienced anything like this one. Dick would not move so Ivan stayed with the horse. He knew he had to find shelter soon or freeze to death. Tying the horse's front feet with one end of his lariat, he took the saddle off the horse. Then he jerked the front feet from under him. When Dick hit the ground, Ivan threw a half hitch around his hind legs leaving that ole pony hog tied down. With more wraps of the rope around all four legs, the horse could not get up. The boy crawled between the legs and the belly, covering himself with the saddle and its blanket. The warmth from the horse's belly sure felt good. It was not long till the snow covered them up.

Being warm, Ivan soon went to sleep. He awoke to Ole Dick trying to get up, so he dug himself out of the snow drift to find the noon day sun shining. He soon had the horse untied and on his feet, but the sight of him made Ivan afraid the old horse would soon die.

As he looked around to see where he was, he discovered he was about a mile from the K ranch on a ridge. Leading his near dead horse, he walked to the ranch house where he put Ole Dick in the barn and fed him. As he finished taking care of the horse, he heard a man say, "What are you doing here?" Turning around, he saw Bart Lewis, one of Hatch's best friends, standing in the barn door.

"I've pulled out and ain't goin' back." "That's what you think," laughed Bart. "Well, I don't have the slightest idea where you could have spent the night with it blizzardin' the way it was, but you are here now and I don't suppose you had nothin' to eat. After you get something in that hollowed out belly of yours, I'll take you to back to your old man so he can beat the hell out of you, then maybe you won't be so fresh." "I'll eat your old grub but no one can take me back," said Ivan. Bart only laughed as the walked to the ranch kitchen.

Bart, who was Doc's foreman had the cook fix Ivan a good meal, which the kid ate like a hungry coyote. When the meal finished, they drank their coffee and enjoyed a cigarette. They talked about the spring work that was about to start at the ranch. When Ivan asked for a job at the K Ranch, Bart only laughed. Bart took Ivan to the barn to saddle their horses they would ride to Vernal. When he saw Ole Dick, he stopped short and studied the ole pony for along while saying nothing. After along while, he said, "Well kid, the old man must have really been rough on you this time, that old pony would not make it out the corral gate, you better take that bay over yonder."

over the Rim

Mustanger

Chapter 13

Ivan hurried as fast as he could to get the bay saddled before Bart could get his horse ready to go. When Bart finished saddling his horse, he turned around to face the barrel of a thirty-thirty loaded and cocked rifle with the kid at the other end. "I told you no one was taken' me back to the old man. I mean it, I am trading you horses, the worn out one for the bay, so get your saddle off that roan and turn him loose," ordered the kid. "I can't believe any man could rough a boy up like you must have been. I'll give you a job catching horses so I can keep an eye on you," was the foreman's reply.

In a few days, Ole Dick was able to travel if allowed to follow along loose. While Ole Dick was recuperating, the ranch foreman put together a camp outfit and a string of old horses that Ivan would use. Bart took the kid to Blue Mountain where he showed him good camp sites and wild horse traps. He knew this tough gutsy kid had been doing a man's work for several years and could catch and break wild horses.

The canyon had a fence made of poles with a gate at the upper end. Through this gate Ivan was to leave all the horses he caught and broke to ride. This canyon was the K Ranch's horse pasture. Bart told him if he turned the broke horses in the pasture nobody would know from where the new ones came. Ivan promised the foreman he would stay and not run off if he would not tell the old man where he was. "I'll bring you grub every now and then, and I shore won't tell your old man," said Bart as he rode away.

Ivan soon found an attractive spot under an over hanging cliff that had a spring of water running from it. Here he set up camp. It would have a good supply of water for cooking, bathing and for his horses to drink. He could picket his horses along the stream that flowed away from the cliff where there was plenty of grass for them to eat. This cave like overhang extended back over seventy-five feet and was one hundred feet wide. The roof was about fifteen feet high at the front and six in the rear. Without a tent, the deep recess under the cliff afforded the protection to stay dry and warm.

From this camp, he could see several miles in three directions. In a few days, Ivan had settled into a regular routine of life, though he was always watching the landscape to make sure no one slipped up on him. When he finished setting camp, he started looking over the traps that he intended to use, along with looking to see which band of horses he would capture first.

His new found freedom made him think there was not any thing he could not do. He was alone now. He could cook and eat whatever he liked for his meals whenever he was hungry instead of when the clock said it was time to eat. Rolling and lighting a cigarette, he sat and smoked it. He felt like a king on his throne. Before cooking supper, he washed his clothes and took a bath in the stream that flowed from his camp.

Wanted Dead or Alive

Chapter 14

The morning after Ivan left home, Hatch went to his room to see why he had not come to breakfast. When he looked in the room, Hatch found only the three little boys sound asleep. He went to the barn where he saw Ivan's horse and saddle missing. After more checking, he realized the boy had run away.

After breakfast he sent Milt and Penny to milk the cows while he questioned Merle, to see if she knew anything about Ivan's leaving. Merle told him all she knew was that when Ivan kissed them good night, he acted as if he were going to cry. While Hatch was doing the morning feeding, he became very angry thinking that a smart aleck kid would have the nerve to disobey by running away from home.

When he finished the morning chores, Hatch went straight to the newspaper office where he had posters printed. They read:

WANTED DEAD OR ALIVE!

NELSON IVAN MURRAY

FOR STEALING A HORSE

A REWARD FOR HIS CAPTURE WILL BE PAID

SEE THE UINTAH COUNTY SHERIFF

Then he spent the rest of that day riding to nearby towns to put up the posters.

While Hatch was sitting at his desk the next afternoon, his half brother Jerry rushed in waving one of the posters he had put up the day before. Laying it on his desk, he said "Hatch, whatever way they bring the boy in, that's the way I will bring you in," he said in a very cold and hard manner. Then he added, "That old black horse I gave to the kid, not yours. IT IS HIS, so he could not have stolen it. I hope for your sake they do not bring him in dead." With that, he left.

Hatch sat there in a daze for a few minutes until it soaked in what Jerry had said, then he sprang into action. He reached home long after dark but he had all the posters, which he burned in the cook stove.

Olive Reeder Murray did all she could to comfort the brothers and Merle when they would cry for Ivan. When Grandmother Mary heard of Ivan's leaving, she came to visit the children and tried to give them comfort. For many months when Merle went to bed, she cried herself to sleep wondering where her brother was, or if he were still alive. Olive was extra kind and helped the boys with their chores. The children soon came to love this good woman, though Hatch made life hard for all of them. Merle's heart saddened when she thought of her Sky.

The wild Charge   D S Murray

Back on Blue Mountain, Ivan started chasing wild horses, but it was not as easy as it had been when he helped Hatch. His saddle horses would tire quickly because he pushed them too hard. The wild horse could out run a ridden horse. It took him three or four days to figure out that he had to out smart those wild broncos. He learned to move just close enough to make them move away from him. Then he stayed on the opposite side of the way he wanted them to travel. He soon found it was easy to let his horse graze along while moving just enough to keep the wild ones drifting toward the trap. The traps were generally in a deep draw or canyon with a fenced area making a corral.

The first bands he caught in his trap were a lot of trouble and hard work. In the trap, he caught them by roping their front feet and jerking them to the ground. When the horse hit the ground, he spun a half hitch in his lariat, catching the horse's back feet. This left the animal with all four feet tied together. With that ole pony tied down, he put his hackamore on their head, and then put his saddle on the horse. Then, he then stood a straddle of the down horse, putting one of his feet in a stirrup. In this position he would remove the lariat from that bronc's feet. When the horse rose to his feet. Ivan was in the saddle with both feet in the stirrups. When the bronc was on his feet, it generally exploded with Ivan spurring as well beating it with his quirt. With this type of punishment, the horse soon started running and forgot the bucking business. Within an hour, those ole colts would be doing what the man was showing them.

Most bands of wild horses had from three to a dozen horses in them. The Western rancher never used mares for saddle work. The Mustanger caught every horse he could. Sometimes he turned the mares and young ones loose. The Western rancher knew that color came from inbreeding so when they captured an Appaloosa or a Pinto they treated them like the mares and old ponies. They considered them as jug heads. This meant they were unfit for hard cow work. The ones not turned loose went to Eastern markets. These horses went to Chicago, Kansas City or Omaha where farmers bought them for plow horses. Although they were small, the farmers knew of their great strength and endurance. Some went to the Denver market. Other buyers bought them to slaughter.

Ivan soon learned to run the smaller bands to his trap, making fewer horses to break at once. When Bart showed up in the middle of the summer with supplies, he was pleased with the number of horses Ivan had

Ole Nimius

put in the horse pasture. He complimented him on the quality of horses he was catching and how well they were broken to ride. With a laugh, he told Ivan how often people asked where he got the good broke un-branded horses. As he left, he told the kid to keep up the good work and he would see him in the fall. Ivan was too busy to get lonely or home-sick although he often thought of his brothers and Merle.

As the Aspen leaves turned golden and the days had a chill in the air, Ivan wondered if the foreman on his return trip that fall would bring him some warm clothes. The wild horses got used to seeing him and never paid much attention to him as he rode through the hills. He was using more of the traps the K Ranch had built. This made his captures much easier. When he found a horse that suited his fancy, he would break it for himself, which soon gave him a good string of his own young horses. He left the horses brought from the ranch, in the horse pasture when he no longer needed them.

With complete rest and good pasture, Ole Dick soon recovered from the blizzard ordeal. The only effects were the loss of both ears and his tail that froze. Ivan never rode Ole Dick again. He turned the faith-ful horse loose to be free. Although free, that old horse never strayed far from camp. Some days he followed his master as he went about his work. When Ivan returned to camp, the old pony was always there to welcome him home. Dick would stay under the cliff when the boy was there. This old horse remained part of his life for several years to come.

When Ivan worked the range eight or ten miles east of his camp, he saw signs that other mustangers were working in that area. The horses there were much wilder than near his camp. He saw one stal-lion with a band of a dozen mares he wanted to capture for they were the finest horses he had ever seen. They had been chased so often that when they saw a man they would flee, never letting the man get within a mile of them. Ivan spent several weeks trying to get close enough to herd them to a trap. As the horse got used to seeing him and not be-ing chased, they allowed him to get close enough for Ivan to have a chance of capturing them. He studied their pattern of fleeing and knew where they would circle back to their home range.

After being confident he could drive the herd to one of the nearby traps, Ivan planned for the day they would be his. Early one morning, he hobbled all the horses at his camp except Ole Dick. Hobbling con-sisted of tying the horse's front legs with a short piece of rope. This left just enough slack so they could take only six inch steps without being able to run. As he set out to make the much coveted capture, it was a near-perfect day, which gave him an extra helping of confidence.

Mounted on his fastest horse, he soon covered the two-hour ride to where the stallion and his mares were grazing. After resting and giving his horse a drink at a nearby spring, he charged the band of wild horses. As the wild chase ensued, they ran the route he expected them to run. His horse could stay close behind the band causing the stallion to turn from his driving the band to fight Ivan and his horse. The man rode hard at the stallion with lariat swinging, which soon put the stallion fleeing to catch up with his mares.

After ten miles, the lead mare doubled back toward the home range. Seeing her way blocked by the rider, she ran over a hill and followed along the top of a cliff. Not knowing the country, Ivan charged over the hill to intercept her path. Loose shale covered the hillside so when he came over the crest his horse could not turn nor stop. That ole pony slid over the cliff, which was about twenty feet high, with another three hundred feet of bare loose shale before the slope ended at the bottom. Things happened too fast for the rider to get out of the saddle. When the horse landed, he was turning and rolling end over end until they reached the bottom where Ivan was left under his mount.

Ivan was hanging onto the hackamore lead rope when the horse got to his feet, if he had not, the excited animal would have fled in terror. When he tried to stand, he discovered his left leg broke three inches below the knee. Dragging himself to a nearby Juniper tree, he tied the horse to it. Using the tree, he pulled himself to a standing position on his right leg. This enabled him to unsaddle the horse. Then, he fastened his lariat to the lead, giving the ole pony more room to graze.

To Busted To move

With the left leg broken, he knew he could not mount the horse, as no Western horse would let you near the right side. They had landed by a small creek that the horse could reach from his picket. On his hands and right knee, he dragged his saddle to a nearby rock that was out of the horse grazing area and made camp. Finding four sticks, he cut the string from his saddle, which he used to make a splint for the broken leg. Though the leg was beginning to hurt, Ivan knew he had to straighten and set the leg. After cutting his trouser leg to expose the break, he found the bone protruding from the skin. With a lot of pushing and tugging, he succeeded in getting the bone back under the skin and nearly in place. He then bound it with a splint. (After the leg healed, you could see and feel a sharp point of the bone just under the skin.)

The next six weeks would be a time of starvation for both man and beast. During this time he would kill one small rabbit, catch a horny toad and one small fish. The pain was so bad at first he became delirious. In his delirium, he thought people were there talking to him. As the leg began to heal, the fever left, leaving him very weak and hungry.

When the leg healed enough to stand on, he tried to pick up his saddle to place on the skinny starved horse and found he did not have the strength. His horse had eaten every growing thing within the circle of his picket. This included the bark from the tree as high as he could reach while standing on his rear legs. After tying the horse close to the tree, he dragged the saddle beside him. Then he tied the end of the lariat on the saddle and threw the rope over the branch of the tree. He pulled until he had it on the pony's back. That ole pony was so near starved the cinch was now too large. It took him many minutes to get the saddle tight.

Because of Ivan's depleted condition, it took him along time to get set in the saddle. The horse was so weak it almost fell down when it started to move. After he untied the horse, it started to grazing and the rider let him. Tying himself in the saddle so he would not fall, he remained there for three days until the horse grazed his way back to camp. It should have taken only two hours to make the trip.

When he reached camp, Ole Dick was waiting for his return but the rest of his horses were not in sight. Just seeing the old horse made Ivan feel happy to be back at camp. When he looked around his camp, he found a pile of gunny sacks piled by his bed roll. In the sack that was on top of the pile was a heavy winter coat, a pair of new Levis along with other clothing that would keep him warm. There was a note left from Bart written on a page torn from a tally book. It said, "sorry I missed you. I will see you in the spring. Thanks for the fine quality of well broke horses you kicked down in the pasture." The note had no date so Ivan had no idea when Bart had been there. In the other sacks,

"Ole" Dick
was shore Happy to see him

DF Murray

he found cans of fruit and vegetables, matches, coffee, bacon, tobacco, salt and pepper as well as a pint of whiskey.

Ivan spent the next two weeks in camp growing stronger. He left only twice. He went to find his hobbled horses. Also, he went hunting and killed a deer for fresh meat. By eating whenever he was hungry, he soon regained his former health. With hobbles on, the starved saddle horse began to strengthen and fatten up. After reaching camp, the boy realized the precarious position he was in after the fall over the cliff. As his health and strength returned, he became restless and started taking short rides to find out the condition of the horses. The Winter snows had come shortly after his arrival back at camp. He hoped the deep snow and the shortage of feed would weaken the band of horses that had caused his wreck. This herd had become his nemesis. This made him determined to capture and make the stallion his saddle horse.

He rode to the area where he last saw the herd but could not see any signs of them. After searching several days, he decided to move camp to a location near where he had last seen them. Taking only a bed roll with a few groceries and his Dutch oven, he set out with his saddle horses to find a new camp. Riding a few miles East of the camp where he stayed when he broke his leg, the country began to slope to the East and the snow was not so deep. Finding a cliff that would provide shelter for him and his horses, he set up camp. The nearby stream had plenty of grass along its bank to feed Ole Dick and the rest of his cavy. With camp secure, he started looking for his herd and a nearby trap.

Ivan Building His Trap

The country was full of wild horses that would spook and run when he was within a mile of them. He found several well-built traps that someone recently used. At nearby streams, he found someone else's recently used camp sites. At these sights, there would be supplies, cooking equipment and bed rolls. He soon figured out the men that used them never packed any thing along while running the wild horses. This made him extra cautious to make sure no one saw him.

One day he found the old lead mare that had led the band for which he was looking. There were three small colts with her and she had a broken front leg. As Ivan rode close, she acted as if she would fight him, but hopping on one front leg, she was easy to stay clear of. Because of the colts, he did not destroy her, but wondered, who would leave a broken legged horse to suffer. He also realized a crippled mare and three small colts were no match for mountain lions. Before the winter was over, the lions would get them. That day he also noticed fresh signs of two shod horses so thought it best to move back to his home camp.

When Bart arrived in the spring, Ivan asked him if he would bring him more camping equipment. He told of his broken leg, of the fine stallion, the broken legged mare, of the traps and camps. Then the foreman asked where he had seen all this. Bart listened intently as the boy told of his adventures. Then he said he had probably made a big mistake in bringing him to Blue Mountain to run horses. He explained he wanted to keep track of him and not let the boys' father know where he was. He then added, "Guy McNurlen and his brother Pat ran horses in that area and on east of where you broke your leg." Then adding, "Don't let anyone see you."

Silver Saddle and Trap

Chapter 15

One summer day when Ivan reached camp after trapping a large band of horses, he found Bart and a stranger waiting there with a new tent all set up. Ivan noticed the man's saddle had a lot of silver mountings and very fancy tooling. After the man went to bed, the foreman took Ivan to check the picketed horses and explained this man had won the bronc riding events at Cheyenne Frontier Days. The man asked Bart for a job breaking horses. He told him he was tired of the gypsy life of the rodeo. Bart hired him because he could make such a perfect ride.

Bart stayed with Ivan and the stranger for a few days until they finished breaking the horses in the trap. As long as the man was in the corral, he could ride anything but as soon as you opened the gate he fell off. He could only ride in the arena. He was scared when he got in the open. For two weeks, Ivan spent most of his time chasing the horse that had just bucked the stranger off to retrieve his saddle.

One morning, Ivan woke up to see the stranger saddling Ole Dick. As Ivan was standing in the tent door, he asked, "What are you doing with that old horse?" The man sneeringly replied, "I am leaving this God forsaken country and no one can stop me! This is the only horse gentle enough for me to ride." Ivan informed him that "'the old horse is mine and no one will ride him again." With that, the man sneeringly said, "No snot face kid can stop me." Ivan reached in the tent and took his rifle that was leaning just inside, and as the man mounted and started to ride away. Ivan told him to "stop!" He turned Ole Dick around, facing the kid and said, "You can't stop me." With that, the rifle barked and the saddle was soon empty. Ivan dragged the man's corpse to a secret place where he buried it with the fancy saddle and all the man's personal belongings.

The stranger talked a lot about the country along the Tongue and Yellowstone Rivers in Montana and the large amount of horses there. Ivan thought about leaving before, but he figured now would be a good time to go where Father and no one else could find him. He took all the horses he had except two and turned them in the K Ranch pasture.

Back at camp, he packed his belongings on one of the horses and started north riding the other, letting Ole Dick follow along. He slept most of the time just in his bed roll under the stars on the ground. If the weather was bad, he put up his tent.

As he traveled, he did as any other Westerner did by starting about daylight. They would have to pack and load their tent and belongings on their horses before they started. After traveling for about six hours, they stopped, unloaded their belongings, unsaddled, hobbled the ponies and let them rest and eat for four hours. Then he saddled his horse and put the pack back on the pack horse. Then he went for another six hours and unload again. They went through this to let the horses back cool and dry so they would not get raw and sore. If they were pushing hard, they never stopped as long or unloaded. They just let the ponies eat with the saddles and packs on their backs.

Staying clear of settlements and ranches, he rode for six weeks. He stopped only long enough to catch a horse that he would pack his camp on until the horse was gentle broke. By the time he reached Miles City Montana, he had fifteen to sell. He asked around town if anyone was hiring cowhands, to which the answer was always we don't know of anyone.

Discouraged with the answer the town's people gave, he packed up and started on down the river. Two days later he made camp on the edge of Glendive Montana. There were other men camped nearby, so he asked them what the chances of finding work would be. These men said they were looking for work and could not find any in this part of Montana, North and South Dakota or Wyoming. They asked if he had been in the country long because they had never seen or heard of the old bob-eared and tailed black horse. Ivan said he had been on the trail for about two months and that ended the questions. Feeling he could do nothing but work in the hills catching horses, he decided the best thing to do would go back to Blue Mountain and work for the K Ranch. The young man liked the country around Glendive and took a few days riding through it before starting back to Blue Mountain.

Back at his camp on Blue Mountain, he worked extra hard to catch as many horses as he could before Bart's fall visit. He had not chased the horses for more than three months. Now, they were not as afraid. This made it easy to catch a large number at one time. By leaving them in the trap so they were suffering from thirst and hunger, they broke out much faster with a lot less fight. As the Aspen began to change, the Boss rode in one day with supplies. He was happy with the large herd of horses that were ready to take to the ranch. He made a comment about what poor shape they were in, but the Mustanger never gave an answer. When Bart inquired about the stranger, Ivan told him the man rode north toward Browns Hole on his way to Rocks Springs. Bart's only comment was, "He was not any good anyhow. I'm glad he left."

Ivan spent the winter riding farther from his main camp to find good horses to trap and break. He was working farther north and noticed the horses in that area were not as spooky and there were no traps or signs of mustangers. When he found a large wide valley filled with good horses, he set about looking for a camp and trap site. In the head of the main canyon, he found the perfect place. Just below the rim, near the trail leading out, was a spring in a well-grassed meadow. The sandstone cliff had an over hang under which he set his tent and camp.

While in this camp, he awoke one morning to a raging blizzard. He did not mind because under the cliff there was room for him and his horses to be out of the storm. For a few weeks, he caught many horses because they were weak and the snow was deep. This made it hard for them to run. In the deep snow, they could not buck hard and many never even tried. There were several blizzards that winter and Ivan got caught out in some but always made it to camp safely.

When Bart arrived with the spring supplies, Ivan told him of the plan to move his headquarters to the canyon. He told the foreman of his plan to build the perfect trap in the side canyon with its spring and large meadow to pasture his cavy. The kid asked if he could have the time to build a new trap on the mesa where the trail reached it. "How will you build the perfect trap?" was Bart's only reply. The young Mustanger excitedly told of the two long fences that would be wide where the trail reached the mesa and how it would narrow to twelve feet wide at the entrance of the trap.

The trap would be heart shaped covering three acres with the bottom point leading into a round corral. The smaller being about forty feet across with an eight inch wide post buried five feet in the ground and five feet above with which to snub the bronc's. He would dig a trench where his fence would be. Then, cut juniper trees about twelve feet in length to stand in the trench, filling around the post with dirt. He explained the posts would not stand straight up and down, but lean to the outside so a horse could not damage his legs against the fence.

Ivan told of the horses that roamed on the mesa near the trap and how he would drive them into the canyon. At the lower end of the canyon, it narrowed into a gorge leaving no way for the horses to escape. If he placed a fence in the head of each side canyon with a gate, he could have a large number of horses in that canyon most of the time. He would break several to ride at the same time. Then turn the ones that were broke back in the main canyon until he had a large herd to take to the K Ranch's pasture. This would save him many trips.

There would be gates where the horses he did not want could be let free to roam the mesa. The ones he wanted to keep would roam the canyon pasture.

As Bart sat listening, he got caught up in the young man's excitement and said they would move camp the next day. Before daylight the next morning, the two men were starting to pack the camp and its supplies on horses for the move. When all was loaded, they went to the nearby trap and chose the horses that would be kept for ranch use. They soon caught and tied these to the pack horses and the rest were set free.

As they rode along, Bart told Ivan the trap he would build would be his and would not belong to anyone else. This added to the excitement Ivan felt, his own trap! When they arrived at the new camp site, they quickly set things in order. Then the men started cutting poles for the cavy pasture fence until it was too dark to see.

They were back to cutting posts when the sun came up the next morning and by mid day had enough to fence the mouth of the little canyon. By dark, they finished the fence and all but one of the horses were loose grazing in the new pasture. They always kept one horse on a picket so they would have one to catch the others. Bart spent a day with Ivan looking over the canyon and surrounding mesa, before taking the extra broke horses and going back to the ranch.

In a month's time, Ivan had the side canyon fences built with four poles at each entrance to serve as a gate for blocking the trail when needed. Ivan spent the next three months' cutting posts and dragging them to the trap site with a rope tied from his saddle horn to the post. When he had enough posts to make the fences, he started digging the trench. He dug the trench a foot wide and three feet deep. He would dig a few feet and then set the post. Then he dug some more. When the aspen leaves began to turn, Ivan finished the trap.

When Bart arrived with the fall supplies, there were several head of newly broken horses for him to take back to the ranch. He stayed a few days at the wild horse camp looking over the new trap and the wild horses that were in the large fenced canyon. As the two men visited, he told Ivan how proud he was to have such a good man capturing wild horses for the K Ranch.

Also, he suggested Ivan make a visit back home. This got Ivan to thinking that maybe the foreman was right and he could go home and stand up to his old man after all. As the winter months passed, Ivan often thought of home with Merle, his three little brothers and Grandmother. He became homesick and made plans to draw his wages when spring came and go home. He got caught out in a blizzard where he had only some rocks to hide behind. Here he built a fire that kept him warm enough to keep from freezing. The blizzard raged all afternoon. About the middle of the night, it blew its self out. It turned very cold with a northwest wind. He had been wet most of the day and all night when he reached camp where he had shelter from the wind and cold.

In a few days, his lungs felt as if they would burst and he was burning with fever. He knew he had pneumonia because he felt as he did when he had it while Mother was still living. During this time, he never smoked because it brought coughing spells that made him pass out. He missed about a month's work with this illness, but he eventually got to feeling better, and started catching the horses close to his trap.

When the snow began to melt, Ivan drove all the horses from the canyon to his trap.

There, he separated the broke ones into his small breaking corral. Then after turning the wild ones back in the canyon, he rode to all the side canyons where he opened the gates. Arriving back at the trap, he caught the broke horses and tied them together so they could lead them.

Back at camp, he packed the camping equipment on pack horses. Catching his strongest horse, he tied the string of newly broke horses to it and started for the ranch headquarters. With the herd of horses and Ole Dick following, it made a long day. It was long after dark when he arrived at the main K Ranch.

The next morning he turned all the ranch horses and camping equipment into the foreman and drew his three years' wages. He took his seven personal horses when he left.

As he rode West toward home, his thoughts were on how he could now stand up to the old man. He felt he could even whip him in a fight. He did not mind the idea of whipping his father when he remembered all the times Hatch unjustly punished him.

"close ties"

Home Again

Chapter 16

When Ivan reached Vernal, he stopped by Newton's Saddlery where he bought a new saddle, a bridle and blankets. His next stop was at the General Mercantile store where he bought boots, clothing, a Stetson hat, tent, cooking utensils, horse halters and pack saddles with which to haul his new outfit. As he rode leading his pack horses down the street toward the edge of town, people looked at him as if they did not know who he was. He had left a boy and now he was a man with an outfit.

When he arrived home, Merle and the boys were very excited to see him. Merle hugged him and cried saying, "Sky, dear Sky, I thought you were dead and I would never see you again." As he was unsaddling his horses, he asked about Olive, and Merle told him she was very sick. He was soon in the house by Olive's bedside asking many questions. When he asked her why she had not seen a doctor, she told Ivan, "Hatch had said that letting her die was cheaper than to pay a large doctor bill."

When Ivan heard this, he was furious. He told Olive he would take her to the Doctor and he would pay the bill. He then caught a team of horses, harnessed them and hitched them to a spring wagon. Driving the wagon to a hay stack, he filled it with soft hay. Then he drove it to the yard gate. After covering the hay with his new bed roll, he carried Olive to the wagon and drove her to town.

Driving straight to the hotel, he obtained a room where he put Olive to bed. He sent for the doctor. When he arrived, Ivan laid his three years' wages on the table by Olive's bed, He told the inn keeper and the doctor, "Use what you need to doctor this lady back to health. If it is not enough, I will pay the extra when this lady is well." After the doctor left, Ivan asked Olive to divorce Hatch, which she agreed to do. He stayed with the sick lady until he could see an improvement in her condition. Leaving the hotel, he went to visit Grandmother Mary.

When he stopped at the ranch to pick up his horses and camping equipment as well as visiting his sister and brothers, Hatch was home and seemed happy to see him. Things seemed different and Ivan forgot the things he had wanted to say to Hatch. Father asked Ivan if he would work for him. Hatch promised Ivan would get good pay. Hatch told the young man if he would stay, he would buy more sheep. If Ivan herded them, he would give him half the wool and lamb crop. Ivan agreed to work for his father because he thought this would get him a herd of young ewes with which to start a ranch of his own.

Hatch and Ivan soon found a band of sheep that were for sale which father bought. The combined herd now numbered three thousand five hundred making the Murray's one of the larger sheep outfits in Uintah Basin. They took the sheep to pasture in the high Uintah Mountains where the air was cool, the water fresh and the grass lush. When fall came, they would drive them to the Green River Desert where the winters were mild and they would require no hay to feed them. Because of the rugged mountain terrain, Ivan could not use a wagon to live in, so Ivan put his new camp outfit to use.

Hatch and his four sons drove the band of sheep to the high summer pasture as soon as they brought the newly purchased sheep to the ranch. They sold the lambs and sheared the sheep before Ivan came home from Blue Mountain, so he would have to wait for another year to receive any money.

This did not bother him because he owned half the new lambs and was looking forward to having his own sheep. He planned to stay until the sheep sold the next spring. He never planned to sell the ewe lambs so he could start building his own flock. That summer he moved camp every three days so the sheep would always have plenty of fresh grass to graze.

When Hatch visited about the middle of June, he told Ivan about a bucking horse the Ute Indians owned. They were offering four hundred dollars to any man that could ride it to a stand still. Nobody had ridden the bronc. He said Bart Lewis had told him of the wild horses that Ivan captured and broke for the K Ranch. He said, "If you can ride stuff like that you should be able to take the Indians money without a problem." He promised to send someone to look after the sheep so Ivan could come to the Fourth of July Celebration. On the morning of the Fourth, Hatch rode into Ivan's camp, throwing a gunny sack at the young man's feet and said, "There, have your own private celebration." Without saying more Hatch then turned his horse and loped away. In the sack was a new pair of Levis and a fifth of whiskey.

A week later Hatch rode into Ivan's camp with some supplies. He told Ivan that Bart Lewis had been to Vernal for the Fourth and watched the Ute Pony buck. He told people he knew a kid that could ride that

steamboat
and
Ivan

bronc. Hatch said there was a lot of excitement about what Bart had said. The Indians just laughed at Bart. They said they would bring the horse back to Pioneer Days if this great rider would be there. Father said he would send someone to herd the sheep so Ivan could come to town and ride the horse.

A week later a man rode into camp saying he was to take care of the sheep for a couple of weeks so Ivan could go to town and ride the Indians' horse. The first morning of the rodeo Ivan watched every move the Ute Pony made when he sent another cowboy and his twenty-five dollars flying. The Indians charged twenty-five dollars to anyone that thought they could ride their horse, but would pay four hundred if the cowboy could ride him till he quit bucking. Ivan decided he had the broncos bucking pattern memorized so he could take the kinks out of that ole pony in no time at all. Before going to put his money down he went to the blacksmith shop and had his spurs sharpened.

When he went to pay his money to the Indians, no one noticed the sharpened spurs. The crowd was betting on this cowboy, most betting he could not make the ride. Bart and the men from the K Ranch bet large amounts of money that "their man" would at last break that old pony to saddle. The Indians placed so much value on the horse that they would not let it buck out of a chute. They were afraid the horse might get hurt. They pulled and held his head over the back of another horse while the cowboy put his saddle on and mounted.

The ole pony stood quietly while they saddled him and Ivan mounted, getting seated just right. When they lead the other horse away, that old bronc exploded even harder than he had before. The crowd went wild making so much noise Ivan lost his concentration. He knew many of his friend's had bet heavily on him to ride this horse till it quit bucking. He also needed the four hundred dollars. When he felt he might get thrown, he spurred with all his strength, sticking his right spur through the hide and into the shoulder joint. That old bronc folded up in a pile on the ground unable to get back on its feet. The Indians soon helped their horse up on its other three feet and were furious at what they saw.

When Ivan went to collect his money, the Indians said they would not pay because he had ruined their famous bucking horse. Ivan showed them one of their advertisements that read they would pay four hundred dollars to any person that could ride the horse till it quit bucking. He said, "the horse quit bucking, and if you want to let me back on him we will soon see if he will buck," but the Indians said, "no pay." Ivan and his friend argued with the Indian until they agreed to have the sheriff be the judge of the dispute. Not knowing he was the Sheriffs' son, they appealed to the sheriff to make the right call. The sheriff told them the cowboy had ridden their horse till it no longer bucked as the advertisement said, so he ordered them to pay the four hundred dollars.

The world champion bucking horse called Steamboat was at the Pioneer's Day rodeo. Because of the excitement that the Indian pony caused, Steamboat was not in the spot light. The K Ranch men asked Ivan if he would ride that "'old sunfishin' bronc" if they could get the owner to let him do it without a draw, Ivan said he would ride that ole pony if the "boys" wanted him to do it. Steamboat had his head pulled over the back of another horse so they could saddle and mount him. Ivan did not know anything about the horse he was soon to ride except the boys called him "a sunfishin son-of-a-gun."

After they got the saddle on Steamboat, Ivan slid into the saddle and they turned the bronc loose. That ole pony set back on his haunches spun and went straight in the air. When Ivan thought that bronc could go no higher he flipped like he would fall on his side, but just before the rider's head hit the ground the horse kicked the ground with his hind leg throwing himself up and over coming down the other way. This he repeated until he shook Ivan loose and then lit out bucking in hard short spine cracking jumps spilling the man in the dirt. When Ivan hit the dirt, he heard the 20-second gun go off. The boys hailed their friend's ride as if he had ridden the horse to a standstill. They all said now you are a real bronc peeler because you stayed in the saddle after seeing daylight under his belly.

A few summers before, Clayton Danks, the foreman of the L 7 Ranch, headquartered on the Elkhead River in Colorado, had ridden Steamboat for the twenty seconds at the Cheyenne Frontier days. Danks was the only man ever to ride that horse for twenty seconds. Clayton was the world champion bronc rider and Steamboat the world champion bucking horse that year.

Every night, the celebration held a dance with fiddles and a piano furnishing the music. Ivan's Uncles made up the band and they could play for hours without stopping, which pleased everyone. Ivan and his cousin Clarence were the best dancers. They danced every dance with the young and old ladies alike. They sure had a lot of fun.

There was a young man that was slow mentally but he sure could dance and the women liked to dance the jigs with him. He liked beans and that was about all he ate. At the picnic he had eaten an extra large quantity of those good baked pork and beans that only a good Mormon wife made.

When it came time for the dance, Ivan and Clarence asked the fellow if he was going to the dance, to which he said, "no. You see I 'et' to many beans and they are 'distressen' me." Those two young men thinking they could play a joke on him and everyone else at the dance, told him that his distress would not be a problem. When he had to relieve himself, all he had to do was jump, shout and kick his heals together and no one would hear a thing. After much pleading, he finally thought it would work that way and he would go to the dance.

They had been dancing for a while and Clarence asked the Uncles to play a waltz. Everything was going in a very romantic way when all of a sudden Bean Eater shouted real loud and jumped up, clicking his heals together. Everyone stopped and looked to see what the problem was and in the dead silence there was a loud noise. The young man's face turned red. He began to cuss the two young men for the trick they had played on him. He told them he was going to kill them. At that, the crowd figured out the joke. With roars of laughter, the dance stopped until all could get under control. The young man left the dance in a hurry and would never eat beans again.

When the celebration ended, the Shepherd went back to care for his flock. Drinking from streams that flowed from snow banks and eating the lush mountain grass, the sheep soon fattened and grew a fine fleece. When the early winter snows started to fall, Hatch brought his three younger sons to help drive the sheep from the mountains to the desert. After they reached the ranch, Hatch told Ivan he would have to take the sheep on south by himself. This announcement didn't bother Ivan, because he knew the sheep would graze as the walked south. On the morning he started his trek to the desert, Milt, Glen, Nile and Merle helped him to the edge of the farms where the open range began. Ivan told the kid's good-bye and said he would see them in the spring on his way back to the mountains. The four youngsters rode back to the ranch.

As the shepherd kept the large band of sheep drifting south, he let them eat while walking at a slow pace. After a month of drifting the sheep south, they reached the town of Green River where Ivan asked about the best place to winter his sheep. They told him of the San Rafael Valley that was another thirty miles to the South. He purchased enough supplies to last him till spring if he used lamb for meat. It took another five days to reach the San Rafael river. There were plenty of dry weeds and grass if he moved camp every four days.

Ivan often had visitors from other sheep camps that winter and he returned those visits. He and a young Mormon man named Marriott who was herding in another camp nearby became close friends. (This man started the Marriott Hotel chain in later years.) He set up camp in places that would afford protection from blizzards for him and the sheep. He would watch the sky for any sign of an approaching storm. When a blizzard hit with its fury, he had the sheep and his horses in the most protected area available. Ivan did not lose any sheep that winter because of the weather.

With a watchful eye, he found any poison weeds that if eaten would kill the sheep. When he found them, he burned the area so he would not lose any sheep. There were some days that were cold and snowy, but most days the sun shone keeping the temperature above freezing. With his faithful dogs to guard the sheep at night, the predators only stole a few of the old ewes. He enjoyed the desert that winter as much as he had the summer in the high mountains. This life was much easier than that of the Mustanger. With his own band of sheep, he would never have to capture wild horses again.

When the cactus and sago lilies were in bloom, Ivan knew it would not be long until he would start the sheep north to the high mountain pastures. He was starting to drift the sheep north when he met his father. Hatch told him they would take the sheep to the high Colorado mountains between Aspen and Crested Butte. He went on to say the train from Green River Utah would haul the sheep and horses to Glenwood Springs, Colorado. The year old lambs would be sorted and loaded in cars that would take them to the Denver stockyards where they would sell them.

Hatch made arrangements to have the sheep sheared when they arrived at the town of Green River. He had contracted the wool to the church's woolen mills and after it arrived at the mill they would weigh it and send the check to Vernal. When Ivan told father of his plan to take the yearling ewes for his own flock instead of selling them, Hatch told him to pick out the ewes with the new lambs he wanted. They were his and he could run them for that summer with Hatch's.

After thinking about the offer, he finally agreed to the deal. The wool went west by train to Salt Lake City, and the sheep were loaded on another going East. The yearling lambs went to Denver and the ewes with their baby lambs would be left at Glenwood Springs. The train arrived at Glenwood Springs in the middle of the night where it pulled on a siding and unhooked the cars loaded with the horses, ewes and lambs. As it left Hatch was on it because he had to go with the yearlings to see them sell.

Having nothing else to do until daylight, Ivan went to a hotel and got a room for the rest of the night. In the morning, he went to the train depot to check on getting the sheep off those cars. He also asked if the agent knew if there were men available to help drive the sheep to the mountains near Aspen. The agent said he knew of a couple of men that the freight bulls had kicked off a freight train. He would talk to them about working for the sheepman. A yard crew working for the Denver and Rio Grande railroad helped Ivan get his livestock unloaded safely in the yard.

As the Sheepman was loading his pack horses the depot agent showed up with two men who agreed to help drive the sheep if Ivan furnished them horses to ride. Ivan took them to the livery stable and rented them horses for three weeks, which would give them time to get the mountain pastures and back to Glenwood springs.

The trip up the Frying Pan river was hard on the sheep as there was very little grass for them to eat. His two hired men were from an Eastern city and had never ridden a horse before. He had to teach them about horses, sheep and camping out plus how to herd sheep. If it had not been for his four dogs, the trip would have been impossible. The herd moved slowly because Ivan had no wagon in which to haul the small lambs that became too tired to walk and dropped in their tracks. He often stopped to let the lambs and old ewes lie down to rest. It took a week to reach the alpine meadows with this mixed flock.

The trip from the Green River Desert to the mountains west of Aspen had been hard on the herder and his animals. The streams were cold and clear with lush grass in the meadows through which they ran. Ole Dick made the long trip in as good a shape as the rest of Ivan's horses, which made the boy happy. He hobbled the two that would wander from the camping area and on another he placed a cowbell around its neck. After the sheep settled in on the new range for two days, he paid the hired men their wages and sent them back to Glenwood Springs.

Almost every day, it rained, making life wet, cold and miserable for the herder and his horses. When the sun shone, he dried his clothes and bed. On the north slopes, there were ice and snow that never melted, which made crossing them on a horse very dangerous. The sheep would wander in these areas and when his dogs could not drive them from there he would have to ride a horse after them or walk.

One day when he was going along a game trail in one of these icy places, his horse slipped and slid down the steep mountain side. His lariat had gotten stiff in the wet cold climate and he was dragging it on the ground with one end tied to the saddle horn. As they approached a sheer drop off, the rope caught in some brush and rocks, stopping the downward plunge. He climbed the rope to make sure it was secure and found it so entangled it would not come untied. Using his rifle barrel, he twisted the rope until he pulled the horse to safety. When he tried to free the lariat from the brush and rocks, he could not untangle it so he cut it just beside the rocks.

By June 1, he moved camp, traveling several miles south toward Crested Butte to mountains that were not so steep. While at this camp, he was eating lunch when a white man and three Mexicans rode into camp. They told him to "get out of here. This is my camp, sheep and horses. I won them from your old man in a poker game, so get I said."

Ivan asked if he could finish eating, and if they would not like to eat too. The man said they would, but he must fix some more grub. Ivan saw the treachery in this man, so he asked if he could go in the tent to get some more food. Ivan's rifle was just inside the tent and as he reached the door he grabbed his gun, spun around, loading and cocking the gun. He said, "Now drop your guns and back away from them." This they did.

He then took the guns to a safe distance and made the new outfit take down and pack his camping equipment on his horses. After all was packed, he made the most timid one take the bridles off their horses and spook the horses away from camp.

The new owner had been making all sorts of threats while protesting that Ivan was taking his own horses. Ivan told the man this camp outfit and the horses are mine and you must settle your gambling debt with the old man. Throwing the men's gun on top of the largest pack, he mounted telling them they could find their gun where they fell off the pack horse. He had the Mexicans tie the horses together in a line one behind the other including Ole Dick so he could keep them close

Ivan
starting a colt

as he fled. He rode north for a mile or so and then doubled back south toward Crested Butte and Gunnison.

When reaching the Gunnison River, Ivan rode down the valley west past the town of Gunnison trying not to attract any attention. As he came to the Black Canyon, the road around it was hard on his now tiring horses, but he did not slacken the pace for yet another day. For three days he pushed the horses at a very hard pace, making sure the new owner of his sheep did not catch and kill him.

When he came to the town of Montrose, he decided that the gambler was not close enough behind to create him a problem. In the valley north of town, he found a camp site in a secluded spot where the horses could rest for two days. While he was eating supper, a local rancher rode into camp where the cowman visited for a while. When he was ready to leave, he asked Ivan if he would sell the big bay and roan horses. Ivan said he would sell them for seventy-five dollars apiece, to which the rancher took the cash from his pocket and paid for them. This amount of money equaled a years work. Ole Dick was showing signs of wearing out. Ivan did not want to set a pace that would kill the old horse or would leave him behind on the trail. After the much needed rest, he only traveled ten to fifteen miles in any day.

Passing through the towns of Delta, Grand Junction, and Mack he rode north toward Rangley, crossing Douglas Pass. At the summit of

Douglas Pass, he saw a small band of wild horses that he liked. He decided to see if he could catch a fine black that was in it. Finding their water hole, he set up camp near that place and in two days had roped three horses. Tying them to a tree so they would get used to being tied, he left them there for three days before necking them to gentle horses. Thirst had made them easy to handle so after letting all his horses water, he rode onto Rangley.

At Rangley, he bought a large amount of camp supplies. Purchasing extra groceries and cooking utensils so he could have a camping site near many other wild horse traps. This saved the time of traveling back to camp each day. He would cache these in a secure place that only he knew. While riding along, he thought about the easy money he had made from the sale of those two horses. He decided to become a Mustanger that sold his own broke horses. From the Aspen sheep camp, it took three weeks to reach his wild horse trap on Blue Mountain where he felt safe.

The McNurlen's

Chapter 17

Riding into the valley at his trap, he saw evidence that other mustangers had used his valley and trap. He could tell because something ate so much of the grass in his camp pasture, which made him worry if his horses had enough to eat. The three Douglas Pass horses were well broke now because he had used them for pack horses and ridden them. He hobbled all but one horse, which he would keep on a picket rope. The rest he turned loose in the valley. With the one he kept on a picket line, he caught the others each day. He always left a bell on one horse so he could easily find them.

He spent several days checking the traps on Blue Mountain. When on these trips, he took a pack horse along loaded with camping supplies. Finding six cache sites, he decided he could spend more time capturing horses than traveling to and from camp. Arriving back at his main camp after one trip that had taken him four days, he surprisingly found his horse pasture gate closed and two strange horses loose grazing in the pasture.

With loaded and cocked rifle in hand, he rode into camp where he found two men squatted on their heals eating supper. He rode within a few feet of camp before the men knew he was there. They had their backs toward him, but hearing his horse's steps they stood up and turned around holding their coffee cups. "Climb on down and fix yourself a little bit of coffee," said the older man. "I am Guy McNurlen and this other feller here is my brother Pat." Acting as if he never saw the rifle, Guy went on to tell of their finding this camp a year before. They had checked it several times and decided it was no longer in use by the builder. Being vacated, they decided they would catch some of the fine horses in the area.

Ivan decided they were friends instead of foes. Putting his rifle back in its scabbard, he dismounted and turned his horses loose. As he ate, they told him they had seen Bart Lewis of the K Ranch this spring and asked about this trap. Bart had told them of the kid that built it and of him going in the sheep business. They along with Bart figured the kid would not be running horses for some time. The three men visited long after the sun went down.

Pat said, "Kid, we will leave at day light in the morning because we won't use your trap." They told of their permanent camp on Blue Mountain, which was thirty miles east. It was near a trap with a large fenced pasture. They had built a dugout for a cabin. this cabin was half in the ground to give it more shelter. Lying in his bed roll, Ivan decided he liked these men and hoped they would teach him more about running and breaking wild horses.

Long before time to get up, Ivan was awake thinking about the events that had taken place since he left this secure haven a year and a half ago. When the dawn came, he was up, dressed, making coffee and breakfast for his guests when they got up.

While they were eating, he asked the mustangers if they would teach him the easiest way to catch and break horses. "It seems like you got it all figured out from the looks of your set up," Pat said. Guy assured the young man the McNurlen's would teach him all they knew about horses.

Before the sun was up, the three men were leaving the trap to scour the mesas and benches of the surrounding country looking for horses. By the time the sun reached its zenith, a large herd of horses drifted toward the valley trap. The three men had split with one riding along the north, one on the east, the other at the south. They kept a long way from the herd as to not set them in a stampede. The upland horses knew the trails to the valley because they traveled them as they went to the valley for water each day. By supper time, they had the herd shut in the valley. This herd was enough to keep the men busy breaking them for many days.

Getting ready to start work the next morning, Ivan noticed a pile of halters, ropes and hackamores with the McNurlen's other camp supplies. The hackamores were such as Ivan had never seen before. On the nose band there were two large braided knots about two inches across and two inches apart. After they filled the trap with horses, they kicked the mares, colts and culls out on the mesa.

Then the three men started roping, haltering and then tying the ole ponies to the fence. They roped the horses by both their front feet. They threw a large loop over the horses back and the loop caught the feet while they were running as hard as they could. Just as the horse hit the ground in an undignified manner, the man shouted, "WHOA." While all four feet were in the air, the men flipped a half hitch loop in the rope. This caught both hind feet, pulling this loop tight, hogtying the ole pony on the ground.

When they got the horse tied down, the other man took a halter with a long rope attached and jumped on the head, placing the halter around it. Before they untied the horse's feet, they wrapped the halter rope around the nearest corral post. When the bronc got to its feet, the bronc buster took the slack up and he had the horse tied to the post.

Ivan had always roped, saddled and rode one horse at a time. This way of haltering the horses was a new way so he just helped without asking why the McNurlen's did it this way. With a dozen ponies tied to the fence, the two mustangers placed hackamores on many of the horses. Then they saddled three and each man climbed aboard and turned their bronc loose.

As Ivan's horse bucked, he pulled hard on the hackamore he noticed the horse slowed, and soon stopped bucking. When Ivan slackened the rein, that ole pony took in a deep breath and exploded. Pulling hard on the rein, the horse soon stopped bucking and that is when Ivan figured what to do with the knot on the nose band. By keeping pressure on the rein, it pinched the horse's nostrils, cutting off most of his air. In no time, the horse started going around the trap in a gentle manner. It was hard to keep fighting because the harder the bronc fought, the tighter the cowboy pulled on the hackamore, shutting off the horse's air. If a horse had any sense, he soon calmed down.

When the horse tired, Ivan rode him to where they had tied and dismounted him. Pat said, "See you figured out how to use that hackamore." "I see you seen how to place those knots low on the nose so they shut the air off so he could not half kill you when he bucked," said Guy. Ivan asked if they would help him make one of these bosals. Guy said, "We owe you for the use of your trap so you can have the bridle for a payment."

It had been a long time since Ivan had kept track of the days or even months. He only went by the seasons. The McNurlen's knew what day of the week and month it was. On the first of July, they put on their town clothes and asked Ivan to go to Craig with them for the celebration. With two days of hard riding, they reached town where they left their pack and saddle horses at the livery barn while they let off a little steam.

This celebrating business was new to the Kid so he just followed along and watched. Guy and Pat bought a bottle of whiskey that they shared between themselves, and everyone else they met. Guy said, "Kid, if you are going to make a cowhand, you have to learn how to celebrate." The first drink or two burned as the Kid swallowed it, but in a while it went down with ease. It was not long until the Kid was feeling very happy like his friend's. The McNurlen's were soon sitting in on a

Front Scotin + Heckin

poker game at Smokey Kitchens gambling parlor. They tried to get Ivan to play with them but he would not play remembering the game when Hatch lost his sheep. At midnight, Smokey closed the bar and the men went to their room upstairs.

The sun was shining in the window when the Kid awoke with his head feeling as if a mustang had kicked him and his stomach churned as if to make butter. Sitting on the edge of his bed, he swore he would never take another drink as long as he lived. When Guy woke up, he reached for the bottle and took a long swig of the amber refreshment, then he handed it to the Kid and said, "Take a swig of that and you will feel better." They filled the 4th of July with drinking, meeting old friend's and betting on horse races. Also, there were bucking and roping contests. A man named McGonale rode a bucking horse called Nancy Hanks with a blindfold over his eyes. The men all placed bets on this event.

The morning of the Fifth, Guy told Ivan they had celebrated long enough, so they stocked up on supplies and left for camp. From the moment the older man woke up, he went to "refrehen" himself again. A few miles from town, Guy passed out and fell from his horse. The Kid had not wanted to leave the celebration. Seeing the opportunity to go back to town, hobbled all the horses except his. Seeing Guy lying in the road gave him the idea that if the man came to, he might ride on to camp without him.

Cutting the strings from Guy's saddle, he hogtied the older man where he lay. Then He threw the man's slicker over his head for shade. After this, Ivan mounted his horse and loped back to Smokey's bar. There were not many people in the bar when he arrived because it was still early morning.

When Pat came to the bar, he asked the Kid where his brother was. Ivan then told how he hobbled Guy in the road west of town. Everyone in the bar had a great laugh as they thought of seeing Guy hogtied in the road. They told Ivan Guy would kill him when he got loose and reached town. All day they watched the road leading to town for Guy. Thinking it had been a fine joke, the men were going to hide the Kid until Guy cooled his temper toward the Kid.

Out on the road, Guy had slept until about noon. When he woke up sober, he found himself tied and covered in the noon day heat. Not being able to move, he waited for five hours before a homesteader with his family in a wagon passed by and cut him loose. When he had gotten the horses unhobbled, he started to town in a very foul mood. The thing that he was the most angry over was that a lady had seen him tied in the road.

For three days, he looked for the kid but could not find him anywhere. Guy knew the Kid was in town because his horse was in the livery barn. It took three days for the men to get Guy to promise not to kill the kid and see the joke in what happened. Finally having a good laugh with the boys, he asked where the Kid was. The McNurlen's and Ivan were soon on the road back to Blue Mountain.

The McNurlen's rode Ivan's extra broke horses to help him sort the large herd through the trap. They only kept the stallions. They turned the rest out to roam over the benches and mesas. When they finished sorting, they began to rope, saddle, and ride the horses. When these were all broke gentle to ride, Guy asked Ivan to go with them to work on the fall cattle roundup. He told Ivan they could sell their horses to the ranches for a good price. Placing his supplies in a safe cache, Ivan then loaded what the men suggested on his pack horses. With the two men and the herd of horses, Ivan started on a trail that changed his life.

Pat McNurlen

"WILD HORSE SPECIALIST"

Working for the Two Bars

Chapter 18

Reaching the McNurlen camp at the east edge of the mountain, a man was waiting for them. He was Bill Patton, foreman of the mighty Two Bars Cattle Company. As the herd entered the pasture gate, Bill looked them over. The men unsaddled their horses and Bill made a deal to buy the whole herd. With his one third of the money they would receive, Ivan felt he was a rich man.

The next morning Bill told Ivan he would hire him to be horse wrangler with roundup wagon number nine. That wagon was Guy's mailing address and Ivan would always work with that crew when working for the Two Bars. Pat and Bill left for the ranch headquarters at Sunbeam on the Little Snake River, where Pat would break horses. Ivan and Guy started the trip to Powder Wash, Wyoming with the herd of horses. This took two weeks because they rode north through

Ivan working for Two bars

Brown's Hole on their way. Ivan had heard much about this wild country from his father who had helped bring law and order to it. That night Ivan would take his first turn of standing watch over the loose herd. In two days they reached the ferry on the Green River. They would go east from here, but Guy said they would throw off the trail and stay with the "Speckled Nigger" that night. Everyone who knew Albert Wellhouse liked him. He was a kind and charitable man.

At supper, he told Guy he was looking for someone to dig Matt Rash's body up so he could ship it to Cleburne, Texas for burial in his family's plot. One of Matt's brothers and father had come to the Park to take it back home but could not find anyone that would disturb the dead. He was willing to pay fifty dollars to anyone that would dig it up and wrap it in a canvas bag for shipping.

Guy reckoned there wasn't much left after fifteen or sixteen years so he said if the Kid would help him, they would dig the old boy up. Albert lent the two men a team and wagon. He furnished them with shovels and the bed roll in which to wrap the corpse. As they drove to the grave, Guy told Ivan of the trouble that led up to the murder and the war Anne Bassett waged against the Two Bars. This war was part of the financial trouble of the Two Bars. He told how the Two Bars kept crowding cattle into the park. The little ranchers fought back by driving the cattle on west across the river. Also, they hauled loads of butchered beef to Vernal and Rock Springs to the butcher shop where they sold it.

Hi Bernard had met Anne Bassett on Douglas Mesa east of the park and she threatened to kill him if he did not quit pushing his cattle into the park. He only laughed at this young attractive lady. He told her, "If she wanted a fight, she sure had one." That is when he hired the killer Tom Horn to clean Brown's Hole of the "vermin" that inhabited it.

Tom Horn came to the valley using the name James Hicks. He soon hired on a local ranch where he was a good worker and everyone liked him. He worked, ate, slept and played with the local people until he knew every move they made. He gave no hint he was watching them to learn their every habit. This made it easier to kill them when the time was right. He stayed almost a year before he thought he knew them well enough.

Making a big deal about it so everyone would notice, Horn left town claiming that he was leaving for good. Instead, he just went a little ways out of town and hid. A few days after he pretended to leave the country, Horn shot Isom Dart, the black cowboy, in the back. Dart never saw them because the coward hid in the brush and ambushed Dart.

Isom Dart had come to the country from Arkansas using the name Nate Huddelson. He came in the company of Tip Gault and his gang of horse thieves. When old Tip and his gang tried to steal a herd of horses that a man by the name of Anderson and his horse wranglers were driving from California to the United States, only Tip and Isom Dart survived. Despite being badly wounded, Isom escaped and survived.

He later met a Shoshone Indian woman with a little half breed white girl. He fell in love with the mother and child not knowing she was married to the cruel Ute Indian Pony Beater. Tickup, the Indian woman, had escaped from Pony Beater because he was so cruel to her and the child.

When Pony Beater discovered the affair, he went after Isom. Pony Beater jumped Isom and a fight to the death began. Pony Beater sliced Isom's ear off with a stone axe but Isom prevailed by killing Pony Beater. Isom worked for the Middlesex Cattle Company as horse wrangler until he had enough money honestly to start his little ranch in Browns Hole. He sent Tickup and the child to Oklahoma so they could educate the child in the Indian schools there.

After ambushing Dart, Horn ambushed Matt Rash. Nobody found Rash's body for several days. Somebody stopped by Rash's cabin and found him and his favorite horse shot to death. By the smell, they could tell they had been dead for several days. Two Days later Horn was in Baggs Wyoming. He drank heavily and talked about killing those "vermin rustlers." George Bassett and many other young men left the valley never to return.

Finding the grave, they soon had the body exhumed and ready to place in the bed roll. The body was dried and mummified with no smell, which made the job much easier than anticipated. When they arrived back at the ferry, the father and brother thanked them for exhuming the body and paid the men for their work.

They started east toward Powder Wash with their horses and made many miles before they set up camp for the night. A couple of more days brought them to wagon number nine. Approaching the round up wagon, the cook gave a hello to Guy and told them to turn the herd loose while they ate themselves some grub. Guy introduced the Kid to the cook, Bobbie Bowen. As they shook hands, Ivan knew he would like this man.

The good ranches of the West knew if they fed their men well they would get more and better work from them. Most ranches fed in the same manner. Breakfast consisted of coffee, biscuits, cow meat, potatoes, gravy and some kind of fruit sauce. Dinner was about the same but there were vegetables added such as corn, green bean and toma-

The Boys Fed "Ole Dick" Biscuits

toes with some pastries thrown in. The men always liked fruit pies and bear signs (doughnuts). Supper was about the same with things like cooked rice with raisins to which the individual man added sugar and spices to suit his taste. They had milk from the Carnation can or if an old cow with a calf was near the daring young men would rope her to get some fresh milk. In this part of the West, men would not eat dried cooked beans, because of the discomfort they caused. The cook never allowed horses near the cook wagon because they drew flies. The cowhands bathed when they had water every day. They lived in the open but did not reduce themselves to live like a filthy beast. They were loyal to the company they worked for.

As the crew rode into camp, different men asked about the old black horse with no ears nor tail. Guy asked the Kid to tell the men the story of how that ole pony saved his life. Bragging on Ole Dick to the men was not hard. As he finished his story, many coughed or cleared their throats as they sat in silence.

Often, Ivan saw someone feeding Ole Dick a biscuit after a meal. The whole crew looked on that ole pony with favor. The Kid met good men that would take him under their wing and would teach him the cow business. They were men like George Watson who had a small ranch on the west end of Blue Mountain, Alf Christian, Titus and Billie Wear, Emery Clark, Lawrence Toughy Wren and Luther "Lute"

Armstrong. In a few days a crew consisting of thirty-five Two-Bar men and five reps were ready to sweep the country gathering cattle for the fall beef herd.

The seven horses in Lute's string looked like the horses Ivan had caught on Douglas Pass. When he asked about them, Lute said they came from the Bookcliffs and Douglas Pass and Creek area. He said they were the favorite horses among the ranches on the Oil Shale Plateau. They caught most of these horses southwest of DeBeque in Winter Park and Coal Canyon.

Two Half-breed Indian brothers, one named Dave Knight, the other Charlie Chipman, came to that range a few years earlier from Oklahoma. They brought a Steel Dust Stud with them and turned him loose to run with the wild horses that were all old mares. Most of the horses in that area descended from that old Steel Dust stud and mares the old Ute Indian Chief Coloro had left behind on his last hunting trip to Winter Park. These horses stood fifteen hands or more, being of a refined sturdy build. Although they would buck unexpectedly, they considered these horses the best cow pony a man could fork.

The afternoon before the roundup started, Bill Patton and Sol Pucket rode into camp. When the men gathered for supper, Bill told the crew Sol would run the wagon on this gather. Bill was usually the boss on wagon number nine but this fall he was running a wagon on Fortification Creek thirty miles to the southeast. From the first night at the wagon, Ivan night herded the remuda. Sol told him he would continue to be the night hawk. This job was to herd the remuda for the night. At four in the morning, the nighthawk brought the horses in and put them in a rope corral.

After breakfast, the men would catch the horse they were to ride. Then, the day herder took the horses to graze while moving toward the noon campsite. When there was a herd gathered, the night hawk had the remuda corralled at supper time so the men could catch and picket the horse they would ride on their shift of night herding. They divided the night into three equal shifts, which all but the cook and the horse wrangler had to work.

During his time off in the day, Ivan could catch some sleep and help the cook move camp. Each man would roll and tie his bed, leaving it in a neat bundle by the wagon. The men all knew if they wanted their bed at night camp they had to have it rolled and stacked. If anyone did not roll their bedroll in the proper manner, Bobbie tied it to the wagon and drug it through the sagebrush to the next camp. Some men had to ride back along the trail looking for their things as the war sack soon was in shreds from being dragged.

To help the cook, Ivan loaded the men's bed rolls on a wagon and put the stove on its cart. Then he harnessed and hitched the four mules to the bed wagon. After that, he followed the cook and his wagon to the noon camp.

Bobbie was one of the many cooks that used the small sheet iron stove to cook with on the open range. In its oven, they baked many delicious pastries. After he unharnessed the mules and turned them loose, he gathered wood for Bobbie's stove. A canvas hung under the bed wagon, making a sling that they kept filled with wood as they traveled along. They only used this wood when there was no wood near a camp site. With his camp chores completed, he could get some sleep until the cook was ready to move after dinner. He would help load the stove, hitch up, move to the night camp and then get some more sleep.

One dark rainy night, something spooked the remuda and no matter how hard Ivan tried he could not hold the horses in a herd. When he thought he was about to get them under control, his horse would become unmanageable making all he could do to stay on his back. When daylight came, he was in a country where he didn't recognize any land marks.

Just after sunrise, eight cowhands showed up from camp on their tired night horses. They helped Ivan collect the horses that were near him and all roped a fresh horse and started on the trail that the others had made. As they rode along at a fast lope, someone said it must have been a big bear after the horses from the looks of the tracks. It was only then that Ivan noticed a large set of bear tracks on the old pony's tracks.

After thirty minutes of hard riding, the men caught up with the horses and a large sow bear trotting along behind them. Most of the men took down their ropes and charged the bear. Some horses would not get close enough to her but those that did found themselves tied to her. One man roped her head and two others roped her hind legs. They stretched the bear among the three horses. The men shot the bear many times in the head and killed her. Rounding up the tired horses, they eased them back to camp. They all took the rest of the day off.

During the first thirty days of the roundup, the weather was warm and dry. Unfortunately, for the last thirty days, it rained every few days and sometimes it snowed, making life very uncomfortable. As they continued the gather, men from other associations stopped for a meal or stayed the night. Sometimes they borrowed a fresh horse, leaving the worn out one to pick up later. Ivan met many good men like those with which he was working. Some of these men were Smalley and Streeter Reinhardt who were brothers working at the L 7's. From the Snake River Association, there were men like "Doc" Chivington, Al McCarver, Harry

moving Camp

Laremore, Crawford and Hubert Beeler, Dan Howart, Dee and "Toots" Montgomery, Jesse Adams, Walt Yost, Obie Farnsworth, Jim and Bill Banks to name a few of the true old time cowmen.

The last two weeks of the gather Bill Patton came to the wagon and fired Sol Pucket. Patton claimed Pucket should have had a herd at the train stockyards at Wamsutter Wyoming by that time. Guy told Ivan that was old Bill's way of being mean to the men. Only a few of Bills cronies were not scolded. He always made the reps ride farther each day than any of the Two Bars men. From the start, Bill scolded the Kid for the littlest things, it seemed as if he were unable to please the foreman no matter how hard he tried. Lute Armstrong, from the Square S Ranch headquartered sixty miles to the south on Piceance Creek, took the brunt of Bill's abuse.

At last, the reps finished gathering the beef herd and left for home taking their ranch's cattle with them. Bill pushed the men and cattle very hard as they traveled the sixty miles to the rail head. They drove the herd by whipping them with their lariats and the trip took four days. If they had moved the herd at its proper pace, the trip would have taken six or seven days. With the herd loaded on the Union Pacific train and going east to Omaha, Bill paid the men not hired for the winter their wages. Ivan and Guy got paid their share for the horses sold to the ranch back on Blue Mountain.

Guy and the Kid turned in their company horses and caught their private horses from the remuda. Loading their equipment after buying a large amount of supplies, they started back down the trail from which they just came. Riding along at an easy pace, Guy talked about the reason Bill pushed the cattle so hard. He said old Bill and his cronies would take the cattle worn out or crippled from the hard drive and sell them later as their own. Bill, being the western slope ranch manager, would write them off the books as dead cattle.

By the middle of the second day, Ivan began to see fine horses in small bands. He asked Guy if they could not set up camp and run a few of them. He sure wanted that kind of horse. The older Mustanger replied, "Kid if you want to tangle with Ike Montgomery and his sons Dee and Toots go ahead and catch your self some, but leave me out of it. Ivan never asked about the answer he received.

The morning of the third day, Guy told Ivan to leave the extra horses hobbled, because he knew where a nearby trap was. This trap had a large pasture in a small canyon and a good pole corral in which to catch and ride the horses.

After a week of running horses into the large pasture, the men had captured nearly a hundred head to break to saddle. The frequent blizzards and deep snow made Guy think they should take the horses to Rock Springs and sell them to a buyer he knew. After three days of driving the horses northwest into the wind, the mustangers were glad when they reached town. Here they could pen the horses and stay in a warm dry hotel bed.

At breakfast the next morning, the horse buyer said he would buy all the horses they would bring to Rocks Springs if they had saddle scars on their backs. When the meal was over, the three men went to make a deal on the horses. The buyer talked of the army needing many horses for the war they thought would soon start in Europe. He told them he would pay fifty-five dollars a horse. After spending Christmas in town, they started back to the McNurlen camp on Blue Mountain.

As they were riding south of Rock Springs, Guy told Ivan about a rancher named Stewart who lived near Burnt Fork. He married a woman by the name of Eleanor and they each filed on a homestead right next to each other. They built a house straddle the property line. This way they filled the letter of the law by living on the land. He told Ivan there was many "widder" women with children in the country living on their own homesteads.

Telling Ivan about the country west of the Green River, Guy began telling of the good hunting they could do in the Flaming Gorge. He said if he had the time he would take Ivan there to hunt cats, deer and big horn sheep. The more he talked, the more Ivan thought it would make a pleasant trip to relax and get a winters supply of meat. Finally he said, "Guy what is a keeping us from riding on over there and doing a little hunting now?" Guy's reply was, "I don't rightly know."

Ivan had always heard people tell about the Flaming Gorge but he never imagined what a breath taking place it was to see. When they reached the bottom of the Gorge, he sat on his horse for along time looking at the many bright colored layers of stone and dirt that made up the walls of this deep canyon. It was easy to see why they called this canyon Flaming Gorge. He asked Guy how deep the canyon was and Guy said, "Oh its gotta be a quarter to half a mile deep."

The weather in the gorge was very mild and pleasant during the day but very cold after the sun went down, which was early in the afternoon because of gorge's depth. They rode along the river until they found a meadow that contained several hundred acres where there would be pasture for their horses. The meadow was full of large mule deer and on the rims close to the river they saw many big horned sheep. Guy asked, "Do you think we can find something to hunt here?" Ivan answered, "We sure could get something even if we could not hit them by shooting, we sure could sprinkle a little salt on their tail so they would follow us back to camp, they sure are not afraid."

The men set to making a good camp. They dragged in a good supply of dry wood with their lariats tied to their saddle horn. With this completed, they hobbled the ponies and set up the tent. When camp was in order, the men took their rifles with them and walked up the mountain side to look the country over. Deer were plentiful and so were the mountain sheep. Guy asked Ivan if he would like a little mutton for camp meat. When Ivan said he would, Guy raised his rifle and with a pull of the trigger they had a supply of meat for their camp.

They saw many mountain lions and bobcats in the area where they camped. Guy told Ivan it was because of the large amount of deer and sheep that is the main diet of the cats. The mountain lion did the killing and the bobcats ate the leftovers.

There were many timber wolves in the area but only on one occasion did they see them in the daylight. Nevertheless, the wolves sang them to sleep by the deep throated call in the night. Hunting for a week, the men had a good supply of deer and sheep that would give them meat all winter without having to stop and hunt. They killed a few cats and wolves for their hides that they would sell come spring.

As they left the canyon with their horses loaded, Ivan told Guy he would come back often to hunt in this enchanting place. The older man just shook his head up and down. Although the mountains of the West were full of these kinds of animals, Ivan thought the setting made them more magnificent. Ivan came back many times after to hunt and it saddened when the government built a dam at its lower end flooding most of the canyon.

Back at the McNurlen camp, they spent the winter. When the weather warmed for a few days, they would ride to Ivan's trap and always bring back horses they caught. That winter they placed a rock or stick under the saddle, the first time they saddled the bronc. This left a raw place on the horses back. When the sore healed, it left the horse with a white saddle scar. The army buyers would think they were buying well broke horses. While in reality, they only rode the horses a few times.

When the men saw a coyote in an open area they would give chase and rope it. Then they shot it for the hide that they would sell come spring. A horse could out run a coyote on the level or down a slope but if they went up a grade the coyote always got away. Roping a wild beast was just cowhand fun. A sport entered by all.

On days when the weather kept the men in the cabin, they would talk about the horses they caught. At times Guy told Ivan of the horses that was in the different areas, of Miles City, Montana and its rodeo and horse sale. He talked of the ranches that had as many as three thousand brood mares. He said they would ride to Miles City one day. Ivan asked about the small horses that looked like Clydesdales that were in the area of the fall roundup. Guy told him that ranchers turned draft

Hard fast

118

horse stallions loose on the range trying to increase the size of the mustang. The Two Bars had turned some Clydesdales loose on Powder Wash and Lay Creek, on Green Mountain. Near Casper, a rancher let Belgians loose and by Lander Perchrons was roaming free. These large draft animals produced too large a colt and many mares died while trying to foal.

Ivan asked about the Thoroughbred horses they saw on the Red Desert south of Wamsutter. They told him of an Englishman by the name of Ike Montgomery who came to America to get in the cattle business. Being used to the bigger English saddle stock, he could not adjust to the small Western mustang. Each fall he would go back to England to spend the winter. In the spring for several years, he brought an English stallion to the Red Desert that he turned loose with the mustangs. The horses they saw were the decedents of those stallions. Old Monties sons were now running the ranch, which only ran horses. All mustangers knew of this old boy's reputation and never messed with any of his horses.

When Spring arrived, Pat McNurlen came to camp with a friend named Harold Bathurst. They were going to help with the horse herd Ivan and Guy had caught during the winter. When they trailed them to Rocks Springs, they pushed the horses along at a good pace and were in town in four days. As they drove the horses in the holding pens, the buyer counted them. He took the drovers to dinner and wrote them each a check for the promised amount on the horses. The mustangers went to the hotel where they got a hair cut and a bath. Before leaving town, they bought new hats, boots, clothes and supplies, after which they headed for wagon number nine and the spring roundup.

Back at wagon number nine, they found old Bill in a bad mood and almost a whole new crew. There were reps from as far south as the Grand River. They said their bosses sent them to gather all the stock from down their way because rumor had the Two Bar Cattle Company closing down their Western Slope operation. From DeBeque and Roan Creek, came cattle pools Harvey Scott, Jim Anderson, John and Clarence (Clarie) Armstrong who were brothers to Lute, the square S rep. Another brother named Bill reped for the Oland Ranch. John Baker, the Armstrong boy's cousin, reped for the P. L Ranch owned by the Mager brothers. The last three ranches headquartered on Piceance Creek. These reps told of hearing the same rumor that the Two Bars was shutting down.

All the men from DeBeque and Peiance Creek area were riding those fine Book Cliff horses. John Baker had seven pinto horses in his string and when asked about them he said a neighbor named Shake Coleman raised and broke only pinto horses. Shake and his wife

Mattie came from New Mexico with a herd of these pintos, and John liking them bought a few and started raising them too. He said he would not ride company horses because they were not tough enough to stand up to a days ride. If spurred in the shoulders, these fine ponies would buck in the morning and after forty miles of riding would still buck in the evening.

From up north by Riverton, Wyoming, came Will James and an older man known only as Bearpaw. They told of hearing the rumor the Two Bars was shutting down and they came to gather every hoof that belonged up north. They were reping for the Y. Bench Ranch owned by a man named Montgomery, who lived in England.

Will James was riding the most beautiful smoky blue horse Ivan had ever seen. Will called the horse Smoky and was very protective of him. Smoky had the Rocking R brand on his left lower shoulder. Ivan asked Guy where that ranch was and Guy said somewhere up around Judith Basin Montana. He also told Ivan that the smoky blue horse came from the Pryor Mountains near the Shoshone River. When Will James was resting, he was always drawing pictures of horses and the range life. Guy told Ivan to stay away from that outfit because they were a tough bunch. Ivan asked Guy if sometime they could go to the Pryor's and catch some of those blue horses. Guy's only reply was, "Maybe."

There was much talk about Vol Hoggatt being in cahoots with Frederick Bonfils of the Denver Post. They were trying to bring settlers and homesteaders to the Great Divide. This would take many thousand acres of grazing from the cattlemen. There were long discussions about the large number of sheep just north of the Wyoming/Colorado border.

The cowhands thought the Cattlemen Association was right to hire killer Bob Meldrum to police the border between the two states. They had a good laugh about the cowboys' army that rode to California Park in Colorado last summer to stop the great sheep invasion. A man rode into Craig. He said that he saw ten thousand sheep driven into the Park by many men. They had several wagons and many dogs helping.

Panic spread like a brush fire and telegrams the cattlemen sent to Steam Boat Springs, Meeker and Rifle for armed men to come and fight off the devastating invasion. In three days they had men from the other three towns and many from Craig ready to go fight and repulse the enemy. When the large army of one hundred and fifty heavily armed men rode into California Park, all they found was a seventy-year-old man and fifty sheep. The great army soon disappeared by groups of three or four, leaving the old man to pasture his sheep in that high mountain valley. None at the roundup admitted taking part in that war. Ivan sat quietly and listened while they discussed the sheep business.

Bobbie was still the cook, but he had a new nighthawk, which made Ivan happy. Now he could work the cattle. On the spring gather, they branded all the young stuff and castrated bull calves. They held the herd on the bed ground by spacing men a few hundred feet apart. They rode back and forth keeping the cattle in a tight circle. Men that were handy with a rope rode into the herd roping an unbranded calf by both hind legs. They dragged the calf outside the herd where there was a group of men by a fire where the branding irons heated. One man grabbed the calf by the head, which he sat on and another took hold of the feet. The man on the feet removed the rope as the roper told the man that used the hot iron to burn the figure in the hide.

The man on the iron was an expert. He had to burn the hide perfectly or the brand would do one of two things. If the iron was too hot or left on the animal to long it burned clear through the hide. This caused a bad sore that could get infected by the flies causing suffering or death. If the iron was too cold or not held in place for the right time the hair would grow back and the animal would not have an identification.

Before the ropers flipped their loop, they watched to see what brand the cow was carrying so they could tell the iron man what to put on the calf. These men never swung a rope over their heads or rushed any animal. They moved very slow and quiet among the herd. With their loop hanging from their right hand, all that was to be done to make their catch was give it a flip. They allowed only the best ropers to do the roping. If a man missed three tries in one day, the boss replaced him with another roper. One man would rope as many as three hundred calves a day. Generally three men worked the herd at anyone time. Ivan was one of these men that always did the roping.

The nighthawk was from Vernal. He told Ivan that he and Ivan's brother Milt had stopped at Dragon that winter and old Bill Calthorpe had nearly beaten Milt to death with a pistol handle. He also told Ivan that Hatch Murray had mortgaged his land, sold his cattle and bought a large band of sheep. He took them to the Green River Desert for the winter. The weather warmed early and Hatch thinking it was spring had the sheep sheared along with most sheep ranchers.

A late spring blizzard blew in after the shearing scattering the sheep all over the place as they drifted with the storm. When the snow melted, he found several bunches with as many as five hundred in a wash dead. The nighthawk said, "Rumor had it with the loss of most all the sheep he was broke and was now herding sheep for another ranch."

Bill pushed the men and the cattle very hard. This crippled and wore out many cattle. It was not long until there was a small herd of these. Within a short time, Bill sent this small herd with some of his

stopin the Beefing

cronies to Rocks Springs. The men wondered who received the money from these poor cattle. He seemed to scold and berate Ivan a lot more than he had at the fall roundup. In the evening, Bill would catch the horse he would ride the next day and put him on a picket so when he awakened the cook, Bill would saddle it.

When the nighthawk arrived at camp in the morning, Bill ate. Then he walked through the sleeping men giving them a kick on the feet to wake them up. As they were eating, he gave the day's orders and cussed the men because they were not in the saddles gathering cattle. Each passing day he became more abusive to Ivan. One day Guy told Ivan that if he helped him gather a few cockleburs they would put a stop to old Bills ornery ways.

When they had a few burrs, Guy and Ivan got up early one morning ate and saddled their gentlest horses. While the other cowhands were eating and Bill was cussing them, Guy slipped around old Bill's horse and placed the burrs under his saddle. Bill cussed and harangued the men until they mounted after which he climbed on his horse.

It was always just getting day light when they rode from camp, so it being dark Bill had not noticed Guy doctoring up his ole pony. Guy and the Kid never mounted but stayed on the ground holding their horses because they knew what was going to happen. There was a chill in the air and those ole ponies sure felt lively. When Bill mounted, his ole pony felt those burrs dig in his back. He bogged his head between his front legs and went bucking with all his might through the men sitting on their horses.

When the dust cleared, only Pat McNurlen and Will James had ridden their horses to a stand still. The rest of the men had been bucked off and their saddles fled to another part of the range. Guy and Ivan held their horses on the ground so they didn't escape. This made Bill blame Ivan for the whole affair. The range horse bucked if he saw another of his kind doing it. When Bill's horse cut a path through the mounted men, those old ponies joined the fun, spilling most of the riders in the surprise of the moment. Bobbie Bowen dug in his wagon to find his saddle so he could saddle a work mule to help catch the loose horses. After three days they had enough saddles and horses to continue the roundup. Before the roundup ended, they caught all but three of the horses with saddles. They didn't catch those three until the fall roundup.

On the morning they started working the cattle again, Bill and four of his cronies held Ivan over the back of a gentle horse and started beating him with a pair of bat winged chaps. When the chaps hit the Kid the fourth time, Bill felt a rifle barrel touch his right ear. Guy McNurlen said in a cold clear voice, "Hit the kid one more time and your brains will scatter in the wind." As he let the chaps drop, the cook waved his meat clever near his head and said, "You even look at that boy again and I will lob off your head." Bobbie's meat clever was a famous item through the western cow country. It was eighteen inches long and ten inches wide. Bobbie cut steaks with one chop. He even cut through the bone. He kept it razor sharp at all times.

Kind hands tenderly laid the near dead young man on a bed in the bed wagon where Bobbie and his friend cared for him many days. In the wagon they would not move him around, but he would travel as camp moved. In those four hard blows, Ivan had narrowly escaped death. When he was able to be up and around, he helped with small chores at the wagon. When the roundup ended, Ivan was well enough to work again. Most of his friends were going to take in the Fourth of July celebrations, but Ivan said he had some business to take care of down at Dragon. Before parting Ivan, Guy and Harold Bathurst planned to meet on Raven Ridge, to see if they could catch the old Buckskin stallion, "nemesis" of the West.

Guy Mc Nurlen
&
O.H. Waterhouse
" tyin' him loose"

Bill Calthorpe and the Buckskin

Chapter 19

Leaving the roundup wagon, Ivan went to the McNurlen cabin to check on Ole Dick whom he left behind when he went to the spring gather. Riding into camp, he saw the old black horse coming to meet him. Resting on Blue Mountain made the young man feel like his old self. Loading his belongings on his pack horses, he started the trip to Dragon with Ole Dick going along. While riding along, he thought of what a bad man Bill Calthorpe was. When he thought of Mary Calthorpe's death, Ivan decided to give Bill a lesson that he would not forget.

As he thought of the events that led to Mary being killed, Ivan wondered if there was any justice in the world. Old Bill, His two brothers and sister Jane were the source of the whiskey flowing in the White Rock Indian reservation. Mary worked for Bill, keeping house and driving one of the four horse teams when they went the forty miles to Rangley for supplies. She would not take part in his evil and illegal activities. The Federal Marshals placed an undercover agent in the town of Rangley to find out where and how the whiskey was reaching the Indians. The agent worked three years in the area before they hired him to haul freight from Loma to Rangley. It took him another three years finally to make the connection that would implicate old Bill.

The one hundred eighty-mile round trip took from ten days to three weeks depending on weather and road conditions. Snow blocked the road from October till June. During the four months the trail was open, the freighters had to ship the whole years worth of supplies. The freight outfit consisted of two large wagons hooked in tandem and pulled by a twenty-mule team. The skinner rode in a saddle on the left wheel mule using a jerk line to guide his hitch. These mule skinners were masters with their long black snake whips. They could pick a fly from the lead mule's ears without even touching it. If they wanted, the skinner could cut an animal to shreds. The agent hauled freight for two years before he learned a man named Bill Calthorpe was the owner of the freighting company. Bill had two outfits hauling freight from the Denver and Rio Grande railroad at Loma.

After three years, the freighter was ready to quit and give up on finding the source of the whiskey. Someone always loaded and unloaded his wagon for him. On the last trip he planned to haul, he did his usual check when he stopped for the night many miles out on the road. The top of the load was groceries, but the bottom of the wagon contained boxes of whiskey. He traveled on with hope he was closing in on the whiskey running gang. When he reached Rangley, he watched for several days to see who came to town after supplies. After several trips, he noticed an outfit from the west driving two light wagons pulled with four horse teams. A woman drove each wagon. Both women carried guns. Also, three heavily armed men rode in the wagons. The outfit always came to town in the evening, left their horses in the livery barn, but disappeared before daylight.

The next time he went to the railhead for freight, he telegraphed his office to tell them of his discovery. Then he explained his plan to capture the outlaws. This investigation took more than six years. The government sent five marshals to Rangley when the office received the telegram. The five marshals over took the freighter a few miles north of Douglas Pass where he explained how they would capture the criminals.

On the evening after his arrival in town, the wagons from the west arrived. The agent went to the marshal's secret camp and explained that the whiskey runners were in town. The marshals then broke camp and moved to the road West of town so they would be ready to make their arrest.

As the wagons loaded with whiskey headed down the road in the cool freshness of morning, the people riding in them were happy when the sun began to ascend over the dark form of the mountain. As the sun got higher in the sky, the warmth it gave made everyone feel calm and relaxed. They had been on the road several hours and were making good time, when they ran into some unwanted company blocking the road. They were looking into the barrels of four Winchester rifles with a federal marshal attached to the other end. These bootleggers did not intend to let four men on foot stop them even if they were holding rifles.

Bill and the others lead the way in the first wagon. Mary followed in the other wagon. At the sight of the lawmen, the driver in the lead wagon and Mary laid the lash across the backs of their horses. The tough little mustangs lunged wildly into their collars and were off at breakneck speed. Just as fast, the men in the wagon drew their guns, and lead began to fly. The outburst cleared the road. The lawmen's only chance to stop them were to shoot the horses. They got the lead team on the first wagon, which caused the second team on this hitch to stumble and fall. The wagon ran on top of the horses causing it to wreck.

126

Quickly, Mary pulled along the side of the first wagon, slowing just enough for the people in the first wagon to jump on while the cracking of pistol and rifle held the marshals at bay. With Mary laying her lash on the horses back, the rest of the gang was shooting and unloading the wagon supplies on the trail to slow the marshals.

When the wagon had traveled four more miles, they ran into the second road blockade. The gang rushed head on at a breakneck speed with bullets flying. The two young and inexperienced lawmen standing in the road shot and killed the driver instead of the horses. As Mary fell backwards into the wagon bed, the team of half-broken mustangs, feeling the lines go loose put on a burst of speed, which lasted until they dropped in the harness many miles from where the driver was shot. The lawmen though mounted on faster horses could not over take the gang, because when they were in shooting distance Bill and his gang shot back. They knew their team would run until it dropped, but that would be long after the marshals' horses had. This at last ended the whiskey flowing to the reservation. They never arrested Bill for that crime.

Three days of riding and Ivan was at Dragon ready for a show down for the way Bill had treated little brother Milt. Ivan turned his horses loose in Bill's corral and gave them a good feed of hay from the stack and oats from the granary. Entering the bar, he bought a bottle of whiskey. Seating himself at a corner table, he placed his six shooter in his lap and began pouring the whiskey in the glass.

When no one was watching, he poured it on the floor. As the bottled emptied, he acted as if he were getting drunk. He did not drink one drop because he wanted to be cold sober when he faced old Bill. The bottle was about empty when Bill came into the bar and saw Ivan seated in the corner looking drunk.

A silent hush fell on the noisy, crowded bar as old Bill came over to the table and leaned across it, saying, "You little smart aleck I am going to teach you the same lesson I did your good for nothing brother." Before Bill could move, Ivan had his six shooter barrel touching the end of his nose. Ivan was holding the hammer back with his thumb and the trigger pulled with a finger. The blood rushed from Bill's face as he realized he was not dealing with a small boy. Warning Bill not to move or even blink an eye or else he would kill him, Ivan began telling him the things he did not like about him and his business.

Ivan first explained what he thought should happen to a man that would get his own sister killed. He said, "Mary was the only good one of your outfit." Then Ivan went on telling what he would like to do to a man that would sell his own daughter to a man to use as a whore. After that, he told him he was going to kill him for beating Milt with the handle of a six shooter. The cold hard look in Ivan's eyes told Bill that his life was about to end at the hand of a very angry man. When he finished, he told Bill if he was in sight by the time he counted to three he would get his brains blown out. At the count of two, the coward fled the room.

Ivan sat there in the silence of the crowded bar and studied the stricken faces. Compassion filled him as he saw Edna sitting on the bar. When she was fifteen, her father sold her to Bill for five hundred dollars. Then he took her to Denver and married the young girl. She was a very beautiful young lady and Bill used her as well as selling her to his patrons for a few minutes' pleasure. She still had the look of hope on her face so Ivan thought he would try to get her to leave with him.

Ivan waited for three days to see if Bill would show his face. When he did not, Ivan planned to leave. Ivan never saw old Bill again. He asked Edna if she would like to leave this place. She said if he would take her along the answer was yes. Ivan told her to get her things packed and he would get the horses ready to go. After saddling, loading and packing his own horses, he caught Bill's best horse, saddling it with the best saddle he could find in the storage barn. He then caught six more good horses for the lady to take along, placing a pack saddle on one to carry the lady's luggage. After loading, they left town heading North toward Blue Mountain where she found the man she loved.

After leaving her at Leo's camp on Blue Mountain, Ivan rode to Vernal to visit Grandmother Mary and his brothers and sisters. Also, he planned to buy a new saddle from the old blind saddle maker. The saddle he now used was the one he bought the first time he went back to Vernal after running away from home. With the years of hard use it was worn out.

Grandmother Mary and Merle cried when they saw their dear Sky. How happy they were because they thought they would never see him again. Mary was soon fixing Ivan a meal and telling him of the events that had taken place in the last two years. She told how Hatch lost his sheep in a poker game.

When Ivan asked about his brothers, She told him Nile and his father were up on the Uintah's herding sheep for a big sheep ranch. Glen was working wherever he could find work on farms or ranches. Merle was living with her and working for neighbors doing mostly house work. She helped in the garden and sometimes even in the fields. Uncle Nels and aunt Kate were giving little Ellen a fine home with all the comforts a girl could want. She was not sure about Milt, but she heard he was working for the T. I. Ranch on White River up at Meeker.

Merle asked where he had been since he left with the sheep for the desert. He told her he had just been around working. Mary then asked if he sold his share of the sheep and if Hatch paid him for herding his sheep. "Dad lost the sheep in a poker game, I have not seen him since he left me in Glenwood Springs," was Ivan's reply. "Where have you been living and what have you had for money?" asked Mary. "I was living in my own tent catching a few horses to sell. Also, I worked on roundups for the Two Bars," he told her. Ivan stayed a few days at Grandmothers so he could visit his brothers and sisters.

When he left, Ivan rode to Father's and Nile's camp in the high Uintah's. While there, he decided to hunt moose on the north slope. Upon reaching the north slope, he soon found a lake with many a moose nearby. He picked a fine two-year-old bull that he killed and took back to give part to Hatch and Nile, as well as Grandmother.

Telling Grandmother and Merle good-bye, he drifted east to Raven Ridge to meet the boys. He arrived a few days before they did. He found a fine camp under an over hanging cliff where a spring was flowing. From this high ridge, He could see the country for many miles. While waiting for the men, Ivan rode through the country, looking for the best place to build a trap. There were times when he saw a buckskin stallion leading his large band of horses. This band was different from any he had seen for the fact the stallion lead instead of driving his band. All wild horses have a mare that leads them and the stallion brings up the rear herding the stragglers along. The buckskin allowed another stallion to bring up the rear.

Ivan gave chase just to see where their trails went. The way that band disappeared, it was if they vanished from the face of the earth. Deep, wide, dry washes cut through the country. They only had water in them during a cloudburst or when the snow melted. This band of horses knew this maze of washes so well they could run for miles, staying out of site. The Mustanger knew after a few days why this horse was a nemesis to all who tried to catch him.

When Guy and Harold showed up, they wanted to start to Miles City Montana in a few days. They promised to help Ivan catch the old buckskin before leaving. If they left in a week or so, they could catch horses all the way to Miles City to sell at the big horse sale and rodeo. When they left Miles City, they planned to rent a cattle car on the Great Northern Railroad to haul their outfits and horses to Walla Walla, Washington. They wanted to enter the rodeo in Walla Walla. From there, they planned to ride down to Pendelton, Oregon. From Pendelton they planned to ride to Winnemucca, Nevada, catching horses to sell upon their arrival at the Nevada town. From there they would catch horses back to Rock Springs.

After selling those horses, they would come back to Skull Creek for fall round up. At Skull Creek it would be a clean gather as the Two Bars was starting to close down. They told Ivan about the Nez Perce Indians suicide race that started the Pendelton Roundup Rodeo. He wanted to go, but in the few days he had chased the Buckskin he knew that ole pony had to be his. If he could catch that horse, he would go with them.

Starting early in the morning while it was still cool, the three mustangers rode about ten miles to the west before seeing any signs of horses. The country along the Colorado Utah border was full of large gullies that had seeps and grass in them. While crossing one of them, they rode right into the old buckskins' band. In the excitement and confusion, the herd scattered to the flat above.

The men gave chase only concentrating on the old buckskin. The rest of the horses were soon following in the chase. Riding at breakneck speed while spurring and whipping their mounts, they were not paying any attention to the ground they were passing over. Guy's horse stumbled and fell, rolling him and Guy in a large patch of cactus. The other two stopped and helped him up and out of the cactus. Arriving back at camp, Ivan and Harold began picking cactus thorns from Guy's body beside the camp fire. It was close to midnight before the job was done.

The next morning Guy was up and ready for the day's fun of chasing the old buckskin again. They found him and his band near where they were the day before. The chase was going quite well and it looked as if they might get close enough to herd the wild horses into one of their traps. Going down a steep hill, Harold's horse fell, rolling him into a cactus patch. Helping Harold out of the cactus, they started back to camp to dig the thorns from his body. They had almost reached camp when a desert cloudburst with heavy rain and lighting struck them.

At camp, they quickly unsaddled their horses. Ivan's horse wanted to stay in the shelter of the over hanging cliff, but Ivan drove him away. The horse insisted on coming back so he hit him with the bridle reins. The horse finally started to go to the other horses when a bolt of lightning hit and killed him. Being less than 10 feet away, the lightning knocked Ivan unconscious. His two friends soon had him in the shelter of the cliff.

When he came to, he tried to stand up and found his spurs welded together. He took them off and got to his feet. With a lot of work, they got the spurs separated but lightning welded the rowels solid. He could still use them but when he reached a place where he could get new ones he did. It was late in the night before they got all the stickers out of Harold.

Filled with superstition about the ole buckskin being a horse that the spirits took care of and something bad would happen to those that tried to catch him, Ivan used the excuse he needed to stay in camp for a while and work on his rigging. By the

The Ole Buckskin

middle of the morning from his high overlook, he could see the cloud of dust the running horses made when the two mustangers found and started chasing the wild herd, though they were several miles from camp. Watching the cloud of dust from the running horses, Ivan knew where the horses were going. The wild herd was running a mile a head of the two riders and was pulling away.

When the dust from the wild ones stopped Ivan knew they had reached a deep large gully. This gully only had one entrance from the south side and there is where they had entered. He knew the horses could only go west where they would have to swim the Green River or come east to a juniper covered flat where they could hide. Ivan quickly saddled his horse and started as fast as his horse could run the four miles to the gully. He took an extra sixty foot lariat along.

Upon reaching the head of the gully, he could hear the wild horses running toward him. He tied the sixty-foot rope to a juniper tree beside the trail. As the old leader came out on the flat, Ivan roped him, leaving the old buckskin tied with one rope. Quickly taking the rope from his saddle he roped the horse again. Backing his horse until he had the stallion tied tight between the tree and his horse. With their leader caught, the rest of the herd scattered but stayed close. Taking his rifle from its scabbard, he fired three shots. He waited for several minutes and then fired again. He did this several times hoping this would bring his friends to help him.

It was an hour before his friend's arrived on the flat where the man had the old horse caught. It did not take them long to rope his feet, pulling him to the ground and hogtying him. They soon had Ivan's hackamore and saddle on him and with Ivan in the saddle they turned the buckskin loose.

When the bronc got to his feet, Ivan knew he had never forked a horse that could buck like this one. In a short time, Ivan's nose started bleeding from the terrible beating he was receiving. Guy roped the horse's hind legs giving the rider time to dismount and Harold then roped the horse's front feet. Leaving him saddled and hogtied while the men rode back to camp with Ivan riding bareback.

The next morning the old horse was very angry and bucked with more fury than the day before. They tied the buckskin down and unsaddled him. Then, the men gelded him, hoping that the soreness caused by the castration along with the lack of food and water might make them able to ride the old buckskin in a couple days.

The old stallion's band acted confused without their leader and stayed close not being afraid of the men. They soon had most of the wild herd roped and tied to trees, which they set about breaking to ride.

On the morning of the third day, the men got the near dead horse to his feet and saddled him. He was easy to ride and by noon he gave into the man's commands. Ivan rode the worn out horse to camp where he hobbled and unsaddled the horse, leaving him on a picket rope as well. With water and feed the horse was as good as new the next morning. Ivan walked up to the horse and saddled it and rode him away as if he had ridden that ole pony for years. The horse never bucked again in the rest of his long life. The mustangers soon had camp packed on horses and were driving their new herd north toward Montana.

With the new herd not trail broke, the men pushed them really hard for the rest of the day so the herd would tire, making driving much easier. By mid afternoon, Ole Dick had tired and was lagging behind several miles.

After camp was set up and supper eaten, the old black horse walked wearily into camp. Ivan baked a batch of biscuits. When they were cool, he fed them to the old pony. Each man took a shift night herding the horses so they would not start back home. Ivan also hobbled the old buckskin.

At breakfast, Ivan fed Ole Dick a good helping of biscuits. Traveling at a slower pace, the old black was able to stay within site of the herd most of the day. It was after dark when they turned the herd in the pasture at Guys' dugout. When morning came, Ole Dick was at the corral to welcome Ivan as he went to bring in the herd.

Miles City and Pendelton

Chapter 20

Ivan left the old black and two of the Douglas Pass horses in the pasture when they rode on toward the north. Using the other Douglas Pass horses to pack his camp on and using the old Buckskin to ride, he started to Miles City with Guy and Harold driving their herd. When reaching Greystone, they rode the length of Browns Hole and then straight North to Rock Springs. Crossing that part of the Red Desert, it surprised them not to see any wild horses.

Stopping at a sheep wagon for dinner, the herder told them the country was full of mustangers catching every horse they could find. He said the army was buying anything that could walk. At Rocks Springs, they sold the herd, keeping only three horses apiece. Ivan rode the buckskin all the way from Ravens Ridge. The buckskin was the toughest horse he had ever ridden. He never seamed to tire.

Riding northeast toward Muddy Gap, they found the desert full of outfits trying to catch horses. Traveling light, it took three days to reach the crossing of the Sweetwater River. Up here, they got away from all the people trying to be mustangers. For the next one hundred and fifty miles north to Buffalo they caught many good ponies. This country had only wild horses and cattle roaming over it. Sometimes they met a cowman looking after his stock. The mustangers caught and broke so many horses it took two weeks to cross this prairie. Ivan soon found the old buckskin could out run the wild horses, making him the one to do the roping. The country between Buffalo and Sheridan pleased Ivan so much he said he might come back there to live his life, but for now he continued his adventure. All the horses they saw in this country carried brands, so they traveled as much as forty miles a day. He liked the well-watered valleys that ran west from the road to the Big Horn Mountains. He had never seen such good grass as grew on the prairie along the Big Horns. Sheridan was a very modern city and he thought it would make a pleasant town to spend some time.

From Sheridan, they followed the Tongue River down stream still watching for unbranded horses. Stopping at a ranch for the night, they asked if there were any wild unclaimed horses in that part of the country. The men at that ranch said the ranchers owned all the horses in this country. They said most ranches ran more horses than cattle. They told of a ranch

that had three thousand Percheron brood mares. When the colts reached four years old, they shipped them to the Chicago market where farmers bought them to use as plow horses.

One of the hands told of a ranch farther north that raised several thousand mules each year that they shipped east when the colts reached four. They said Miles City Shipped more horses to eastern markets than any town in the West. From there, the mustangers pushed hard and were in Miles City in two more days.

At the rodeo grounds, they found a pen to put their herd in and bought some hay. They found a camp site nearby and they soon had their tent set and camp made. The only thing they had to do was feed the horses for nearly a week before the sale. There were buyers from all over the United States and Canada looking over the horses brought to the sale.

With time to kill, Ivan and his friend's took in the sights of the city. In one saloon, a man wore a red sash tied around his waist. He bought drinks for many of the boys. When he saw them, he asked them where they hailed from. After telling him they were from Northwestern Colorado, he had the bartender set them up a few rounds, which he enjoyed with them. He gave his name as Charles M. Russell who hailed from Judith Basin and Great Falls. Russell spun many interesting funny stories. In later years Ivan learned that this was the famous "Cowboy Artist."

When the rodeo began, the three Colorado men signed up and paid their money to ride a saddle bronc. Guy and Harold placed in the money, but the noise of the crowd made Ivan lose his concentration. He forgot the rules and spurred his bronc wrong so the judges disqualified him. The owner of Steamboat had the old bucking horse there as well as a big black horse he called Midnight. When he saw Ivan, he asked if he wanted to put on an exhibition ride. He could ride Steamboat whenever he wanted to make the ride. After watching those Ole Ponies put on their show, Ivan told the man he did not care to risk embarrassment in front of this big crowd. He told Ivan that every hand that tried Midnight got dumped before the gun went off. Clayton Danks was the only one successfully to ride Steamboat. He told Ivan, "You rode him at Vernal if the timer had shot the gun on time."

Ivan said that he wanted to ride the black in an exhibition, but the owner said, "You must draw him like the other boys." The man asked Ivan if he was going to Walla Walla and Pendelton. Ivan told him he was and then the man asked him to put on an exhibition ride on Steamboat at those two places.

When the celebration wound down and the crowds left, the three Colorado men rented a box car on the Great Northern Railroad and left for the west, having sold all but two horses each. The train had Steamboat and Midnight as well as many other cowhands and their horses. Ivan and his friend's bought enough lumber to make a gate to fence the old Buckskin along with the other five horses in one end of the car. In the other end, they set up camp.

The train chugged along day and night stopping only long enough to fill with water, coal, and change crews. It passed through Billings, Bozeman, Missoula, across the chimney of Idaho and Spokane Washington. A few miles from Spokane, the Engineer stopped the train on a siding. The mustangers wondered why he stopped at this little burg. They left their car and asked some cowmen about the stop. One of the hands told them the great Suicide Race was about to begin.

Climbing to a hill above town where a crowd was, Ivan looked across to a flat filled with Indians dressed in the finest costumes he had ever seen. The Indian's sat mounted on their ponies in a long line standing side by side. At a given signal, the ponies sprang forward in a wild race.

The Indians screamed and whipped those ponies around a staked course three miles long. The staked track ended at the top of a very steep hill that was over five hundred feet down, with a wide deep river at the bottom. When the horses and riders reached the top of the hill, there was no slacking of their speed. The ponies jumped when they came over the crest where they landed many feet below. There were few of the horses that landed on their feet. The rest slid down into the river in one great mass of horses and riders. The horses who managed to stay on their feet swam across to the other side where they entered an arena with their rider.

The men in the river boats helped those riders that got hurt and could not swim the river. All the horses swam to the arena. The young man that reached the arena first got many prizes and sat with a beautiful dressed young lady for the rest of the celebration. Ivan wanted to watch longer but the Engineer blew the train whistle. Many times after, he wondered where that little town was. When morning came, they pulled on a siding at Walla Walla where the train ride ended.

Walla Walla Valley was a very pleasant place to be. Many streams and rivers ran through the valley. The farmers raised fruit and vegetables that were of a fine quality. The town was home for two colleges. Also, this was the place the Marcus Whitman's Mission to the Umitila Indians had been.

For four days, the cowhands rode bucking horses and roped wild cattle. It was a fun celebration. Ivan placed in the money several times and was happy because this paid for the train ride so he saved the money he received from the sale in Miles City. He hoped he could draw Midnight so he and that old black bronc could prove which one was the best.

The Drumheller livestock company furnished the cattle and bucking horses for the Walla Walla Stampede Rodeo. Mr. Drumheller asked if any of the men going south to the Pendelton Roundup Rodeo would help drive the stock there. The three Colorado men were among the large number that volunteered to help, "Beings they was ridin' to Pendelton anyhow." Ivan entered the Roundup Rodeo and placed in the money, which made him feel the trip was a good paying vacation. While in Pendelton, he went to the Woolen mills and purchased a heavy winter coat and four blankets along with some winter shirts.

Riding southeast from Pendelton, the three mustangers thought the Blue Mountains had no rhyme or reason to the way God formed them. It was cloudy and overcast with rain most of the way to Baker City. Riding south from Baker City, they soon went over a pass that took them to familiar looking country. Two days later, they began to see signs of horses. They did not like the first ones they saw because these horses were large raw boned animals with a large head.

These jug headed horses did not appeal to the men that had been riding the full blood mustangs. These horses seemed inbred with some kind of draft horse. As they rode south, all they saw were of this quality so they began catching them as they traveled. The horses were much slower than the ones they were riding and it did not many take days to have as many as they could drive.

Upon reaching Winnemucca, Nevada, a buyer for the army took the horses off their hands at a good price. Traveling at a steady pace, they made many miles each day. Several times, they stopped for a few hours and caught horses. They tied these horses together for travel, but they never took time to break any as had been their practice in Oregon and Nevada. Never stopping for more than a night at any place, they were soon back to Rock Springs and sold the wild horses to a buyer.

136

Skull Creek Roundup

Chapter 21

The buyer told the men Bill Patton had sent word to tell them they were to go to Skull Creek where wagon number nine would be working the Roundup. When reaching Skull Creek, they found three wagons with seventy-five men starting to make the gather.

Bobbie Bowen was cook on number nine wagon. Cranky old Pat Dawson was the cook on the other wagon. Tug Wilson and his Meeker Association wagon generally worked the area as well.

Pat Dawson seemed to hate everyone including himself. When he talked, it was to complain or to cuss someone. He had been the Snake River Associations cook for many years but was so cranky they no longer hired him. The only thing that he showed any signs of liking was a huge old crooked-stemmed black pipe that always hung from his mouth. It was so covered with nicotine that the hole in the bowl was no bigger than the end of Pats' little finger.

The biscuits and most of the other food had a gray tell tale sign of ashes in them. Pat had a large coffee pot that held three gallons. He made coffee by adding ground coffee each day. He never dumped the grounds or cleaned it until it was so full of grounds there was no room for water.

When he wanted to, he could be the finest chef that ever cooked a meal. His pies and pastries were as good as ones that his mother used to make. Most of the time, he was angry and just threw some grub together.

The DeBeque and Peiance Creek reps were all there. They planned to take all the cattle belonging to the south with them as it was rumored that this was the Two Bars last year to operate. This seemed true because the Two Bars rounded up every one of their cattle, sweeping the range clean. Ivan got assigned the rough string of horses, which consisted of unbroken and outlaw horses. He took these horses without a question because they were like most he had been riding and the pay was a third more each month.

When they gathered in all the cattle on Skull Creek, they pushed east, gathering all the cattle and horses that they could drive in a herd. As they moved east, they cut out the other ranchers' cattle and their rep took their cattle back to their home ranch.

Ed Miles, manager of the Cary ranch and head of the Upper Yampa Association, sent several men from the upper Yampa to work this gather. Ivan met men he would be life long friend's with like Ed and Ray Peck, Harry Ratliff, Bill Brewster and George Salisbury.

The roundup continued east. When it reached Maybell, Bill Patton rode in with orders for number nine wagon to work on northeast to the Great Divide country, taking Harold and Guy with it. Ivan stayed with Pat Dawson's wagon and worked on through Axle Basin. Bill said the Two Bars horses had already been gathered from the horse ranch in Axel Basin and driven to the ranch on the Laramie Plains.

A few days before they reached Maybell, Pats old black pipe came up missing. The nighthawk, Jim Robinson, not knowing any thing was wrong went to the bread box to get a biscuit for a snack. As he reached in the box, old Pat hit him, breaking two ribs with a stick of firewood yelling he would kill him. Jim ran a safe distance from the enraged man and shouted, "What's wrong with you Pat. You told me I could get a cold biscuit any time I was hungry."

With many words of profanity, Pat accused Jim of stealing his pipe. Pat accused every man on the roundup of hiding or stealing the pipe. Even the foreman gave the little Irishman plenty of room. None of the men knew where the pipe was.

Three days after the wagons parted, two reps whose names were Harry Abbott and Harry Armstrong rode in from the Square S Ranch to help clean the Danforth Hills of cattle. They rode in at breakfast time and were told to "belly up and feed your face."

After riding all night, they were not in the best mood. When Harry Armstrong poured and tasted his cup of coffee, he cussed the cook while he got to his feet and said, "No man has to drink this crap." Picking up the coffee pot, he took it to the edge of camp and dumped the contents out on the ground.

As he turned around, he met the meat cleaver swinging cook. Throwing the coffee pot at the cooks feet to trip him, Harry turned and ran for his life. Pat tripped over the pot and fell face down in the pile of coffee grounds.

As he started to get up, he just sat back on the ground and began to giggle like a little girl. The hands thought he had taken leave of his good senses. He reached in the pile of coffee and held up the most

Pat and his Pipe

beautiful hand carved lion head white ivory pipe that any of the boys had ever seen.

The men stood motionless, watching the little man enjoy his discovery. When he at last came to himself, he went to the fire and threw out all the food on the ground. He told the boys, "You come back in a couple of hours and I will have you a good meal," which sure he did. For three weeks old Pat talked and chattered like a school girl. Also, he fixed the best meals the boys had ever eaten and cleaned the coffee pot after every meal.

When the wagon reached the country near the town of Lay, Bill Patton showed up and sent it north up Lay Creek. He sent Ivan onto Axle Basin with Harry Armstrong of the Square S and another rep from the White Bears Ranch. The headquarters of the White Bears Ranch was in Lily Park on the Bear River (name changed later to the Yampa River), which was on the east end of Blue Mountain. A group of small investors comprising of school teachers, college professors and preachers owned this ranch. This ranch was like a town unto itself. It built an elaborate irrigation system that put five thousand acres into cultivation. It raised poultry, garden truck, alfalfa hay, besides grains and many other crops. Oliver Waterhouse managed this large ranch-farm and used the brand W bar B.

When they reached Juniper Springs, the three cowhands stopped for a day to bathe and relax in the hot mineral water. They also took hot mud baths to take the kinks out of their bodies. The hotel resort was an oasis in this bleak and desolate land.

Reaching the T I Ranch's roundup wagon, they met the foreman, a man named Art Amick, who owned a ranch near Meeker. His ranch headquarters was a mile from the T I's. He worked the wagon as foreman so he got paid wages while he gathered his own cows that strayed to the basin.

The T I Ranch was one of the larger ranches in Northwest Colorado. They didn't even know how many cattle and horses they owned. When the ranch was at its prime, they ran twenty-three wagons, many south on the Grand River around Rifle and many on the Roan Plateau.

If a man needed money, he found a few horses with the T I brand on them. After catching them, he rode to the headquarters on the mesa South of Meeker. Then he told the ranch that he had been working at a certain wagon many miles from the ranch. Then, the ranch gave wages to the many scam artists. This soon put the ranch in a bad financial fix that led to their selling out and shutting down.

The new owner of the T I soon arrived in Axel Basin taking over the job as foreman. He had another wagon that he ran but it had finished roundup. The foreman brought two men with him, one of which was Ivan's brother Milton. The brothers were glad to see each other because it had been over to a year since they had both been at Vernal at the same time.

The foreman was a bragger that no one liked. He told how people were afraid of him and no one ever killed or ate his beef. In the West, it was a custom for the ranches represented at a roundup to furnish a beef occasionally for the men to eat. Many times, settlers or travelers also butchered a beef that belonged to the ranches. The men pushed themselves hard to get the roundup finished so they could get away from the old Bragger. When the sweep of Axle Basin finished and the herd cut, the reps started back to their ranch headquarters with their ranches' cattle and any that belonged on their home range.

Harry talked to Ivan about going with him for the winter to run wild horses on Douglas Creek and the Bookcliffs. Ivan did not want to ride the sixty miles back to the Two Bars headquarters in Lily Park. He asked the White Bears rep to take the Two Bars cattle and his string of horses back to the ranch for him. The White Bears man said he would be happy to take the stock with him. Ivan sent a letter to Guy McNurlen asking him to look after Ole Dick and his other two horses. Also, he asked him to collect and hold his fall wages. He told Guy where he was going to run horses and that he would see him in the spring. Ivan decided to go to Douglas Creek because too many people from Brown's

Hole and Lily Park went to Blue Mountain to catch horses to sell to the army. This left a small number of horses from which to choose.

After telling Milt good-bye, Ivan and Harry started back to the Square S. After having been on the trail most of the day, they came to one of the T I's cow camps. They decided to stay the night, giving them a place to shut their stock in a corral and to sleep in a bed for the night. There was a big fat T I steer grazing in the meadow near the cabin. These daring young men thought it would be a good joke on Old Bragger if they butchered it, which they did. Before leaving the next morning, they hung the hide from the ridge pole inside the cabin so when the door opened the first thing you saw was the T I brand.

As they traveled on to Piceance Creek, they gave the homesteaders they passed, some beef from old Braggers Steer. Upon reaching the Square S Ranch, they met their friend Harry Abbott. At supper, Ivan found that Harry Abbott was the Ole Man Sherers personal valet. Harry cooked all the ole man's meals, cleaned the house, washed and ironed his clothes and drove the car for him. When Ivan asked why he had worked the roundup, Harry said the ranch was short of help.

Mr. Sherer talked to Ivan and found out he and Harry Armstrong were only going to run horses for the winter, he asked Ivan and Harry to stay and haul hay to the cattle. When he could not convince the two young men to stay at the ranch, he told them, "I will buy all the horses you boys catch this winter."

The two young men stayed at the ranch until after Thanksgiving. Taking Harry's eight personal horses plus Ivan's two, they rode the twenty-five miles to where they set up camp on Douglas Creek below Cathedral Bluffs. This camp site was in a short canyon next to a south slope where the sun kept most of the snow thawed.

For several days after arriving, they spent their time building traps to capture wild horses. They built them in draws where trails crossed or near water holes used by the wild horses. To build the traps, they cut Juniper posts and fenced the draws above and below the trail or water hole. Also, they made gates to block the trail.

There were more mountain lions on Douglas Creek than there was on Blue Mountain. Being too rugged for good cattle grazing and mustanging, there were only a very few men that worked this area and therefore no one killed the lions.

Because of the lions killing the very young, the sick and the old horses, it made for a high quality of strong horses. While they built their traps, they saw many lions. Harry said, "Where there are a lot of cats, there you will find good horses." Therefore, they never killed the cats.

141

When they had six of the traps built, the fun began. They brought four pack horses loaded with oats from the ranch. They used the oats to grain their saddle horses. These grain fed ponies could run through the snow without tiring too quickly. This made the mustangers job easier. They herded only the best wild horses into their traps. The wild ponies grew weaker as feed became harder to find in the deep snow. In the weakened condition, they quickly tired. This made them easier to ride because they never had the strength to buck hard. The range horses never got hay except at the ranch headquarters. The Western cowman said, "If a horse can't live on the land he is worked on, he ain't no good." The only grass he got he had to find for himself. The snow was six inches to three feet deep depending on elevation or the slope of the mountain.

At camp, the first fence they built was across the mouth of the canyon. They used this for their horse pasture where they kept their saddle horses plus the newly captured ones. By the first of February, they had thirty-five new horses broke. They decided to take them to the Square S to see if the Ole Man Sherer would keep his word and buy them.

Driving the horses around the West end of the bluffs, they cut across the high mesa in two feet of snow to the ranch where they stayed a few days. The Ole Man liked the ponies and paid top prices for them. The mustangers told him they never needed money in the hills and he could pay for the horses in the spring when they came back with more.

Loading up their pack horses with oats, they started back to camp. About half way to camp, a Blizzard struck with all its fury, catching them on the mesa. It was closer to ride on to camp than go back to the ranch. They caught the pack horses, tied them together and leading them arrived in camp after midnight.

In two days, the blizzard blew itself out. Ivan caught a cold that he could not shake. While they were waiting out the blizzard, Harry told Ivan they should pack up camp and go over the pass to Coal Canyon in the Bookcliffs. He said the weather on the South side of the Oil Shale Mountains was much warmer than on Douglas Creek.

When the weather cleared, they broke camp and loaded it on their horses before day light to get an early start. When they struck the Rangley Loma road, the snow was three feet deep. They struggled for the next ten hours to get across the Pass. At the summit, the snow was five feet deep, making them shovel a path for along ways. Two miles down from the summit, the road only had two feet of snow. Here, they set up camp for the night.

Crossing the Pass tired the horses to the point that they were ready to drop in their tracks. The men stayed in camp for two days, letting the ole ponies rest. When they broke camp and started on, they drifted Southeast along the foot of the Oil Shale mountains. The weather was much warmer and there was not much snow on the South slopes, making travel much easier on man and beast.

When they reached a low saddle in the mountain, a large canyon ran off to the South. Harry said over the saddle was Dry Fork branch of Roan Creek and the canyon running South was Coal Canyon. He said down Dry Fork was town and home. He did not want to go home, so they started down the canyon. From Coal Canyon, they could reach Winter Park where there were a lot of horses or go to Soda Springs a few miles farther.

He pointed out Ole Dave Knights main camp. Dave had many places he hid food and kettles. By carrying a blanket tied on his saddle, he would be near a camp wherever he traveled in the Bookcliffs. Ole Dave took the labels from the cans as he cached the food. When he was ready to cook it, he just opened several cans and dumped them in his Dutch oven. He said, "It all gets mixed together any way," Meat, corn, tomatoes, peaches or whatever he opened were what you ate at his camp.

They crossed a well-worn trail that Harry told Ivan was the White River Ute Indians main trail from the Grand River Valley to the White River at Meeker. He said his Grandmother fed the old Biscuit Eater Coloro when he came begging at the Conwell ranch on Roan Creek. Chief Coloro was self-appointed chief to a small band of about a dozen old Indians that came to this area every summer to beg and hunt. The ranchers' wives felt sorry for this band and always gave them some handouts that were mostly biscuits, which the Indians ate with gusto. Because Coloro stopped at every ranch and fed, he gained a lot of weight giving him a very large belly. This short man with a large belly riding on a small pony was a funny site to see, always making people laugh who saw him. He and his band were harmless and when he died the people around DeBeque missed the old biscuit eating rascal.

As they rode down the canyon, Ivan began to see signs that sheep grazed in this valley. By evening, they reached a sheep camp where Harry introduced Ivan to Jim Berry and his son Kenneth who lived in DeBeque. These men had a small band of sheep that they pastured here in the winter and in the high mountains to the east in the summer. The sheep men asked the mustangers to spend the night with them and they could sleep in the wagon with them.

Ivan once saw this type of covered wagon used on the Green River Desert. It set on four low wheels with a four foot wide box that was two and a half feet deep and ten feet long. There was a platform at the top of the box that stuck out two and a half feet that they used to sit on or sleep. The top had eight wooden bows across and slats every eighteen inches running length ways. They covered this with a good duck canvas. A door was at one side in the front. The door was split in two parts, so the driver of the wagon could drive with only the top half open if the weather was bad. Next to this was a cupboard containing cooking utensils and food. There was a small one burner stove that they used for heat and cooking. Across the rear were more shelves for storage and the bottom of the beds hinged up where there were compartments to store many items.

The Berry's were deeply religious people, having prayer and studying the book of Mormon every day. Also, he gave thanks to the Deities before each meal. Kenneth was Ivan's age. He told Ivan that when spring came he was going to Europe on a seven-year mission for the Latter-day Saint Church.

Ivan told the Berry's he grew up a Mormon, which started a friendship lasting the rest of their lives. The horsemen stayed a few days with the Berry's while they looked over the prospect of traps and horses. Jim told the men they would find more horses at Soda Springs or in the side canyons farther down toward the coal mining town of Cameo on the banks of the Grand River. The Berry's asked Ivan to stay with them until his cold was better. Ivan thanked them and said he needed to work and so they left.

Moving down Coal Canyon, they found the valley to be full of wild cattle and horses. Most of the cattle had a big two foot circle branded around the tail. Harry said that was Ole Dave Knight's brand. He went on to tell how no one could ever alter it. The brand was registered the Circle Dot, but Dave had another brand that he used for his horses. Harry led the way to Soda Springs where there was a good set of corrals and a fenced pasture. Here they set up camp under a cliff from which a stream flowed. Ivan became sick with pneumonia and never left camp for two weeks. The sun shone every day. During the warm part of the day, he sat against a sandstone where there was heat from the sun and soon was back to work.

In the lower elevation of the canyon, there was little snow and the horses were in good condition, making them harder to capture. Ivan had never seen better horses in the wild, so he worked extra hard to catch as many as he could.

There were many buffalo in these hills. When Ivan asked Harry about them, he said they belonged to Ole Dave. Dave turned several loose after he came here from Oklahoma. In the protection of the hills, the buffalo increased in number. One day, it started to snow while the mustangers were several miles from camp so they abandoned their work for the day and started back to camp. When turning up the canyon that led to Soda Springs, they met three men, one of which was John Baker the man that reped for the P L ranch at the Two Bars round-ups one hundred and fifty miles north. It didn't surprise him to see Harry, but told Ivan he was the last person he thought he would ever see in these hills. John introduced the other two men as Dave Knight and Kenny Craig who was younger. The three men were on their way to Soda Springs and Winter Park. They said this storm was going to be a bad one and they needed to move some cattle and horses down to Coal Canyon out of the snow.

The five men spent a comfortable night under the cliff. Early the next morning, Ivan and Harry rode with the others to Winter Park to help move the cattle from there to the lower canyon. Back at Soda Springs, they turned the cattle loose to drift with the storm on down the canyon. When the storm blew itself out, Dave and his men left. The old Buckskin horse proved his worth that winter by carrying Ivan on many wild rides that always ended with some horses caught.

As the grass began to grow and the Sago Lilies and Cactus began to bloom, the two men knew it was time to start back to the ranch and spring roundup. They each wanted to stop by home for a visit with the home folks. The winter's work was well rewarded with a fine string of well broke horses. Ivan and Harry drove down the canyon to Cameo and onto Grand Junction. In Grand Junction, they sold most of the horses to the army.

Taking a few days to relax, they each got a hair cut and new clothes. With new boots and a new Stetson hat, the men each started toward home. Harry rode north to DeBeque. Ivan went west to Loma and then north to Rangley. The weather was warm and pleasant, making Ivan glad to be alive.

In three days, he arrived at Douglas Pass where he stopped for a day to let his horses rest and eat. Three more days found him sitting and eating supper with Grandmother Mary. Grandmother was very happy to see Ivan. She told of the happenings in Ashley Valley since he was last there. He told her of seeing Milt at the fall roundup in Axle Basin and how he was getting along. Ivan visited with Merle, Glen and Nile before he started to the Two Bars Ranch in Lily Park.

After two days of traveling the Vernal-Craig road, he was twelve miles east of Elk Springs where he turned north heading for the Little Snake River on which the ranch was located. He arrived late in the night.

While he was taking the saddle and packs from his horses, Guy came to the corral to help him. Guy was quiet at first so Ivan asked, "What's a biten' at you Guy." The older man said, "I have some bad news for you Kid. The old black horse never made the winter, but I brought your other two broom tails with me." The two men stood for a long time in the moonlight without saying a word, but each knew how the other felt about Ole Dick and his passing.

As they stood there, they talked about the ranch being shut down. Guy asked the Kid what he planned to do after the roundup was over, because he figured there wasn't any future in runnin' horses. Ivan told Guy he "didn't rightly know." Then Guy told Ivan the Texaco Oil Company was hiring drivers to drive trucks in the oil fields. "Kid you ought-a go get yourself one of those high paying jobs rather than killing yourself breaking horses," Guy said as he started back to the bunk house.

On the morning the roundup started, Bill Patton sent number nine wagon to Skull Creek to see if they missed any cattle in the fall. While they worked an area near the south end of Blue Mountain, Guy and Ivan saw twenty head of horses in a band and one had part of a saddle on it. The old mares leading the band had a brand on their jaws that the men could not get close enough to read. Only the three mares and the horse with the saddle carried brands. This was sure a fine bunch and they wanted to take time to catch them but the roundup was moving too fast.

It took a couple of weeks to sweep Skull Creek and be back at Maybell where men from the ranch met the wagon to receive the cattle. Next, they sent the wagon and crew to the Great Divide to sweep that range clean. They told Ivan and Guy to ride to Axle Basin and get the cattle gathered at the T I Roundup. The men from the ranch took those already gathered and left for the ranch.

Before they left for the basin, Bobbie told Ivan and Guy that Vol Hoggat and Frederick Bonfils had started a settlement at Great Divide. They were bringing in a lot of settlers into the country. Ora Haley told Bill Patton to hire guns to keep the settlers out as Hi Bernard had done to the Brown's Hole people a few years before. Bill never did any more than have a few fences cut, causing the steers to ruin the Nester's garden. The cowhands rode up to the Nester's cabin, making threats but they never shed any blood. The sheep from Utah were crowding in, making a more immediate problem for the cattlemen.

The two mustangers could not get the herd of horses near Blue Mountain out of their minds. Instead of riding to Axle Basin, they rode west to find the horse with the saddle. A days hard ride took them to where they saw the twenty horses.

After making camp, they rode out to get a better look at the brands. When the lead mares saw them coming, they took off on a dead run toward the south. Being too late in the day to give chase, Guy and Ivan went back to camp. They planned to get an early start the next morning.

The next morning they picked up the trail without any trouble. It was several hours before they saw the band a couple of miles to the southeast traveling at a good pace. Guy told Ivan those old mares are heading back to their home range, which could be a long way away.

That night they camped where Black Sulfur Creek emptied into Peiance Creek. The old mares and their band started growing tired enough that the men could get within a quarter of a mile of them.

When morning came, the old mares were only half a mile from camp and seemed to be content. Pushing on up the ridge east of Black Sulfur, they saw some lot stakes with flags on them. This made the men curious so they went to look them over. They found them by an iron pin with a brass top about three inches across. The numbers stamped on the brass plate never made any sense to them.

Keeping the horses in site, they looked to see how many pins they could find. By noon, the horses let them close enough to them to rope the one with the saddle. They removed what was left of the saddle, exposing the raw bloody back. They were trying to figure out the brand when out of a nearby draw drove four men in a wagon. The man driving introduced himself as Joe Juhann, government geological surveyor. He said they had been working the Shale Oil Plateau for three years. They started near Rifle and were now working in this country. He asked them to come to his camp for dinner.

As the men rode beside the wagon, one of the men asked where they got the horse with the sore back. They told how they came about him and all the men laughed, saying a young man from over by Rifle had worked for them last summer. This horse and the three old mares belonged to him. He was a poor rider and one morning he was bringing in the team and other horses when a bear spooked them and the horse spilled the young fellow. The horses left in a hurry and they had not seen him since. A cowhand from the Square S brought the team to camp a few days later, but said he never saw any more horses. After eating, the men rode out to where the other horses were and soon had two of the old mares caught. The one that led was too crafty to get a rope on so they let her run free.

That night, the surveyors told them the bear that caused the horse problem last summer was bothering them again this summer. They set up camp in an old abandoned trapper's cabin. The cabin sat out on a wide ridge in the middle of a sagebrush flat. There was no door on the cabin so they hung a tarp over the door to keep out the night cold. There was a cooking pit in the center of the cabin where they hung a Dutch oven. They cooked the next day's meal every night before going to bed in this big caste iron pot.

One night the old bear came into the cabin and got the lid off the Dutch oven. He started eating the beans cooked in it. As he moved about the kettle, he stepped on one of the surveyors, which woke him up. The stinking bear had the bale of the kettle over his head. As the men awoke, they started shouting, which scared the bear. The kettle came unhooked from the hook it was hanging on and the bear with his head in the pot took off, trying to find the door while knocking down everything in his way.

Well, they thought Mr. Bear spilled beans all over the cabin and them while knocking them down and walking over them. At last, the bear found the door and sure left in a hurry. Not being able to find any matches in the turned upside down cabin, the men went back to bed although the cabin stunk like a bear's winter den.

When daylight came the next morning, the surveyors discovered the bear had been eating Sarvice Berries and had never spilled a drop of beans in the cabin. The mess came from the opposite end of the bear. Not surprisingly, because of the mess, they moved outside in their tent. They found the licked clean pot a few hundred feet from the cabin. They never saw Mr. Bear again. Leaving the horses with the surveyors, the cowmen started riding hard for Axle Basin, laughing about their great wild horse chase and the bear in the cabin.

Two days ride brought the two men to the T I's roundup wagon and old Bragger. A rep from a ranch near Craig rode in shortly after them. While eating supper, the Craig rep who was very talkative, rattled on about how good the food was. He told how his ranch never ate their own beef but figured if they fed someone else's they would eat some of it.

At this point, Old Bragger broke into a tirade about people who went through the country killing another man's beef. He never said anything about anyone being afraid of him. Ivan and Harry never showed any sign they knew what he was talking about, but gave each other a knowing look. When he finished, he sat quietly listening to the other men talk. In the morning they made the cut. Then, Ivan and Guy left with the Two Bars stock.

The Changing West

Chapter 22

At Lay, they met men with a herd of Two Bar cattle and threw their stuff in with them. As they rode to Great Divide, Ivan told Guy about the T I steer butchering. In the country around Great Divide, Guy and Ivan were sure set back at what they saw in the middle of the best range to feed a cow in the whole country. One day as Guy rode by a nester's cabin, he heard a woman screaming for help.

Spurring his horse, he soon was at the cabin where the man sat on the woman beating her unmercifully. From time to time, the man jumped to his feet and gave her a few kicks. Then, he sat on her and started to beat her again. Guy had a mighty good helping of respect for ladies and he was quickly working on that bully. He was working him over right good when something hit him along the side of the head. Squaring off to protect himself from the other person, he found himself face to face with the broom wheeling woman. She was yelling, "This is a family fight so get on out a here." That old cowhand sure did oblige the old gal.

As Ivan searched down a draw for cattle one day, he saw a well-built log house with a man nearby grubbing sagebrush and a woman piling and burning it. He rode on over to get acquainted with them. They said their names were Lum and Lucinda Pankey. The couple came with their children came from Missouri to homestead on Great Divide. They invited the cowhand to have a little lunch with them. They told him they had three sons who fought the Kaiser in Europe. Ivan sure took a liking to the Pankey's because they were just plain, hard-working home folk.

When he left, he noticed the fine mules and horses in Lum's corral. Also, he noticed the large pair of oxen they used for breaking the land for the first time. It made him think of Uncle Jake Workman and his one ox that pulled the cart back home in Vernal. Ivan knew these were some of the last men that would ever use the oxen for draft animals. As Ivan rode on, he saw many more people making homes and clearing land in which they planted potatoes and wheat.

Back at the wagon, the boys talked of the fast changing world and what they were going to do when the open range ended. Many talked about the oil fields and the big wages paid there. With fewer cattle on the range, it did not take long to finish the roundup. The weather turned cold. It rained or snowed most of the time they made the drive to Wamsutter with the cattle. At Wamsutter, they loaded them on the train for Omaha Nebraska. What horses the Two Bars had, they shipped them with the wagons to the Laramie Plains.

Rumors were that Ora Haley was about to quit the cattle business for good. They paid the men off when the train left with the cattle, horses and wagon heading east. Many hands found jobs in the oil fields and never worked cattle again. Some staked a claim and started a farm or small ranch so they could marry and raise a family.

As Guy and Ivan traveled back to Craig, they saw the many new homesteads and small ranches filling the country. Guy said he could work for the White Bears where he would have to do some farm work besides horses and cattle. Ivan said he might herd sheep or work in the oil fields. When they reached Craig late in the evening, there was a message for Ivan that his Grandmother was very ill. If he could come home, she would like to see him.

It was three o'clock in the morning when Ivan rode from the livery stable driving his three pack horses along with the extra ones he had not sold. The wind blew a newspaper across the street under one of the pack horses and that set him to bucking. This started the other two pack horses and the other loose stock to bucking. They all felt good even the old Buckskin who made a few short crow hops. The Ponies soon quit bucking and broke into a long slow mile eating lope led by the one wearing the cowbell. This lasted for seven miles and as they slowed to a trot, Ivan kept them at this pace for many miles.

Five miles east of Elk Springs, Ivan could hear a car coming from the west before he could see it. He drove his horses off the road and let them slow to a walk. The tired horses never shied as the car passed.

The car had a glass wind shield. It was all enclosed with a canvas top having windows made of ising glass. The wind blew and it was cold. Ivan wore his heavy sheep skin coat to keep warm. When the car slowed to pass, the driver waved and Ivan saw he was not wearing a coat. It lay on the seat beside him.

His horses were all worn out except the old buckskin. When Ivan reached Elk Springs, he asked the owner to take care of the worn out ones and his camp equipment. After they stored the equipment in the back of the store and turned the ponies to pasture, the men warmed themselves by the stove.

150

Homesteaders
Barbed Wire
and
Cow hands

D.F. Murray

Ivan told of seeing a man driving a car and not wearing a coat. The owner said the man stopped to fill with gas and showed him this new invention that heated the car with gas. The owner said he did not believe it so the man said, "Sit in the car and see for yourself." "Well, I sure did and you know the contraption sure did make that car warm. What do you reckon they will think of next?"

Ivan reached the Green River Ferry at sunset, leaving eighteen miles to ride to reach Grandmother's. He reached home and put the old buckskin in the barn. That ole pony was near dead. His ankles and legs swelled to twice their normal size by the next morning. The horse never ate or moved for three days after the long hard ride.

In a few days, he was back to normal and Ivan gave him to Uncle Jerry who needed a gentle horse to herd his sheep. He told Uncle Jerry about Ole Dick dying and the horses he left at Elk Springs, Uncle Jerry offered to buy the horses and equipment from Ivan. This made Ivan decide to see if he could get a job driving truck in the oil field, so he sold his outfit to Uncle Jerry.

Ivan stayed with Grandmother taking care of her needs until she was up and around again. Then, Uncle Jerry and Ivan took the stage that went to Craig. When it reached Elk Springs, Ivan paid the store owner for the keep of his horses and equipment. He helped Uncle Jerry pack the equipment on the pack horses.

When the stage left, Ivan started on a new way of life. By changing teams at regular places, the stage reached Craig after two days of travel. When the weather and road were dry, they used a truck as the stage. If it was wet, the faithful horses pulled the coach. It took as long to make the trip in a truck as when they used horses. The freighters still used twenty mule teams to haul freight over the road in this part of the West. From Craig, he took another stage to Casper, Wyoming, where the Texaco Oil Company had an office for hiring men.

Texaco hired Ivan and sent him to school to learn how to drive the big trucks used in the oil fields. Texaco paid him wages plus room and board while he attended the driving school in Casper, Wyoming.

After completing his training, the company sent Ivan and seven other drivers to Rawlins to get their new trucks that came from the East on the train. They loaded the trucks with pipe that came on the train. Then they hauled the pipe to the Tea Pot Dome oil field near Midwest Wyoming. There were not any cranes to load the pipe, so the men took the pipe off the train by hand and placed it on the trucks. It took all the men lifting at once to move the long pieces of pipe.

These new modern Coleman trucks were the best equipped trucks that money could buy. The wheels had wooden spokes with an iron rim. Hard solid rubber three inches thick and five inches wide covered the iron rim. They had a cover over the motor with the exhaust ending just behind the driver's seat. It had no muffler. There was a box seat for the driver to sit on. The seat came equipped with a wide leather belt that had a harness buckle to hold the driver in his seat. Behind the seat, there was an iron plate as tall as the seated man to protect him if the load should shift.

Because of the danger of rocks breaking the windshield, the trucks used in the oil fields never had one. They had no floor boards, leaving no place to catch dirt. The driver sat on the seat behind the steering wheel where he could reach the clutch, brake pedals and the gear shift. The throttle was a lever attached to the steering column that you operated by hand.

The company furnished the driver with clothing. They made the hat out of a heavy horse hide with no brim. It fit tight to the driver's head and had a pair of goggles attached. They wore a heavy horse hide coat over a brown shirt made of cotton. Their trousers were made of brown canvas and they tucked the legs in leather boots that laced to just under the knees. To protect their hands, they wore heavy gauntlets made from a horse hide.

When the men had all the trucks loaded, they hooked them in a line, using a four-inch pipe twenty feet long with a chain running through it. They connected all the trucks in a line. Then they fastened their loads so it could not move. The reason they were hooked in the line was they could help each other through mud holes or over hills. The roads they drove on were just trails used by wagons pulled with teams. There were a few bridges built on the main trails. They were the first in that country to use trucks instead of teams and wagon to haul freight. They still passed many freighters on their trips.

Texaco would not allow any hooks used on chains so they fastened the ends of the chains with a bolt clamp. After the men cranked and started their engine, they got buckled in their seat and at a given signal all started moving together. They traveled at the unheard of speed of twenty-five miles per hour.

Sometimes when the front trucks got stuck in a mud hole, the rear trucks kept pushing. This folded the line like an accordion. They upset a few of the trucks this way. When this happened, the rear trucks backed up, pulling the stuck ones out. Then they unloaded the ones that upset and the men set them back on their wheels after which it was loaded again. Ivan drove one of the middle trucks. This made it very noisy and dirty.

On the morning after they loaded the trucks, the drivers set out for Casper at three-thirty in the morning. It was an exciting time for the new drivers as they tried to keep their truck at the right speed and follow the one in front of them.

By lunch time, they reached Muddy Gap where they went to the boarding house and ate dinner. Also, they filled their trucks with gas. After dark, they reached the terminal in Casper where they stayed the night in company barracks.

The next morning, they left after day light for Midwest and the Tea Pot Dome oil field. They unloaded their trucks and were back in Casper for the night. The next day, they went back to Rawlins for a load of lumber for derricks and drills with their motors with pumping equipment.

Ivan liked the fast travel of the trucks and decided he needed one of the new automobiles that he saw in the towns and along the lonely trails he traveled. He was saving his money to get a start in ranching, but figured he could afford to buy himself a new Buick automobile now that he had such a good paying job. While on the road and not using the automobile, he would leave it in the carriage shed at the livery barn.

At breakfast one morning, Ivan met a waitress that served them. He asked her if could start calling on her when he was in town. She told him that it would be all right with her if he called on her. He took her to the Saturday night dance and picture shows where they had a lot of fun together. When she asked him to go to Sunday Mass with her, he became silent. Finally, he told her that all a preacher wanted was a person's hard earned money and the answer was no.

They continued to see each other for the time he drove truck for Texaco. She gave him her Rosary telling him it would protect him and bring him good luck. He kept it for many years, but felt it did nothing for his protection or luck.

During the first year with Texaco, Ivan hauled mostly from Rawlins to the oil field around Casper, but after that he went on other hauls. By then, the oil company let the trucks be unhooked from each other unless there were very bad roads. They now went in groups of three, so if they broke down or got stuck, they could help each other. New oil fields started at places like Powder Wash, Craig and Axle Basin to which Ivan hauled supplies to build derricks and the drilling equipment.

On a trip west of Casper to Riverton, he stopped for the night at Shoshone and in the saloon there were three outfits of freighters. The freighters all bragged about their teams and how good they could drive them. One said he could bring his team of twenty horses with two loaded freight wagons and the camp wagon hooked behind in at a dead run. Then turn a corner to a side street leading to the livery barn.

The bets were about even on the driver's ability and those that said he could not. Ivan knew those men were good but passed on the betting. At daylight, people lined the streets waiting for the show to begin.

Coleman Motor Truck

It was not long until the freight outfit rolled in from a side street from the livery barn and drove out of town where he turned around. The rules were that he had to turn the corner at a dead run and go back to the livery barn.

Outside town where the driver had room to turn around, he did so and then laid the lash to those ole ponies. They didn't allow him to have his brake man or helpers on the wagons. He had a fine team of Hamiltonion's who were very much alive on their feet. As he came down the street, there were those that bet on him who changed their minds because of the speed he was traveling. He was riding the left wheel horse shouting orders to the team as well as whipping them.

Without letting off, he swung the lead team around that corner with the other teams swinging so close to the far building that it looked as if they would crash into it. Shouting and swearing instructions to the team, he rounded the corner with his wagons in the middle of the street. The freighters never left town for four days because of the celebrating they did.

While Ivan was there, he heard the freighters talking about a freighter and his helper they called the crazy Dutchmen. These two men got their wagons stuck in the sand and buried the wheels about two feet deep. They set the wagons a fire thinking this would lighten them, but their freight only smoldered, creating a large plume of smoke.

Three cowhands working in the area went to see what the smoke was about. Coming to the top of a rise, they saw the two men just finishing chopping the lower legs from the team. As they rode on toward the outfit, the Dutchmen grabbed their pistols and started shooting at the cowmen.

Staying out of pistol range, they carried on a long distance conversation with the two crazy men. The freighters said they cut the legs from the horses so they would be closer to the ground and that the horses could pull more that way. One cowhand rode to Lander to get the sheriff. The other men went on about their work because the Dutchmen would not let them close enough to put the poor horses out of their misery.

When the Sheriff reached the wagon, the team had bled to death. Only one man was there and he was just wandering around the outfit talking to himself. The freight outfit's owner came with another team, unloaded the wagons and got them out of the sand. It made Ivan sick along with the others at the saloon when they thought of the horrible waste of eight good horses. The sheriff took the one he caught to the insane asylum in Evanston Wyoming. Later, someone found the other man's body in the desert. He died of exposure to the desert heat.

The first winter was a hard winter with a lot of snow and many blizzards. When Ivan and the trucks he was with got caught out in the open, he tried to find a hill or bank to stop near to provide shelter. He always gathered a good supply of wood and had a big fire to keep him warm. They put chains on the truck's wheels and with a lot of shoveling always made their run.

Al Ayers was the mail carrier between Rawlins and Craig. He carried a pair of snow skis and chains for his car. He fixed the skis so they fit on the front wheels of the car. Al put the chains on the rear wheels and the skis on the front. With this setup, neither snow nor mud stopped the mail from going through. Al passed the trucks in fine fashion without even needing to stop.

When Ivan was in Craig, he saw many of his friends'. On one trip, Guy told him that Oliver Waterhouse manager of the White Bears Ranch would hire him to help catch horses. Ivan said, "Maybe at some other time Guy, but this trucking ain't half bad." Guy sure acted disappointed with that answer.

When spring came, there were so many changes that comprehending it all was hard. Craig was a fast-growing town with new people arriving every day. George "Smoky" Kitchens built a new hotel with a new gambling parlor and a fine saloon. The railroad reached Craig from Steamboat Springs. It was supposed to be on its way to open the Mormon country of Utah, but it never went past Craig.

There were whole train's loaded with immigrant families with their household and farming equipment, cattle, poultry, pigs and horses. Each trip, Ivan saw more of the fine range land being lost forever to the plow. It made him sad to watch it all happen.

On one trip, he stopped at a lone wagon camp where there were some milk cows along with many small lambs. When his truck stopped, a pretty young lady and a small child came from the tent to see what he needed. He told her he just wanted to rest a while and thought he would pass the time of day with her old man.

As he visited, he learned she was a widow and did not have an old man. She told him her name was Grace and the little girl's name was Mable. Grace's parents were the Pankey's over at Great Divide. She told him she worked for one of the new preachers and his wife caring for the small children and keeping house for them in Craig. When she had enough money, Grace bought the team, milk cows, wagon and the camp outfit.

She went on to tell how she got started in the sheep business. She met a sheepman in Craig who offered to give her his bum (orphan) lambs if she came to his range on the little Snake River in Wyoming at lambing time. She took him up on his offer and made the same deal with other sheep rancher's. She took as many lambs as was possible for her and her little girl to handle.

With her fine outfit, she was doing very well and had a nice flock of lambs. She said she filed on a homestead on Brown's Hill where her brothers' Emmet and George were building her a cabin by the big spring. They had just returned home from the war in Europe. As the lambs grew, she slowly moved toward her homestead where she lived for the required time each year until she proved it up. Then, she filed on more land. She filed on the section with a spring. In this dry country, this spring was the only water for miles around. This gave her control of a large area of land. Thus, she had plenty of pasture for her sheep. Although, this meant she had no close neighbors.

Ivan hauled many loads to the new oil field in Rangley, Colorado. Also, he went to the oil field on Wilson Creek near Meeker, Colorado. Much of the land that the oil companies now owned, Ivan could have bought for one half cent an acre five years before. He had the money to pay for it, but like many other people he felt the land to be worthless. He hauled many supplies from Casper to Craig where the oil company was in the process of building a new oil refinery. A new pipeline was under development from Sinclair, Wyoming to Los Angles, California. To this project, he hauled many loads of pipe. He spent many hours driving, but the pay was good so he never minded the long hours spent on the road.

That summer Texaco Oil Company bought a new fleet of the most modern trucks available. These new trucks came equipped with dual wheels on the rear so they could haul bigger loads. They had a cab for the driver to sit in with doors and glass windows that you could roll up and down. Also, they had a heater to keep the driver warm. The drivers no longer had to wear the heavy gear to drive them. The trucks were very enjoyable to drive on good dry smooth roads. If there were just wagon ruts or mud, the dual wheels were too wide for the wagon ruts. Mud oozed between the dual wheels and covered the tires. This resulted in the loss of all your traction. You just set there with your wheels spinning and you sat stuck. After a few months of fighting the trucks over the impassible roads, Ivan quit his job.

He went to Vernal in his own automobile. At Vernal, he bought a new saddle and camp outfit along with bridles, ropes and anything else he needed to run horses. After a visit with Grandmother Mary and the rest of the family, he went back to Craig where he caught a ride to Lily Park and the White Bears Ranch. He left his automobile with a friend to use and care for while he was out in the hills. Oliver H. Waterhouse put him right to work helping Guy catch and break wild horses.

As manager of the White Bear's Company, O. H. Waterhouse built wing dams in the Bear River that converted water into irrigation canals that made it possible to bring thousands of acres into crop production. Along with hay, the ranch raised many diversified crops, such as potatoes, garden produce, corn, wheat and oats. They also had a large flock of chickens as well as a dairy herd and many pigs. Diversification made the ranch able to survive the changing times. They still ran a fine herd of beef cattle. Also, they kept a large herd of saddle horses to use in handling the cattle. In addition, they owned many draft animals to pull wagons and farm equipment.

When haying time started, O. H. Waterhouse asked Guy and Ivan to help in the fields as part of the hay crew. Ivan enjoyed working in the hay fields and could run the mowing machines or dump rakes. He preferred to run the bull rakes that pushed the hay from the windrows to the stacker. He never minded working on the stack to make the hay in a neat stack that looked like a loaf of bread when completed.

The hard work gave the men a good appetite to which the cook fed them fresh fried young chickens, new crop potatoes, green peas, along with other vegetables and fresh-made fruit pies served with ice tea. Sometimes the cook made ice cream using the ice from the ice pit.

During the winter they cut blocks of ice and stored it in the pit, covering the ice with sawdust to keep the ice from melting. When they finished haying, they had several hundred stacks of hay containing forty tons in each one.

When the farmhands started the irrigation water in the fields, the two mustangers went back to the McNurlen camp on Blue Mountain. They took a large herd of donkeys with them along with several horses packed with camp supplies and oats to feed the donkeys. Ivan and Guy used these donkeys to teach the wild horses to lead.

After capturing a horse, the mustangers roped it by the front feet, throwing it to the ground. Then they hogtied it and put a halter on him. Next they tied the mustang to a burro's neck. They untied the horse's feet and turned him and the burro loose. This method saved much time because the burro taught the horse to lead and gentled it. The burro braced its feet and leaned away from the horse and with this constant pressure on the halter rope the horse soon learned to follow the little burro.

The horse soon learned to eat, drink or rest when that stubborn little creature did, although it was three times bigger. The donkey always went back to camp to get its feed of oats. This took as long as four or five days, but the little burro's always got the mustang back to camp and the bronc was broke to lead.

With the amount of horses captured by many different men during the time just before and during the war, there were not as many horses to choose from as when Ivan first started running wild horses. Many of these mustangers ran the horse down not using traps as good men would. This was a very cruel method used by the Indians and adopted by the white man. They started the horses running and never let them stop until they dropped from exhaustion or died on their feet running. To accomplish this, they set up relays of men stationed along the path of the mustangs. When the men and the horses they rode in the chase tired, another group was waiting with fresh horses to take up the chase, keeping the mustangs on the run. The mustangs never got a chance to stop. This method crippled, injured and killed many horses. They easily followed the trail littered by the dead, crippled and little colts left behind. Guy and Ivan never used this method because they said it made no sense to them. Also, the helter skelter pace killed or crippled many a man when his horse took a spill in the rough terrain. Most horses caught on these wild senseless rides were not any good for riding because the torturous pace damaged them.

There was a much better quality of horse now than earlier because the less experienced Mustanger caught the old, weak and slow horses. Riding the W bar B grain fed horses the two men had to ride harder and farther to get the amount of ponies they wanted. They left the donkeys in the McNurlen camp pasture while they went on their trips looking to find good animals to catch. When they reached Ivan's trap, they discovered that someone else used it to catch most of the mustangs in the area. There were only a few small herds left in the valley. The men spent several days repairing the gates on the trails that led into the valley before they started driving horses from the nearby mesa's into the large valley.

In two weeks, they had enough horses shut in the valley to start making the selections and capture. Picking out some of the best horses, they caught and broke themselves a string of saddle horses. After which, they rode back to the main camp where they packed their supplies on horses. Then, they took their saddle horses and burros back to Ivan's trap.

They filled the large corral with all the horses it would hold. Then they started sorting the good mares and colts out on the mesa to run free. Also, Ivan and Guy let some of the better stallions loose to insure a crop of good colts in the future. They also kept the poorer ones in the trap to improve the quality of the range. They drove these poor old crow baits to Wamsutter. There they sold them to buyers for the glue factory, fox farms, hogs and chicken farms.

By the first snow fall, they had nearly seventy-five head of horses ready to take back to the ranch. When they didn't have enough donkeys to neck all the captured horses to, they tied three horses together. With three tied together, the horses would not all get to doing the same thing at once and make an escape.

Many mustangers in the West took baling wire with which they wired the nostrils almost shut, leaving only a very small amount of air to get through. When the horses started to run, they went a short distance and collapsed from the lack of air. After dropping from the lack of air two or three times, these poor creatures quietly submitted to go with the herd.

Ivan and Guy would not stoop to this low, inhumane, cruel and cowardly way of abuse. They figured their Creator gave them a bigger helping of brains than He did the horse so that made them responsible for the way they treated the dumb beast. They saw many and varied ways of clogging horses, to which they never stooped. Some men took a forked tree limb. They placed the V over the withers and the two ends down along the legs. Then they tied them solid to the sticks so the legs could not bend. This made the mustang have to hop when he moved. Others fastened a large log chain on one of the front legs just above the hoof around the ankle. Dragging this made moving very difficult. Other mustangers bent a horse shoe around the front ankles, leaving it loose but so it would not come off. If the horse ran, the shoe soon rubbed the ankle raw from sliding up and down. The ankle was soon sore and infected, making it painful for the old pony to run.

The clogging that made Ivan and Guy the angriest was the old Comanche trick of twisting raw hide through a hole cut between the nostrils, leaving it to dry into a long, hard, twisted rope with a stick for a handle at the end. When the poor beast's nose was swollen and weakened from thirst and hunger, the men took the handle and made the horse do anything his cruel and deranged mind could imagine. Most of the time, one man lead the horse with the rawhide in the nose from another horse while three our four persons took turns riding the poor creature. White men used the same method but they were even crueler because they used barbed wire, making this instrument of torture about two feet long.

The trip back to the main camp was slow because the horses were not broke to lead very well. One man rode in front with the pack horse loaded with grain so the burros would follow. The other man brought up the rear driving the best he could. Reaching the McNurlen camp, they never grained the donkeys but let them all loose so they would start back to Lily Park and the ranch. The donkeys knew a good meal and rest awaited them at the ranch. A couple of day's rest refreshed the men.

Now rested up, they packed up and started driving the herd of old crow baits and pack horses toward the ranch. On the way, they caught up with the burros and their horses. A drive of a day and a half had the new horses in the fenced pasture at the ranch. When O. H. Waterhouse saw the fine horses necked to the burros, he told the mustangers they could have the old crow baits if they wanted to take them to the railroad loading pens. He said this would be a bonus.

The boss asked the men to go up to Green Mountain in Wyoming and catch some wild horses in that area crossed with Belgium draft horses. He said they could take the crow baits to Wamsutter as they went. He sent a wagon along to haul their camp and oats for the horses and donkeys. He sent a W bar B cowhand by the name of Douglas Chews to drive the wagon.

They decided to spend most of the winter in Wyoming capturing the larger horses. Taking extra saddle horses, they turned the crow baits loose in the herd and started for the railroad pens. The trip was easy and relaxing because the donkeys followed the wagon with the other horses following them.

With three men, the hours of night herding were not so long. The trip took five days from the ranch to the railroad pens. The buyer paid them twenty dollars a head for the crow baits and said they all went to the glue factory.

Three days later they set up camp in a sheltered canyon and were ready to start their winter work. By graining the saddle horses and the donkeys they only had to hobble a night horse and bell two or three others. This eliminated the dreaded night herding. Most mornings the horses came to camp when the men called and strung out some grain. These larger Belgium crosses were much slower than the horses Ivan normally caught, which made them much easier to trap. The size made them harder to handle. They had to be careful when roping them to make sure the rope was just behind the head and not low on the neck. If you got the rope to low around the neck, it wouldn't choke the animal and they could drag you along. They called this a work horse pull because the horse could pull you as if hitched up.

Time flew by as the men worked hard each day, leaving little time to be idle. Meeting another mustanging outfit one day, they spent time visiting. The other outfit told the W bar B men if they really wanted good draft horses they should move their camp over by Lander in the open country where there was a large amount of wild horses crossed with Percherons. These made a much better horse.

By Christmas, the three men were close enough to Lander to spend a few days in town. They went to the hotel and rented a room so they could live in luxury for the holidays. They turned their horses out in the livery barn's pasture. The first night in town a blizzard struck with a fury that lasted for three days. The men never left the hotel for a week. When the storm was over, they headed south of town some twenty miles to the range of these fine draft horses.

The country was open without any mountains or deep canyons, which made the work much easier than normal for Ivan. The snow was between two and three feet deep on the level, making it hard for the horses to get forage, which left the wild ones in a weakened condition. By graining their saddle horses, they had the strength to ride close without much effort and rope the wild ones in the deep snow. Sometimes they chased a mustang into a deep drift where he got stuck. Then the men could walk right up to the poor stuck creature and put a halter on him. By using a long rope, they would pull it out of the drift and tie it to another horse. When a blizzard blew in, the men stayed in camp until it blew out and warmed up. The wear and tear of the storm weakened the mustangs and made them easier to catch.

Around March 1, they started back to Lily Park. It took three and a half weeks to reach the ranch because the wagon in the mud slowed them to a snail's pace. During this time they would put new horses in the harness and make them pull the wagon. By the time they reached the ranch, most of the wild horses were broke to harness. Because of the heavy pull, they sometimes used as many as six different teams in one day.

Back at the ranch, they set about breaking the horses to ride they caught on Blue Mountain last fall. The first thing was to run in all the horses and catch the wild ones and neck them to the burros again. The manager of the ranch said it saved a lot of time and that is what he paid them for was to get a job done quickly. With the fine set of corrals and building at this ranch the work was much easier than at a trap out in the hills. The boss's wife or daughter was always taking pictures with the Kodak, which made Ivan nervous at first, but he soon got used to it. They took one picture Ivan wished to have, but he never asked them for it. He rode a fine horse that bucked so hard that all four feet were three feet off the ground in the picture. The horse had his head down between his front legs and Ivan had one hand up in the air. They were in the breaking corral with its high pole fence and the snubbing post in the middle.

Ivan soon saw the wisdom in having the horses necked because there was no time lost in catching another horse when you finished with one. The mustangers rode the new broncos on spring roundup, which finished them so well even the farmhands could ride them. During the branding, Ivan was one of the ropers that brought the calves

162

to the fire. He had one horse that was one of the best rope horses in the country. One day Ivan was riding alone on this horse looking for some cows when he spooked a yearling bear that was feeding in the bushes. Being a good roper he thought it would be good practice for the horse if he roped this bear.

Getting the horse to chase Mr. Bear was not hard. Only after Ivan's rope was around the bear's neck did he realize the predicament he was in. He had left his guns at the ranch house that day and now he could not figure out how to get the bear off the rope. He decided maybe he could drag it back to the ranch and someone could shoot it there.

However, the bear had different thoughts about what was going to happen. He began to twist the rope in his paws and mouth until he started climbing up the side of the horse. Of course that ole pony was not standing like he was in a church parade, he was bucking and jumping with all his might. With bat wing chaps on, Ivan was having trouble getting to his jackknife that was in his trouser pocket while staying in the saddle of the bucking horse.

The bear meant business and Ivan had one foot against him keeping him at that distance. At last, he got his knife and cut the rope. Mr. Bear left in the opposite direction and never looked back. That one time ruined a good horse. Whenever someone took a loop down, the poor creature stopped and trembled. You couldn't move him until they put the rope away.

After the roundup was over, the boss laid Ivan off. He told Ivan if he came back to the ranch when haying time started he would give him a job on the stacks. Ivan drew his pay, loaded his pack horses and took them and the rest of his string back to Vernal to visit his grandmother and Merle. This visit was the first time in his life Ivan noticed that grandmother Mary was looking and acting old, which saddened him deeply. He wondered how long his dear sweet grandmother would live. She was still active in the church Relief Society and taking care of Uncle Bill's small children. Everybody he asked about a job in Ashley Valley told him there was a job for him come haying time.

Miner, Arizona and Nevada

Chapter 23

One day Ivan was talking to a freighter. The freighter told him the Gilsonite mine over south of Dragon was hiring men to load coal on the burros, who took the Gilsonite from the mine to the new narrow gauge railroad. The Uintah Railroad Company built the narrow gage line over Baxter Pass from Mack, Colorado to Dragon, Utah. He said they refined the Gilsonite at a retort in Mack.

Selling his extra horses, Ivan kept one to ride and two to use as pack animals, which he used to carry his camp equipment. When he reached the mine, they hired him. They let him turn his horses in the large pasture with the mine's burros and horses. He found a place to set up his camp where he lived rather than pay board and room in the mine's bunkhouse. He decided that paying for his meals at the cookhouse was easier than cooking his own.

Most men working in the mine were from Greece. These fine honest hard-working men came to the United States leaving their families behind. They planned to bring them to America when they had enough money. They saved all the money they could. When they had enough, they sent it home so another man from their home village could come and work in the mine or find a job herding sheep.

After three years, these men sent for their wives and children. Along with the money they sent home, they saved and when there was enough to buy some sheep they started their own flock. They saved their money in a cooperative manner. They staked a homestead on which they had some milk cows that they used to feed orphan lambs given to them. Ivan soon became good friends' with Andrew Manus and his brother Chris. Andrew had been in a fight and had his left eye poked out so his friend's called him Ole Good Eye. When Nick Nicholson came to work in the mine he and Ivan soon became friends, along with Angelo Pulous who was one of the men taking care of the bum lambs.

The work in the mine was cold and filthy, but it paid the best wages Ivan had ever received. They worked six days a week twelve hours a day. They scooped the oil filled sand into bags they loaded on burros. Then the burros took the bags down the mountain to dump in the rail cars.

Ivan soon learned how to load the bags so they had seventy-five pounds in them. Before they could be loaded on the burros, they weighed them so the little animals would be packed evenly and not over loaded. Each burro had a bag hung on each side from a little pack saddle that had an X tree for the pommel and cantle. When there were twenty of them loaded, they took them down the mountain to where they would unload them at the railroad. The mine had six of these pack trains handled by two men on each pack train. A crew unloaded them, dumping the Gilsonite in the open rail cars.

One morning as Ivan was going to the mine, he passed the train waiting to take a load to Mack. As he passed the train, someone hollered from the cab of the engine. When he looked to see who was hollering, he saw his cousin Sam Murray. Sam climbed down from the cab and told Ivan he had married and was soon to be a father. He said that when he went to the railroad superintendent looking for a job, the man said, "You are just a seventeen-year-old kid and the fireman's job takes a man to shovel coal all day." Sam told that superintendent, "Maybe I'm just a kid but I have a wife and she is going to have a kid." After hearing that, the man said, "Well fellow, if you are married you can sure have the job."

The cousins saw each other every time Sam's train came to the mine. Sam got Ivan a pass on the railroad so when Ivan wanted to go to Grand Junction he never had to pay for the ride on the train.

On these trips as the train climbed over the pass, Ivan got off the train and climbed the mountain. He waited at the next switch back for the slow train to come. Sometimes going down the grade, he would scurry down the whole mountain side. At the bottom, he rested in the shade of a tree by the track until the slow-moving train came by.

When winter came, the snow blocked Baxter Pass so the mine shut down the digging until spring. The Greeks went over to central Utah and found work in coal mines. Ivan loaded his camp and drifted south to Moab because he heard there were many sheep wintering in that area.

At Moab he found a job herding sheep and the owner sent him and the sheep on south to an area just north of Blanding. Ivan liked the country and the very mild weather where they had sent him to herd the sheep. The cattlemen were all Mormon and they never bothered the sheep outfits like they did up in Northwestern Colorado. The man that controlled the cattle in that country was Al Scorup who had grown up in Central Utah herding sheep. Though he never cared for sheep, he never bothered them whether owned by the Navajo Indians or a white man. Al and his brother Jim had discovered three large stone natural bridges, which they showed to an engineer by the name of Long. The warm winter made Ivan think he would stay in this country because they had no blizzards that winter.

Hearing from other sheep herders that there was work in the mines at Telluride, Ivan decided to go there when spring came. He hoped to get hired to be a hard rock miner. When the owner of the sheep came in the spring taking the sheep to the high country, Ivan went to Dolores Colorado where he left his horses and equipment. Then he took the Galloping Goose to Telluride.

The Galloping Goose was a narrow gauge railroad. This railroad never had a regular train with an engine and cars, but used three little machines that looked like trucks mounted on small steel wheels similar to those on a regular train. Two of them were larger with a cab that had two seats and behind this was a large truck delivery box that hauled freight. The small one looked similar but was much smaller and traveled much faster. The Railroad used it mostly to haul mail.

When there was a problem on the road bed or rails, the driver stopped. He and the passengers got out and took shovels or the necessary tools to make repairs. In the winter, they shoveled a lot of snow, but in the summer it was mud slides that caused the most problems. On Ivan's first trip, they shoveled for two hours at a spot where the rain washed two feet of mud on the road bed.

Arriving in Telluride, Ivan was delighted with the high beautiful mountains that surrounded this town. The town got its name because of the difficulty of getting there because it was so high in the steep mountains. The miners said they were riding to hell. The name stuck but they cleaned it up for respectability. Ivan quickly got a job working at the bottom of one mine as a mucker. They rode down the twenty-three hundred foot deep shaft in a little cage carrying eight men so fast it seemed to be free falling.

Down this shaft at every three hundred feet were side tunnels called stopes. Some stopes were thirty feet high and some were three to four feet. They went back from the main shaft several hundred feet.

Donkeys hauled the ore from theses stopes to the buckets in the main shaft where they lifted it to the surface. Once on the surface they ground and processed the ore. Once these little animals went in the mine, they never saw day light again. They used them until they died.

In a few days after he started to work, they asked him to be a powder monkey. The powder monkeys set the blasting powder with its caps and fuses so when all was ready they set off the blast. These men worked behind the machinist that drilled the millions of holes in solid rock. They pumped the water continuously or the stopes soon filled with water. They worked in total darkness with the only light coming from a little carbide lamp on their hard hat. The temperature stayed about forty degrees. This made it necessary for them to work in heavy clothing. At this high altitude sometimes it was warmer in the mine than outside.

The men worked twelve hour rotating shifts. When time came at the end of the week to rotate, they worked double shifts. Every three weeks, they got four days off. On Ivan's days off, he rode the Galloping Goose down the mountain to Dolores to spend his time in a warmer climate and check on his ole ponies.

When the fall roundup started in the Paradox valley, Ivan was ready to work outside in the sun light again. He quit the mine and hired on with a cow outfit called the Lavender Ranch whose headquarters were at Paradox and Uravan. The outfits in this country worked the cattle differently from the way they did in the country up north where Ivan had always worked before. They were much smaller ranches. They had between five hundred and two thousand head. They used fewer horses. Because of the rugged terrain, they built cabins and corrals throughout the area where they could stay each night. The deep red rock sandstone canyons fascinated the young man by their awesomeness. They ran the cattle on the summer range that was the Uncompahgre Plateau that was between nine and ten thousand feet above sea level. He was not used to the steep narrow trails that they traveled, nor the change within just a few miles from barren deserts with their alkali flats, to the high alpine meadows with their ferns and lush mountain grass.

As the roundup proceeded, Ivan realized that the cattle in this area were of better quality and had a gentler nature. The thing that he missed the most were the wild horses because there was none in the area. At the home ranch, the wife did the cooking and the hands all ate in the kitchen with the family. There were things about this type of ranching that made Ivan homesick for Grandmother Mary and Merle. Also, he thought of his brothers and wondered how they were doing. It had been two years since he had seen Milt and he sure missed his brother.

At this ranch, it was like everywhere in the West. A man never pried in another mans business, if he told you only his first name, you never asked any more about him. Up North, Ivan knew the men by their full names because most had been there for many years and had nothing of their past to hide.

Galloping Goose #7

These ranches furnished three or four good stout horses instead of the six to eight they used in the Northern Country. A few of the hands were from Texas and New Mexico. Some of the ranch hands lived in their own little shacks. Many kept them so clean you could eat off the floor, but some lived in such filthy conditions that Ivan never even got close to them. The boss told Ivan the filthy ones could track man or beast with the uncanny scent of a dog. They never fed them at the ranch house nor did anyone stay with them.

One of these filthy men had a licence to hunt and trap predators. When he trapped an animal whether a bear or a mountain lion, he teased and tortured the poor creature to death, instead of shooting it like a normal man would.

They used a different type of outfit than Ivan had ever seen. They had a different way of handling the cattle and used shorter ropes. While gathering the cattle in the higher elevations, they rode in wet rainy snow. When they got the cattle back down to the ranch, it was warm and sunny. When the gather ended, the work of sorting and culling took but a short time. This was done at the ranch corrals. They trailed the ones ready for slaughter to Grand Junction. There they loaded them on the train for the market in Denver.

By Thanksgiving, the roundup and shipping were done and they paid off the extra hands. One of the hands said he was going to Arizona to work for the winter and to get out of the bad winter weather. He asked Ivan to ride along with him. Riding southwest, they went through Blanding, Utah, onto Flagstaff, Arizona, where the other hand decided to stay with a friend. He told Ivan that down in the Phoenix area there would be a lot of work Also, his friend said that was true.

Ivan reached Phoenix by Christmas and found a good camp site where there was feed for his three horses. Ivan found a job picking lettuce that paid by the baskets picked. He was glad to find work in this strange and enchanting land. When the lettuce harvest was over, they told him he could help plant and hoe the new crop. When they told him how little the pay was, he decided to see if he could find a cowhand job.

He talked to some of the other laid off cow men in the camping area. They told him that on south and west he could find a job running wild cattle. They told him he would have to hire on a ranch because the ranchers never took kindly to anyone that just ran wild cattle on their own. Also, they said there were few wild horses left in the wild anymore.

Five days riding, took him to a very wild, rugged country that they could only reach on horse back. It was too rugged for wagons. When he reached the ranch that they had told him would hire him, it surprised him to see a man from Northwestern Colorado whom he knew as a rep for the L 7's north of Steamboat Springs.

The cowboy poet J. Harl Siser was as surprised to see Ivan as Ivan was to see him. Harl told Ivan not to ask questions of anyone in this country because most all came here to leave a past somewhere else. They were very touchy if they thought you might be snooping. He said they looked upon everyone as a possible bounty hunter. He said very few gave more than just one first name. Harl introduced Ivan to the manager as "the Kid" from Utah. The boss hired him to help capture wild cows. Harl had come to this country because he said this was the only place that homesteading could not ruin and the only place a man could remain a true cowman. The horses used in this country were small and very tough. The never seemed to tire. Harl said they were the little Indian ponies and they could not ride them into the ground.

When they started to go catch wild cattle, they took a large number of donkeys with them to neck the captured cattle to. Ivan, Harl and two other hands one they called Pete and the other Bob left for three weeks in the back country. The cattle were so wild that if they saw a man they ran and hid. Therefore they had to sneak up on them. They used a pair of field glasses so they could spot the cattle from far away.

Camp was set up in a long narrow canyon with a fence to keep in the donkeys and saddle horses. Each day they would take three burros with them as they left to look for cows. Working hard from daylight till dark, they were lucky to capture three to five of these little beasts. If they caught more than three head, they drug the extra ones back to camp on the end of their riatas.

Ivan could not believe the size of these little cattle and how it paid to catch them. Their head was the largest part on their small thin bodies. They had a horn spread of two to three feet depending on their age. The men never used a trap. They snuck up close and then rushed them, using their riatas to catch them by the horns and hind legs. Harl told Ivan these cattle were Corentias. They used them in the new rodeo sport to rope and bulldog because they were so tough and indestructible. He said their necks would almost turn completely around and never break.

Ivan was not used to using horses as hard as the men in this country used them. As in Southwest Colorado, they only had three or four horses in one man's string. Harl said it was because there was not a good supply like in Montana, Wyoming and Northwest Colorado.

One of the men called Bob, said he would be going back to the country around Elko Nevada when the spring lay off came. They only worked the cattle in this Southern Country when the weather was cool. He said that neither man nor beast could take any working in the hot summer here.

When spring came, the boss told Ivan he was pleased with the large number of cattle that the men captured. If he wanted to, he could stay on the year around. This country was too rugged and hard to work in and with the poor horses they had to use, Ivan decided to go to Nevada to look that country over. He was not at this ranch long enough to get to know the men's real names.

Riding north, Bob tried to avoid any settlement or ranches they passed. He told Ivan he never cared to be near people he did not know. He said, "You can't trust anyone that you ain't been around for a long time." It took six weeks of hard steady riding to reach the country that the cowhand always worked in sixty miles southwest of Elko, Nevada. Ivan liked this country very much because it had many horses in it and no homesteaders. They told him that all traveling was done on horses because it was very hard to travel in wagons. The many washes that run through it made it almost impossible. When they reached the ranch, the old rancher hired the two men. He told them they would be starting on the spring roundup when the men came in with the remuda, which should be any day now. This ranch had no cattle and ran strictly horses. They sold up to three thousand head each year. The owner had been one of the first white men to see the area and settled here at the time he arrived.

When Ivan turned his horses in the pasture, he saw a smoky blue horse that sure looked familiar. The brand on the horses was a blotched wagon wheel. Ivan recognized they altered the brand. The boss saw Ivan looking it over and said it belonged to one man that was after the remuda. He told how the owner had appropriated a few cows that never belonged to him and spent time in the pen. Then they sent him to the army to fight in Europe. While the man was away the livery barn man tried to use this horse to rent but soon found no one could ride him. Not knowing the owner was in prison, he took the smoky blue to rodeos where no one could ride the vicious bronc. He said that old pony would try to kill anyone that rode him.

When he no longer bucked, they sold him to a chicken farm to pull a wagon until such a time he no longer could. Then they planned to kill him and feed him to the chickens. When the owner came home from the army, he had found the smoky blue and bought him back to let him live out his life in ease. Ivan's thought went back too good Ole Dick and knew how the owner must feel. It sure bugged him because he sure had seen that horse somewhere before.

While eating supper with the family in the kitchen, the boss talked a lot about the country and the men that lived in it. He seemed proud of the fact most of them had a past that they never wanted to catch up to them. He said it was three days ride to the nearest settlement. If a man didn't know the way, he could perish from the heat and thirst. He came right out and asked Ivan from what and whom he was running. When Ivan said he had nothing to hide, they all laughed for a long time. They seemed proud of their disheveled past.

Bob bragged of the things he had done. He worked so far out in the hills a sheriff would die of old age before he reached him. That night as Ivan lay in his bed roll, he wondered what he had gotten himself into. He thought of the words Guy had once said to him, "Kid stay away from that tough outfit." He now realized what good Ole Guy meant. The next morning men began to gather at the ranch to start the spring roundup. Ivan soon learned from these new men there was no cattle and they ran only horses here.

About the middle of the morning, six men rode in driving nearly two hundred head of horses all with saddle scars showing they were the remuda that all had been waiting on to arrive. As the men drove the horses in the large corral and Ivan saw the men, he knew where he had seen the smoky blue horse before. The man that was in charge was none other than Will James who was a rep for the Y Bench up near Lander, Wyoming. When Will dismounted, he came over and shook Ivan's hand and said, "Well Kid, there ain't no Bill Patton's in this country, and every man is left alone. You don't need to worry about any one picking on you here, but what kind of a jam did you get into that made you to come here to save your hide." Ivan said he was just "site seeing" to which all had a big laugh. Will said, "No one reaches this country unless they are desperate to save their hide." Ivan said he had come with old Bob from Arizona, which brought even more laughter.

After the laughter abated, Will introduced Ivan as the Utah Kid. Ivan had noticed they called Will by the name Slim so that is what he did too. Ivan could not help but notice how heavily armed these men were, they all carried two pistols fastened around their waist and a rifle on their saddle.

Ivan stood at the corral gate as the horses were drawn for the men's strings and he was surprised how few had been in that country very long. Those that were regular hands picked their horses first and the boss caught each man a string of ten horses each. Ivan liked these ole ponies because they were big strong horses fifteen hands and weighing between eleven and twelve hundred pounds. They told him the horses on this ranch was not of mustang decedents. The rancher here raised only well bred horses from California or somewhere back east. They rounded them up twice a year at which time they branded the young. They sorted the ones to sell and drove them to the rail road sixty miles away to ship east.

There was much preparation put into the packing of the cook supplies and camp outfit. It was all packed on horses that made a long pack train as it left this little oases they called the ranch. The Boss's wife and kids left in one direction taking the camp and cook pack horses with them, while the buckaroos went in another in search of horses. There was a girl about Ivan's age that seemed to take a shine to Will, also a smaller girl and a small boy. He would learn in the next two months what good camp roustabouts these kids and women were.

He thought of the old buckskin as he rode the fine horses that were in his string. All of them seemed to have an unending amount of strength and energy. There were few that bucked. When he asked Will about them, he told him that once they were broken to ride they always stayed gentle because of there being no mustang in them.

As the gather continued each day, Ivan realized these horses worked quiet and easy like beef cattle. At night, it did not take many men to hold them on the bed ground like it did a herd of cattle. Some mornings, Will and a couple of other men would saddle a horse for the first time and ride it for half a day at a time. One day Will said, "Kid why don't you saddle one of those four year olds and help us get them broke, I know you can ride cause I seen you at other roundups." The boss said he would pay him a higher wage for doing it.

Ivan never liked the way most of the men started these young horses. Several would beat the horse on each side of the neck while tied until the neck was swollen and raw. They said that was their way to teach the horse to neck rein. It sure worked. When the bridle rein touched the sore neck, the ole pony would spin like a top. They used other cruel methods that made Ivan sick to watch. One was the huge double ring bit that went in the horse's mouth with the slightest pull those horses would run backwards. Ivan used his hackamore and seemed to break his horses just as well.

The camp traveled in a very wide circle always working to the northeast. When they would sweep an area before leaving, they would cut the herd, turning back the young mares and breeding stallions. In two months time they had a herd of nearly two thousand head carrying five-different brands.

At supper one night, the boss asked who planned to work for the summer and who was going to drift on. He said by noon the next day they would have the horses in the rail yards in Elko. He paid all the men that night so those wanting to drift would not have to go to town.

When morning came and the herd started for the railroad, only half the men were left to help. As Ivan left Elko riding back toward Colorado, he felt relieved to be away from that outfit. He vowed he would never get mixed up in an outfit like that again. He sure never did.

Sheep War

Chapter 24

As dawns first light appeared, Ivan traveled about six hours. Then, he stopped for four hours to let the old ponies rest and eat their fill. Then, he saddled up and rode till dark. Traveling this schedule, the horses never wore out and he averaged thirty-five miles every day.

When he reached Ashley Valley, he went to Grandmother's house to stay a few days with her. It saddened him to see this dear sweet lady failing. She still was taking care of uncle Bill's little girls. Her steps were slow now and she seemed to tire easily. Ivan asked her if she was sick. She said, "I feel all right but I just tire out real easy."

The valley was buzzing with news about the government's proposed fifteen mile wide driveway for sheep up the White River through Rangley, Meeker and to the White River National Forest near Trappers Lake and Sleepy Cat Mountain and south of Glenwood Springs toward Gunnison. If they made the proposed driveway law, the Mormon sheep men would save one hundred and fifty-miles of travel to the National Forest in Colorado. Many ranchers said they would go into the sheep business.

The Northwestern Colorado Cattlemen's Association was fighting this driveway in courts trying to get it stopped. They were also using bullets and ropes. Cattlemen along the Utah border were even killing sheep and their herders if they crossed over the line. Rumors had it that old Tom Berry, a cattle rancher north of Rangley, was the one who clubbed a fifteen-year-old boy to death after the boy wandered a mile into Colorado. Tom and his cowhands also clubbed the three hundred sheep the boy was herding. The federal marshals could not prove this to be true.

East of Powder Wash, cattlemen hanged. a young boy. Then, they killed his sheep and horses, leaving his dogs to howl by the hanging corpse. There was never a rumor or clue to this terrible crime. The harder the Colorado cattlemen resisted the more money the Mormon Church lent its members to buy sheep. The Church wanted to gain control of Northwestern Colorado by populating it with their people.

They were sending families on missions to file on land that would control the water holes and springs. Many small ranchers switched from cattle to sheep. The country was swarming with federal marshals trying to protect the homesteader and the sheep men.

The Greeks like the Manus brothers, Angelo Polous and many others had sent for their wives and children. These good men were running large bands of sheep in defiance of the Cattlemen. For some unknown reason, the cowman left the Greeks alone although they despised them. The cattlemen might have left them alone because these men moved their sheep in areas were the oak and service brush was too thick for cows to graze. They grazed many bands on the shale oil plateau on the head of Roan Creek above DeBeque.

Louis Visentyner and Stan Wyatt found financial backing in Denver and bought thirteen thousand head of sheep that they ran in the summer near Rabbit Ears Pass, east of Steamboat Springs. Brothers Alfred and Bill Jensen were hard-working men that lived north of Meeker. They bought a large band of sheep, which they ran on Sleepy Cat Mountain in the head waters of William's Fork River.

In the winter, Louis, Stan, Bill and Alfred along with the Greeks wintered their flocks on the desert in Eastern Utah. These men never looked for trouble but if it came they were capable of making the cowmen back down. These sheep men were in the very heart of cow country and planned to stay for the rest of their lives.

The Jensen's left the desert before the other sheep men did. This made it necessary to lamb on the trail. This gave them the best grass along the road with which to graze the sheep. When they started east, they moved about eight miles in any day. When the lambs started being born, they hobbled the old ewes by their front feet and left them tied to a bush to have their babies along the trail.

The main camp wagons moved with the sheep. The Jensen's had two large wagons with racks to haul the mother and lambs that followed two hours after the main band moved on up the trail. They pulled these wagons with six horse teams. By night when they reached camp, the wagon was full of new lambs. By morning, the mothers and babies would walk with the main herd. When they reached Sheep Creek southwest of Meeker, they would drive south to Fourteen mile Creek where they waited for the Ernie Sandivol Family from New Mexico to shear them.

Old Bill Calthorpe had been reduced to working a ranch since he no longer had the Ute Indian whiskey money to support himself. Over the years, he had made enough enemies that the cattlemen swore they would kill every sheep he owned and break him financially.

When he started his herd to Trappers Lake, the cattlemen sent word to him they would never let him nor his sheep travel one mile in Rio Blanco County. This meant two hundred miles of extra travel. Bill started trailing his sheep east toward Maybell where the government promised to furnish him a guard as he traveled south to the White River and Meeker.

When his herd reached Maybell, there were four marshals riding motorcycles and four in a car saying they would stop any violence the cattlemen could throw at Bill. After four days, the outfit reached the county line and found a fence with the County Sheriff and a large deputized posse.

Farrington Carpenter, a rancher lawyer from Hayden, held an official document stating that the road was closed and the land in Rio Blanco County was private land. There was nothing to do but turn around and trail for two hundred miles to reach the pasture that Bill could see across the valley twenty five miles away. Bill finally reached the National Forest but the cost left him broke the rest of his life.

As Ivan listened to all this talk, he also learned the sheep men paid three times more a month than the cowman. He knew it would not be long before the sheep would start their trek west to the desert so he decided he would ride to Meeker. He wanted to see his brother Milt who lived at Meeker and see if he could get a job with one of the big sheep outfits.

When he reached Meeker, he heard many stories of killings of both men and sheep. They did not fool him into thinking that if he went to work for the sheep men all would be peace. After visiting Milt who was a vowed sheep hater, he went to Bill Jensen who hired him to herd sheep.

Bill told Ivan to keep his guns oiled and loaded because the cattlemen would kill any sheep men they could. When he arrived at the wagons on Sleepy Cat, he found more men guarding the sheep than herding. The cattlemen hired whores to travel to the sheep camps to get the herders drunk and keep them busy. While the sheep herders partied, the cattlemen mixed the herds of sheep and scattered them for miles. The only way these mix-ups could be straightened out was to gather all the sheep in pens and sort them one at a time by checking every animal's ear mark. This took many days and many men. Bill's sheep had been involved in one of those mix-ups and he told Ivan to run off any women that showed up.

One day, Ivan saw a wagon driven by a man who had three women with him. These degraded creatures repulsed Ivan so he met them before they were ever near the sheep camp. These people sickened him from the way his father had acted with them.

As the man and his three whores came to a stop where Ivan sat on his horse blocking the trail, they were looking down the barrel of a Winchester rifle. He only told them to "get mighty pronto," which they did almost up setting their wagon as they turned around. He never saw them on that range again.

With the country filling with people, many cowhands filed on claims where there were good water holes. Many started in the sheep business. The cattlemen treated them as traitors and increased the killing of their sheep.

With the National Forest Service protecting the sheep men while they were in the high mountains, the cattlemen turned on the forest officials. They framed good men like Harry Ratliff for stealing. The cost of defending himself ruined Harry financially. Cattlemen like Patrick Cullen and his wife Anne came to their defense. She lent them money and even paid for their lawyers' fees of those who went broke.

Patrick took a gamble when he stuck up for the men wrongfully accused. Life long friends' became mortal enemies. Towns, railroad, mines, trucks and cars, the development of oil fields, homesteaders, National Forest Service, and the sheep scourge brought a climax to the great cattle country that almost overwhelmed the stoutest of heart. Across every old trail, there were fences built that made travel much harder. This upset the cowmen as much as the sheep problem.

With all that was happening in Northwest Colorado, the big cattlemen were being choked and squeezed to their death. Farrington Carpenter told the Associations they would have to join in the movement or DIE. Carpenter filed on many sections of land by hiring cowhands to file and then he would buy their filings. He filed on and fenced land that the Cary Ranch had used for years as open range. He told the cowmen there would be laws passed in Congress within a few years that would end the open range and free grazing. So he felt he was justified to file on all the land he could and encouraged them to do like wise. With the Two Bars gone along with the Middlesex, those men of all rank had to agree with Ole Ferry Carpenter.

These changes did not affect the ranchers on the upper Yampa River as soon as those near Craig because the high altitude was not good for growing crops. Because of the fight over the fifteen-mile driveway up the White River, homesteaders and those that could buy land went to Meeker bringing their sheep with them. The Mormon church lent them much of their money.

As the Aspen leaves began to change colors, they brought the sheep to corrals where they sorted the sheep, separating the lambs and ewes from those they intended to sell. They drove the ones to sell to

Steamboat Springs where they shipped the sheep by rail to the Denver stockyard.

The railroad furnished a place to ride in the caboose for the rancher and his hired men. Ivan was one of the men sent to look after the sheep on the way. They made the rail cars with two decks so they hauled many sheep on each. Whenever the train stopped Ivan, Bill and the other men looked in each car to check the sheep. Sheep will pile up on top of each other, suffocating the ones on the bottom. If the sheep were crowded close together, the men entered the cars and separated them.

When the train reached Tabernash, they hooked two engines to the rear of the train to help push it over Rollins Pass east of Fraser. Ivan had never seen such huge machines as these Mallets, or affectionately called Malleys by the train men. They had three sets of drive wheels that were taller than a man.

One of the engineers was a tall thin man who said he could push any train he had ever hooked on over the mountain. He said the only thing that ever stopped him was the snow. He pointed to the mountain and said, "Young man, see the road up there, well that is where we are heading." With that he climbed back in his cab. While the engines were being hooked to the train, the sheep men checked the cars for downed sheep.

When the rear engineers blew their whistles, the train started its climb to Fraser and Rollins Pass. The conductor that got on the train in Tabernash told the sheep men about the tunnel Mr. Moffat was going to build. As the train started up the pass, Ivan stood on the platform of the caboose to watch the scenery, although the noise from the pushers was deafening.

When the train reached the Loup bridge, the conductor told Ivan to look down below them at the gondolas, freight cars and even engines that snow slides derailed and swept down the rocky slopes. He said he knew men who had lost their lives by being buried in those avalanches that swept trains off the rail as if they were a match box.

Climbing higher, the train passed under a snow shed that held the train smoke until the men thought they would suffocate. At the top of Rollins Pass, the train stopped and all got off and ate supper in the restaurant owned by the railroad. They called this place Corna. As the train went down the east side of the pass, the two rear engines served as brakes to keep the train from running away.

Arriving late in the night in Denver, they scuttled the sheep cars on the siding at the stockyard. The men unloaded the weary animals in pens where feed and water waited for them. Most of the sheep laid down for an hour or so just to rest.

Bill told the men to be back at the train depot in four days where they would catch a train for home. A few days vacation in Denver made the sheep men forget the trouble brewing back home.

Arriving back at Sleepy Cat, Bill sent Ivan west to the desert in Utah with several bands of sheep, herders, horses, dogs, and wagons. When they got to the desert, Ivan would divide them in smaller bands for the winter.

When all the sheep were in their small bands and settled for the winter, Ivan settled the sheep he was herding on pastures near his Uncle Jerry's winter camp. Ivan and Jerry spent as much time visiting as possible that winter.

One cold day, Ivan built a good fire in his stove so he could leave a large pot cooking some stew in it. He was nearly half a mile from camp when he noticed the wagon cover was burning. He had walked with the sheep to stay warm, instead of riding a horse. He was a fast runner so he ran to camp where he thought he could put out the fire.

When he reached camp, he saw that the wagon was going to be a total loss. Remembering the rifle his father lent him the summer he went to Aspen was just inside the door, Ivan reached in the fire where he found it and pulled it to safety. The Governor of Utah had given that

30-40 Winchester to Hatch when old Bill Calthorpe was selling whiskey to the Ute Indians. The stock was burning and the barrel so hot it burned Ivan's hand through his gloves. Before he got the fire out, it burned 3/4 of the stock.

Uncle Jerry had seen the fire and rode the old Buckskin horse he had gotten from Ivan the two miles as fast as the old pony could run. The wagon was a complete loss and Ivan only recovered the gun and his saddle and horse equipment that were outside covered with a tarp. His tent had been placed in one of the storage compartments under the bed, leaving him without even shelter.

Like most cowhands, he kept all his personal belongings in his warsack that held bedding, clothing, ammunition, extra guns, spurs, shaving mug and razor along with many other personal items including his money. Living the life of a stockman there was no need to spend money only on clothing, saddles, hat, boots, playing cards and tobacco. He kept his money in a buckskin poke (a little bag made from deer skin with draw strings) like most men of the times did.

In a man's war sack, the money was safe because the men of that time respected each other's privacy and never snooped into what was not his. If something came up missing, it was not long until all in the outfit was on the lookout for whatever was missing. It wasn't Sunday School when the guilty were found. The guilty party received severe punishment. Often, it meant death to the guilty.

All of Ivan's money that he had saved was gone. He was broke, except for his wages coming from the Jensen ranch that he hadn't drawn yet. The two men looked through the ashes when they were cool and found some useable cooking pots. Also, they found the melted gold and silver coins. He accepted the loss as all part of life without indulging in any pity or complaint.

He and Uncle Jerry moved the two bands of sheep together so they could use Jerry's wagon until Bill could bring another. They could sort the sheep when Ivan had his own camp wagon again. Uncle Jerry had an old worn out 45-70 rifle so he cut the burned part from the 30-40 and cut the old gun's stock to fit. Using screws, he fastened them together, making Ivan's gun as good as new.

Uncle Jerry watched Ivan's sheep while he went to Vernal to get a tent and supplies. Jerry told him to spend a few days with the family while back at Maeser Ward. Taking all his horses he figured he could sell what he needed to get money for his camp needs.

Grandmother Mary was happy to see Ivan and was glad he would stay for a week or more with her and the little girls. The weather was cold and it snowed often but there had been no blizzard yet. Ivan had a good visit. He enjoyed seeing his younger brothers and sisters. He told Mary it would be very easy just to stay with her until the grass greened.

Ivan sold one of his horses and purchased a tent and other camp equipment while enjoying the days at his grandmother's. While there, he always milked her cow and did the other chores. Mary really appreciated this.

One morning it was snowing hard. When Ivan went to do the chores, he told Grandmother it was not a fit day to be out as he left her kitchen. Returning to the house with the fresh milk, Mary was cooking her usual breakfast of coffee, bacon, eggs and flapjacks. Ivan helped her by setting the table with plates, cups, silverware, butter and honey. She had a fine stack of flapjacks in the oven with the door open so they stayed hot while she cooked more. Ivan was straining the milk when he heard a noise at the stove and looked around in time to see Grandmother fall across the oven door dead.

He picked Mary from the floor where she had finished falling and carried her to her bed. He went to the neighbor to get someone to help him with the children and to take care of his dead grandmother. The storm soon blew its self out and Mary's children soon made the funeral arrangements. She left nine children and sixty-eight grandchildren to mourn her passing.

After the funeral, Ivan headed back to the sheep camp to finish out the winter. The winter was cold and had many blizzards, but the sheep men were watchful of the weather and were never caught in the open with their bands. When there was a weather change that looked like snow, they moved camp to a sheltered valley where they could keep the sheep from drifting with the storm. The men sorted the sheep and Ivan said good bye. Then he started drifting east to meet the rest of Bill's sheep for the long drive back to Meeker.

When the grass began to grow, Bill arrived on the desert with a dozen heavily armed federal marshals. They stayed with the outfit most of the summer. He had two new pistols that he gave Ivan. He told him they would probably have to use them because the cattlemen won in the court fight over the driveway up the White River. He said they would not have any trouble until they reached White River City, but the cowmen like the Magers, Olands and the Square S on Peiance Creek vowed they would stop any woollies that passed there. Bill Jensen had told them he would take his sheep up the river and if they wanted to fight he sure knew how.

Angelo Polous and the other Greeks stopped by Bill's camp on their way to their winter sheep pastures. They said they were going to the shale oil mountains on Roan Creek. They would travel to Douglas creek south of Rangley where they would shear and lamb the sheep. When the snows were gone, they would go to the Pass then east across the range claimed by the Square S Ranch to the long mountain ridge above the High Moore store that was ran by Julia Latham.

Angelo knew what the DeBeque people thought of sheep and the men that owned them. He remembered them running over three thousand head over the rim in Boudish Run a few years earlier. Bill asked if they thought the cattlemen would let them pass. Angelo said, "This is America and he had the right to use those pastures too. If there is a fight, so be it."

The federal marshals told Angelo they would come to Douglas Creek and help him after they got Bill safely to Sleepy Cat. However, he told them, "No, this was his decision where he would run his sheep and the cowmen needs to know he was not going to be shoved around." He got his point across, the cattlemen never did shove Angelo or the Greeks around.

It took two and a half months for Bill's sheep to reach the high mountains. During this time there was not one threat from the cattlemen as the sheep lambed on the trail and were sheared before passing on to the high pastures.

The cowman talked a lot but the violence was not as frequent this spring. Without the violence of the previous summer, Bill laid off a number of his men and one of them was Ivan. Drawing his wages, Ivan rode down William's Fork River to Craig where he bought himself a new camp outfit including a good tent.

One day, he was talking to Louis Visentynre. Louis asked him if he would help them drive a band of sheep to Rabbit Ears Pass. He said the job would only last until the sheep were at pasture. Ivan heard there was work up in North Park around Walden so he thought this would be away to get paid for going there to look for work. In three weeks, he was in Walden looking for the much talked about work, which was not there.

modern Farm Machinery
was plowing the west

Jailed Sheep Buyer

Chapter 25

A farmer asked him if he would work on his farm where he raised lettuce. Ivan was glad to find any work so he started irrigating and hoeing lettuce. When harvest time came, he took a load to town and the sheriff arrested him. He accused him of being another man by the name of Herb Coats. Herb got drunk and gave the sheriff's brother a good beating. This made the sheriff very upset and he was going to teach him a lesson. He held Ivan in jail for five days until Herb got drunk and beat the sheriff's brother again. When Herb arrived at jail, Ivan saw why he had been mistaken as the criminal. Even the Sheriff said, as he apologized, that the two men looked alike. The sheriff promised he would leave Ivan alone as long as he stayed out of trouble, which he sure did.

While sitting in jail, he got to thinking of his friend Guy and the freedom that he always had at his wild horse trap back on Blue Mountain. With nothing to do he became homesick for the wild fresh country and his best friend, so he decided if he got out of this mess he would finish his job and then head west once more. Ivan stayed at the farm until the harvest was completed.

Drawing his wages, saddling, and packing his ole ponies, he was soon pushing toward home. As Ivan passed through Craig, he loaded his pack horses with enough supplies to last two men until next spring. Five nights later, he was sleeping in the bunkhouse at the White Bears ranch in Lily Park next to the bunk in which Guy was sleeping. When Ivan told Guy what had happened to him since they had last seen each other and that he was going to the trap to catch horses, Guy said, "I'll draw my pay and go with you," which was what the young man had hoped he would do.

The mustangers stopped at the McNurlen camp for a few days just to get the feel of the country. Riding at a leisure pace, they checked out the country and the horses as they jogged along toward the hidden valley and its trap. The security of the valley made Ivan feel as he did when Bart had left him on this mountain so long ago. The men spent several days repairing gates and fences in the trap and trail leading into the valley. Guy said he would like to go hunting in Flaming Gorge before they started breaking horses.

The men shut their extra horses in the camp pasture, packed a small amount of camp supplies and rode north toward the gorge. As they traveled at an easy pace, Ivan told Guy of his hunting trip on the north slopes of the Uintah's. He told of the moose he had killed and how pleasant that high country was. When he finished, Guy said, "Lets go and see how good we can do hunting there." They rode on through Brown's Park and onto Burnt Fork where they started the climb to the snow capped peaks. The rabbit brush was so thick at times they had to ride along the edge of the valley to get through the miserable stuff.

In a valley near a group of lakes, they found an abandoned trapper's cabin in which they set up camp. With a fine camp, they spent a few days site seeing and fishing. They decided to see if they could get a mountain sheep, elk and moose. Riding high on a peak, the met a Southern gentleman with several fine hunting hounds. He gave his name as Zebalon Pike Parker, a "genteel man" from Arkansas. After visiting with him for a while, the Mustanger figured this ole gent had spent more time away from the Ozarks than in them. He said he had a cabin up in a valley near timberline where he could see the open peaks.

The fall snows began to fall as the men left with their packhorses loaded with sheep, elk and moose. They had quartered the animals after hanging them in the cold to freeze solid. In the lower country they gave most of the meat to homesteaders they passed. When they reached the Green River, they rode north into Flaming Gorge where they spent two days hunting the large mule deer that inhabited the canyon. With all the meat they would need for the winter, they headed for the trap and a winter of horse work.

When they were within a day's ride of camp, they came across a band of twelve head of fine horses. Liking these ponies, the men started drifting them toward camp. One fine bay horse kept wanting to turn back but with a little effort they persuaded him to move along with the others.

Coming in from the north, there was a long valley. When the horses were in this canyon, the men stopped and built a fence so the horses could not go back to their home range. While they built the fence, the big bay stayed close and would try to break past them. The men talked about the qualities of this fine animal as they worked. They flipped a coin to see who would own it and Ivan won the toss.

No one had run the horses in this area since the two men were there last. Those old ponies were not hard to drive in the trap. For two

The ole Pony
was goin Home

weeks, they filled the valley with horses from the mesas not thinking about the ponies in the north canyon. Winter chill was in the air as well as snow when the men went to bring those horses to the trap and start riding them. The big bay was at the north fence and looked like he had not eaten a bite since he was shut in, but the others had fattened. They were sure fine to look at. They could not drive the bay from the fence although the men whipped on him.

Finally, Ivan said, "If that old boy is that gentle, I'll just saddle him and ride him back to camp." Tying his saddle horse with his lariat he walked up to the horse and put the hackamore on his head without any trouble. Guy said, "He sure is broke, but I can't figure why they never put a brand on him."

He let Ivan saddle him as easily as he had let him bridle him. As the Mustanger stepped on the ponies back, he stood as gentle as a school marms' Sunday horse. When Ivan touched him with the spurs, he walked a few feet from the fence and then back to it and stood looking north. Guy tied his lariat around the pony's neck and tried to drag him south toward camp, but that horse was soon dragging Guy's horse back to the fence. It took an hour for the men to tire of this game and decide to let down the bars and just ride along with the bay.

When the bars were down, the old bay started up the trail toward his home range just walking. Ivan thought when they reached the mesa he could start turning that now worn out horse. Using spurs, quirt, pulling his head around till it touched the rider's leg and Guy riding his horse in the path did not help. This went on for seventeen miles. Guy was so angry he took his knife and cut the horse's throat.

When the horse dropped, he was near his home range. Ivan saddled his horse that Guy had led along on this crazy trip. Riding away Ivan looked back at the dead horse and wondered what made him so determined to reach the home range that he never ate for two weeks. This was all new to both men that the old pony would not buck and was not afraid of them. They dropped in to silence with each lost in his own thoughts as they rode back to camp.

As the weather became cold with many blizzards, the men spent many days in camp where they were sheltered from the winds. With the first long break in the weather, they took six pack horses and rode to the White Bears Ranch and bought a load of oats to feed their saddle horses.

Back at camp, they grained the saddle ponies twice a day. This gave them the strength needed to run in the deep snow. With grain fed horses, they would run the winter weakened wild horses in the deep snow until they tired from exhaustion and could be caught without having to use the rope. They would saddle these worn out creatures and ride them back to camp.

Their saddle horses always came right back to camp for their generous helping of oats. The snow was deep in the valley near camp and the horses there were wintering hard which kept them gentle. Every few days the men would drive their herd in the trap where they saddled and rode every horse for a few minutes to keep them well broke.

Although the winter had been a hard one, the men had good success at their work. By the middle of March, they had more than two hundred seventy-five head of horses carrying saddle scars. They planned to drive the herd north to the railroad pens where they could sell them to an Eastern horse buyer.

Guy told Ivan there would be problems when they reached the mesa and the loose horses felt freedom. With only two men, the herd would soon scatter and their winter's work would be lost. They decided they would neck three horses with short ropes. If they tied two horses together, they soon got to doing the same thing, but tie three together and the beasts never get to doing the same thing at once. It took several days to get this job done so the trip north could begin. While they were necking those ole ponies, Guy's brother Pat rode into camp saying, "I had just come to see how you had survived the long winter."

Pat told them he had been running horses on the head of Lay

Creek, just inside Colorado. He had talked of seeing the Montgomery outfit several times that winter. He said they had a tiny little woman running wild horses with them that was "sure fun to watch catch and ride a horse back to camp, while demanding they bring her saddle horse along when you come."

Pat also told them he was going to take the Montgomery's and Duffy McAllister's advice which was to drive to Wammsutter to ship. He said the rumor was that the buyers all got mad in Rocks Springs and moved their headquarters to Wammsutter. The men broke camp when the ole ponies were necked for the trail. Pat said he would help them along if they would stop at his camp and throw his broom tails in with theirs.

It took four days to reach Pat's camp as they let the ponies just graze along so their old ribs would cover up. With what Pat had at his camp, they had a nice herd of over three hundred head they would sell at the railhead.

Just south of the Montgomery horse trap, the mustangers were letting the herd spread out and graze when they spotted four riders pushing hard on half a dozen head of horses. Pat said, "If we want to see the fun we had better get to high tailing it," as he stuck the spurs in his ole pony's ribs. All three men were riding at breakneck speeds when they over took the outfit in hot pursuit.

Ivan noticed how little the rider out front carrying his loop down was. When the lead rider roped the front feet, tripping a big black thoroughbred looking horse, that ole bronc hit the ground as the roper flipped a half hitch loop in the rope, catching both hind feet. This left the struggling horse tied tight on the ground.

When the other men all rode to where the down horse was, A tiny, very pretty lady looked up from her work of taking the saddle off the horse she had been riding. She said with a twinkle in her eye and a large grin, "This horse, I have tried to catch before but he always out ran me." Ivan noticed no one dismounted to help her change saddles, so he sat on his horse and watched as this tiny creature changed saddles. She was as quick as a cat after a mouse while she saddled the fighting horse. Ivan knew that it was easier to get the rig on if the downed horse continued to fight. After borrowing Duffy's rope, she placed it around her horse's neck. Then she handed the other end to him saying, "Pick up my rope and bring my Cayuse to camp." With that, she put her hackamore on and straddled the down saddled horse while untying his feet.

When that ole pony got on his feet, he sure exploded in the worst bucking Ivan had seen in along time. That rider went to work on that ole boy with her quirt and spurs more vicious than Ivan had ever seen.

It did not take that bronc long to figure it would be better to run than buck. As he lined out in a hard run she circled around and as she flew by she shouted, "Bring my horse to camp, I'll see you there." Dee asked the Blue Mountain men to come on into camp and rest until morning. Duffy and the Montgomery's helped them bring their herd to a pen at the trap.

When the men arrived at camp, dinner was cooking in the pots on a fire. The big black was standing head dropped and legs spraddled tied to a cedar tree. The quick spoken little lady told them to "get down, wash up and belly up if they wanted to eat."

The woman turned to Duffy and said, "Aren't you going to introduce these fine men to me." Her name was Norma Pankey, she came from Missouri with her family who was homesteading on Great Divide. Ivan had met many of her family and told her so. He asked her where she learned to run wild horses. She said, "It looked like fun so I just started doing it." She said her sister Grace had an outfit over on Browns Hill and she had watched as Duffy and the Montgomery's ran the wild horses. She liked the wild free life that went along with it. As the mustangers sat by the fire that night, they talked along time about the way the West was changing. They wondered how much longer there would be a need for their line of work.

Dee asked Guy if he minded if they threw their herd in with his for the drive to the railhead. He said they had about a hundred and fifty broom tails wired shut for the trail. The Montgomery's would use baling wire to close the horses' nostrils. This was done by pinching each nostril in the middle and sticking a wire through both sides. Then they made a twist so it would not come out. This left two small holes, one at the top and one at the bottom, that restricted the air flow. With each nostril shut, the horse could only run a short distant before it ran out of air and dropped until the lungs could refill. Three maybe four times is all it took for that pony to figure it never paid to light out for his home range and was soon trail broke for herding.

The Montgomery's had sold by contract this herd of brightly colored horses to a movie making company in Los Angeles, California. The movie buyers wanted the Pintos, Appaloosas, Palominos and any bright colored horses they could catch. They would sort the McNurlen's and Murray's colored horses at the rail pens giving them fifteen dollars a head more than an Eastern buyer would. Dee told the Blue Mountain men he would start his horses an hour before they did. This gave him and his men time to get the broncos trail broke.

The next morning the Wyoming men herded their horse herd out of the trap and those ole ponies lit out as hard as they could run and were all soon lying on the ground struggling to catch their breath. Ivan had never seen a sight like this before and wondered how many would lay there and die. It never took long for the horses to get enough air in their lungs to revive them. When they were on their feet, they started to run for their life, but in a few seconds they were all on the ground out of breath again.

The seven riders placed themselves on three sides of this herd and as they struggled to their feet this time, they started moving north. After a mile and another time on the ground, those ole ponies started walking north like they had trailed them for months.

The Blue Mountain men went back to the trap and turned their herd loose, driving them north to catch up with the Wyoming herd. When the two herds mixed together, there was a good mix-up because the horses necked together soon tangled with the one with the wired nostrils. The men stopped pushing them. After a while, the herd got over its excitement and started drifting on north.

With the herd drifting along at its own pace, they would soon fatten on the lush spring grass. They stretched the trip that normally took three days into more than a week so the horses would graze. The broncos quickly started putting some fat on, make their ribs disappear.

When they safely locked the horses in the shipping pen, the Blue Mountain men set about taking the neck ropes off their horses as the Wyoming men and lady removed the wires from their horse's nostrils. They ran each horse in a chute and used a pair of pliers to cut the wire and pull it from the flesh.

The movie men soon had their horses on the first train heading west and the Wyoming outfit left for their trap and more work. A buyer from Omaha Nebraska liked the well broke horses that the McNurlen's and Ivan had and paid them top prices, which made the mustanger feel rich. This was the first money Ivan had to save since the sheep wagon fire. He now had money to get a good start in life again.

After buying themselves some new cloths, the men cleaned and oiled their guns. With the large amount of money they were carrying, they did not want to be caught unprepared if someone decided to try and take it from them. They set out for Craig pushing hard so they could get their money in the bank so it was not lost or stolen.

As they rode by the many new farmsteads, it surprised the men to see the tractors being used on gang plows to summer fallow the fields as well as break the sagebrush land into new fields. They could not just cut across the hills like in times past because of all the fences that blocked the old trails.

After depositing the money in the bank, Ivan took a few days to relax. He thought that going to Vernal would be pleasant, so he started west. By late that evening, he was at uncle Bill's. He enjoyed seeing the home folk again. When he went to a dance with a young lady, everyone admired his automobile. Ivan was like all young cowhands. He went to every dance he could, even if it meant an all night ride. He sure loved to dance.

There was not any work in the valley, so he went back to Craig to spend time and see if he could find a job. He was playing cards in a joint one afternoon when Louis Visentyner and Stan Wyatt came in and asked if they could talk to him alone for a few minutes. As the three men sat on a bench in front of a store, the sheep men asked Ivan if they could hire him to go with them to the Spanish Peaks country in Southern Colorado to buy sheep.

Some outfit had come along and wanted their sheep, making them an offer that if they turned down would have left them looking insane. Ivan was well aware of the feelings and problems in the country that sheep caused, but he figured this was America and the big cow outfits never owned it. He had been caught in the sheep war before and felt he could handle more if the occasion would arise. They said they would pay more wages each month and all expenses until the sheep were on a pasture in Northwestern Colorado.

Ivan remembered what Harl Siser had told him about the country around Walsenberg and thought this would be a good time to go look it over. He found a place to pasture his ole ponies and store his camp outfit while he was on the sheep buying trip. He left his automobile with his friend Lee Keeling to use while he was gone.

Boarding the Denver, Northwestern and Pacific Railroad, the three men set out on their trip to buy sheep. The train was buzzing with the news about Mr. Moffatt's Tunnel and the excitement was catching. Ivan had seen the round house and very large ice house that they filled each winter in this high cold valley to ship to Denver in the summer. There was nothing new about the ride over Rollins Pass under the snowshed at Corona, around the loop and through the needle's eye. Ivan saw the wondrous view of Yankee Doodle lake. looking down Boulder canyon, Ivan could see the wide expanse of the Great Plains east of Denver. He enjoyed those things again but thrilled at the thought of speeding under a mountain at a high rate of speed.

He liked all the new things that was going on around him. It would be a while longer before those brave drillers, powder monkeys, shoring men and muckers had the tunnel open. He had worked in the mines at Telluride and he wanted no part of that cold, dark, and con-

Va+c-h-h-h   00-00-t-tt

fining life underground. He knew many hard-working brave men who had given their lives in the building of the tunnel thus far. Ivan wondered if he would ever get a start ranching as he watched, from the train car window, all the new farms and ranches that were filling the country since his first trip over this railroad.

When the train reached Tabernash, they unhooked and took the engine to the shop for some work on it. Ivan stepped out in the cold clear air of the night as two men were approaching the large Malley engine setting on a side track. One was the tall slim man that had driven the pusher the last time Ivan had went to Denver with a load of sheep. The short man in the conductor's uniform and another man stopped and talked with him. The other man introduced himself. "I am George Schyer, the engineer and this is George Barnes, the conductor. We always conquer the hill and take this train onto Denver."

Ivan asked, "How much longer it would be before the tunnel would be opened?" They replied, "If they keep killing men like they are up there, it will never get finished." They told of a terrible cave in that had just occurred a few days before and how the women of Fraser led by Doc Susie had talked to old Bill Freeman. Freeman was as hard as train rails. He just laughed in their faces. They said old Bill was only interested in the Tunnel and the Gore Canyon cut off west of Kremmling that would connect his line with the Denver and Rio

Grande at what was to be called Dotzerio, west of Minturn. He felt this would at last bring him the Mormon business from Salt Lake City, making his road one of the most powerful in the West.

The train was soon hooked on the new engine and was steaming up toward the hill and Denver. In Denver, the sheep men boarded a train that would take them to Colorado Springs, Pueblo, Walsenburg and Alamosa. At Alamosa, they planned to meet a buyer who would take them to the ranches with sheep for sale.

The train arrived in Alamosa shortly after midnight. After getting off the train, the three men walked to the hotel to get a room for the rest of the night. Arriving at the hotel, they gave them a telegram stating the buyer was sorry he could not meet them, but if they would wait for six days he would be in town at that time. Upon reading the telegram, the men all cussed, rented a room and went to bed.

After breakfast the next morning, they walked to the livery barn to rent some horses and find out where a sheep outfit could be located. The man at the livery barn listened to their plight. He told them he would rent them his automobile if they knew how to drive. He said the nearest sheep outfit that could sell them any sheep was a day's ride into the hills. After Ivan proved he could crank and start the shiftless Ford, he took the proprietor for a ride. Ivan passed the test and they had the car for as long as they needed it. They just had to keep the tires repaired and the motor full of oil.

Stan thought this was really the way to travel because they sped along on good roads as fast as a good horse could run. Louis would say in his heavy German brogue when the roads got bad or he saw an animal in the way, "VATCHHH OOUU-TTT!"

Ivan could not help but notice the many tractors beings used by the farmers to plow their fields in San Louis Valley, as they sped along to the hills where they would find the ranches. There were several hills that the car would not pull going forward, so Ivan just turned it around and backed up those hills. The old shiftless Fords pulled better in reverse than going forward because the shift bands were not as worn.

Arriving about dinner time at the first ranch, the men ate at the cook house and were told a boy would be sent with them to where the boss was working sheep. As the Ford climbed high, it had to be stopped and let cool because the men were climbing steep trails. At these times, they enjoyed this fine rugged country. They spent over a week looking at bands of sheep. At last, they arrived near Wolf Creek Pass where a deal was finally struck to buy four thousand five hundred two-year-old ewes with lambs at their sides.

Back at Alamosa, the sheep buyer was waiting for them to return the automobile, so he could take them to Taos, New Mexico, where he had a "fine flock of old ewes on a meadow filled with the finest grass a sheep ever ate." At the fine meadow, they found a herd of near starved to death young ewes with lambs. If there was any grass in that meadow, the Northwestern Colorado men must surely have been blind. The owner was sure in a hurry to get rid of that fine flock because he and the buyer almost gave them to the sheep men, if they just took them off their hands. Stan said he had to stop at the bank to get the money, but he thought he would take them off your hands.

He sent Ivan and Louis to see if they could rent some good pasture or get hay to feed the sheep while he checked with the sheriff and the banker on the legitimacy of the herd. The sheep were legal and had no mortgage so they bought them and fed them for a few days on some hay they bought.

With feed, those ole ewes sure began to look a heap much better, so Stan called the rancher west of Alamosa to see if the sheep they bought from him were ready to load and move. The rancher assured Stan they would be in the stock pen at Walsenburg on the agreed day. Also, he had a friend over by Trinidad that wanted to sell his whole sheep outfit. If Stan was interested, he would have the sheep at the Trinidad stock yards, so they could scope them out.

The starved ewes were looking much better when they were loaded on the train in Taos for their long trip to Steamboat Springs. The sheep were loaded loose so they could lay down and not be trampled. The lambs were left with their mothers. They would be unloaded once to be fed, watered and given some rest on the long slow ride north and west. The railroad soon spotted a train of sheep cars at the pens in Taos. The men hired a few Mexicans to help them drive the ewes to the railhead and load them.

The train left about the middle of the night. By daylight, they were slowly inching their way up Raton Pass. At times, it moved so slow the sheep men would get out of the caboose and walk along the train, checking the cars with sheep in them. After making the check, they sat beside the road and waited for the caboose to reach them. Then they stood on the platform to watch the scenery. By sundown, the train had their sheep on the siding in Trinidad where the tired sheep were unloaded, watered and fed.

The sheep rancher that wanted to sell his whole outfit had the sheep and horses in the pens with a good feed of hay for them. The man said he had eighteen hundred head of ewes plus rams, Judas goats and seven middle aged horses, which were broke to ride as well as harness. There were two covered camp wagons plus a good utility wagon that could haul supplies or sheep. With this mixed herd of young and old, Stan asked Ivan if he would look them over and set a price on them by the head in the morning. The rancher took them to supper and had a room for them at the hotel.

In the morning, it did not take Ivan long to see these sheep were in top condition, but set a fair price a little lower than market so the men would have a little "dickering to do." It did not take long to make a deal, hire the rancher's Mexican herders and get all the sheep, horses and wagons loaded for their long trip to Steamboat Springs. While traveling to Walsenburg, Louis said he would take this trainload on while Ivan and Stan loaded the ones in Walsenburg.

As the train passed through Walsenburg, it slowed just enough for the two men to roll from the caboose platform to the ground. Checking at the depot, the agent told them he would send word to the rancher they had arrived in town. He said the sheep they bought were at the edge of town grazing, so it would not take long to pen them. He said the rancher ordered a train that had passed through Pueblo about a half an hour ago and would be there in time to load the sheep.

Ivan and Stan went to the hotel to get a bite to eat. When they returned to the stockyards, the sheep were penned and ready to load. The train soon arrived and left the long line of double deck sheep cars and steamed on south. A section crew from the railroad showed up to help get the sheep loaded. They said a freight coming in from Trinidad would pull the sheep to Denver if the sheep were loaded. It seemed those train men could get those sheep to load faster than anyone they had ever seen. As the last car was rolled to the loading chute, the north bound freight train rolled to a stop at the depot. While the paper work was being completed at the depot, the engineer hooked the cars on the rear of his train. When the train left town, the sun was setting over the peaks to the west.

Six hours later, the sheep train was unhooked on a siding in Denver where the big Malley engines of the Moffat line were hooked on the front and rear for the hard climb over Rollins Pass. The ride to the top of the pass at Corona was the most deafening experience the two sheep men had ever lived through. The large Malley engine hooked directly behind the caboose was so noisy the only way to communicate was to write notes. The men sat holding their hands over their ears. The sun had been up a couple of hours when the train reached Corona where it stopped so the crew could eat breakfast.

After Ivan ate, he walked a ways from the train and enjoyed the great panoramic view to the east and west from this spot at the top of the world. He felt at peace with the world and was happy to be alive in this very modern times when animals were loaded and hauled rather than trailed a foot. When the train whistled, he ran to the caboose and was soon creeping down the west side, over a rail bed that looked as if it had not been repaired in a long time. He wondered if they would make it safely to Fraser.

At Tabernash, a different crew took over the train as it was being filled with water and coal. The men checked the cars to see if there were any sheep down or if there was a problem. Not finding any, they went to the caboose and were sleeping when the train pulled out from the siding. At Kremmling, the train pulled on a siding to wait for the east bound train to pass, so the crew and the sheep men ate their dinner.

It was after dark when the train arrived in Steamboat Springs. The sheep had to be unloaded, so Stan said he would go to the depot and see if there was any men available to help. Ivan had just finished unloading the first car when the section crew came and bared the cars ahead. When the last sheep was going down the chute, Ivan heard a man say, "What are you doing here?" He looked to see who had spoken that and was surprised to see Hatch, along with a young man by the name of Sam Steele as well as six other men. By midnight, the sheep were all penned, fed and watered, so the men could go to the hotel for a few hours sleep.

At breakfast the next morning, Hatch told Ivan, Louis had sent a telegram to Craig from Denver asking the depot agent to find some men to work and have them come to Steamboat Springs as soon as they could. Upon arriving, they would wait for the arrival of the two trains of sheep. He and Sam had been looking for work so they came to Steamboat in time to help Louis unload and get the first load trailing towards Rabbits Ears Pass. Louis had purchased some camp outfits along with horses which were in the yards waiting Stan and Ivan's arrival.

The outfit laid over one day while Stan found two more men to herd sheep. Daylight found the sheep strung out for several miles as the different herders and their bands started for the high mountains south of town. Hatch and Sam were given the largest flock, which they would work together for the summer. With Stan and Ivan mounted on good fast horses, they spent the day helping the different shepherds move their bands along.

By the middle of the day, the forest ranger, Ray Peck over took the lead band that Ivan was helping drive. These two men had a good laugh as Ivan welcomed the Quarter Bushel to ride along side. They had met before several times and were good friend's. (They remained good friend's as long as they lived, Ivan always called Ray the Quarter Bushel, which always brought a hardy laugh.) Ray and Edward Peck were the head forest rangers after good ole Harry Ratliff. The cattlemen did not seem to bother them so much after Harry had won his case in court. The cattlemen still looked upon them as traitors, but as time went on and they saw the fair way the Pecks treated all, a shaky peace finally settled over the forest in the West.

A little green fly that was found above the ten thousand foot elevation would drive cattle mad and back down the mountain but never bothered sheep so this high elevation made a fine pasture for sheep. The Forest Service never let sheep bed on the same ground two nights in a row so they would not eat the grass bare. With proper management, sheep improved the range because they ate more weeds than grass. Ray Peck spent his summer months checking to make sure the rules were enforced.

Within a week, the five thousand sheep were scattered in the high mountain between Gore Pass and Steamboat Springs. Stan and Ivan checked on all the bands before riding north to find Louis and the other forty five hundred sheep they brought from the south.

At Rabbit Ears Pass, the two men found Louis waiting for them at the camp where the fine young ewes from New Mexico were gaining weight so fast they couldn't recognize them. Louis was sure proud to tell how he got those old "Yoes" to pasture with no losses. The three men loaded a pack horse with supplies and rode on north to the Wyoming border, checking on the rest of the southern sheep. They were very happy with the way the Mexicans handled the sheep and how carefully they looked after each one.

After they had seen the last band they rode to Columbine, Steamboat Springs and then to Craig where Ivan was paid for the time he worked for them. The sheep men wanted him to stay in the high mountains and herd, but the young man was homesick for Blue Mountain and his friend Guy. He thought he would hang around Craig for the Fourth of July Celebration hoping Guy would show up.

While waiting, Ivan met his friends Lee Keeling and Roy Mienke. Roy was working on the Carey Ranch and Lee had the Lower Elkhead Ranch leased. As Ivan hung around the joints, he heard that Texaco was looking for a qualified driver to haul between Craig and Casper. Texaco had just built a new oil refinery at Craig so Ivan drifted over and asked about the drivers job. He was soon hired to drive one of the new dual wheel trucks. Ivan was to start work after the Fourth of July celebrations were finished.

Goodbye Blue Mountain

Chapter 26

Ivan was about to throw in his hand in a game of Pitch when from behind him some one said, "Raise the ante." Ivan raised and no one called, leaving him the winner of a few dollars. When he looked around, there stood Guy grinning as if he were the happiest man on the earth. The two friend's shook hands and drifted outside where they had a place to catch up on the happenings since they last saw each other.

Guy was working down in Lilly Park doing general ranch work. He said it looked like the old way was all gone, with so many new things like tractors, automobiles and trucks. He said he had drifted back to Blue Mountain and had run a few broom tails with Ole Ernest Lange, but the prices were going down all the time, making it harder to sell them ole broncos. Ivan told of seeing the large tractors with their gang plows on the plains east of the mountains. They discussed the sheep business at some length, but Guy said, "Kid you can herd those wool-lies if you want, but I will starve a-fore I get near one."

The two friend's enjoyed a few days just loafing around the joints in Craig. There was a lot of talk of what this world was coming too. They ran into a fellow that said he was a horse buyer looking for any kind of a horse that could walk. He said he bought them for the glue and dog food factory and was willing to pay top prices. He had heard they were the best horse runner's in the country and would like to strike a deal with them.

They took in all the activities of the Fourth of July celebration, which included bronc riding, wild horse races and roping wild cattle. The last day of the celebration Ole Bill Jensen was talking to Ivan and said he had a few train cars of sheep he was sending to Kansas City Missouri and wondered if Ivan would go with the sheep to care for them. Ivan thought about it for a while and decided caring for sheep was easier than driving those miserable dual wheel trucks, so he told Bill he would go. As the sun rose the next day, it found Ivan and Bill driving an automobile South from Craig to William's Fork. At William's fork, the Jensen's had their feeder sheep in a meadow waiting to be driven to Craig to be loaded for Kansas City.

When the train left at midnight, it carried Ivan and four double deck cars of sheep on their way to far off Kansas City. When the train stopped in Tabernash to change crews, Ivan went to the cafe to eat breakfast. There the talk was about the progress of the tunnel. Old Bill Freeman was not the most popular man in Colorado, he was pushing the men in the tunnel to their limits and never spent a dime on the road over Rollins Pass. The train men were worried they would lose a whole train because of the poorly maintained tracks.

As the train left town, ole George Schryer had his big "Malley" in it's place on the rear as pusher. In the caboose where Ivan rode, the noise and vibration from that huge machine made the trip on to Denver a miserable one to live through. At the Denver yard, a much smaller and faster engine took over. Eighty miles east of Denver the cars hauling livestock were shuttled on the siding at Fort Morgan where all the animals were unloaded, so they could rest and eat for twenty four hours.

There was a crews from the railroad that did all the work of unloading the animals, so Ivan looked over the sheep to make sure they had traveled well. The pens had troughs with water running through and the bunks were full of bright green alfalfa hay. The sheep lay down for a few hours and then started filling their bellies with water and hay.

As they started to lay back down to chew their cuds, Ivan went to the hotel where the trainmen told he would have a room waiting. After checking in his room, Ivan went to the dining room where he ate and listened to the talk. The main part of the conversation was on the methods of farming and the new machines that had revolutionized the industry. Many thought that Eastern Colorado and Western Kansas were the bread basket of the world. Hundreds of thousand of acres were being brought into cultivation. Wheat was the only crop to raise according to those present.

After eating, Ivan walked around town to look it over. He had never seen such a large factory as the Great Western Sugar Mill, which covered many acres and was several stories tall. The thing that fascinated him the most was all the businesses that were selling new modern farm machinery and tractors. As the young man looked at those fine modern machines, he wished he could own a fine farm. The next day the sheep were loaded and the train headed east for Kansas City.

Ivan spent most of the day on the caboose platform looking at the new plowed fields and those with ripened wheat ready for harvest. He saw the new powerful tractors pulling the barges and the forty-two horse hitch cutting the wheat. There were smaller units cutting grain pulled with as few as six horses, but those poor horses were badly over worked which disgusted him.

George Schryer
engineer for Dave Moffat

D. S. Murray

At McCook, Nebraska, the train changed crews and filled with coal and water. This gave him time to check on the sheep and get a bite to eat. He was told the train would be in Kansas City before morning. He could hardly imagine the fast speed they would travel. The conductor pointed out the window at an airplane and said that is the latest way to haul U.S. mail. Ivan went to the platform and watched as the train moved away from the two winged airplane. Ivan saw three more airplanes before the sun went down. Ivan felt it was great to live in this modern time when life was sure getting easier. As the highball freight train sped on east, Ivan fell into a comfortable sleep because outside was nothing but darkness, except when they passed through a town.

He was awakened by the bumping and jolting of the train and was surprised to see from the window they were entering the rail yards at Kansas City. It was not long until the cars with livestock were on the siding and large numbers of men were unloading the animals and sorting them in the different commission companies pens. The pens had good water troughs and bunks filled with hay to which the animals took advantage.

After all the sheep were penned, a man gave Ivan a pass to a nearby hotel where there was a room waiting for him. He also told him what time the sheep would sell. Before sale time, he went to the pens to check and count to see how many had died in route. He counted twice and was pleased to see he had not lost any on this long trip.

As he was looking at the sheep, he noticed several men looking them over with much discussion. He drifted over to the group of men and showed them his letter of identification Bill had sent with him. The men ask many question about the origin, pasturage, transportation to market and their age.

One man told Ivan he was a buyer for a hide company who bought the hides from fine sheep like these to make sheep fleece lined coats. The hides would not have to be shorn or cleaned until they were ready to be made into a coat. Most hides would have to be shorn and this is why they were premium hides. He said these lambs had premium pelts and he would see they brought top prices. When they sold, he sure kept his word.

Ivan spent a few days in Kansas City enjoying the sites and sounds of a large town. He wondered if he would be not be better off staying and finding a job in this large city. When he began to think about being confined in this town with its sights and sounds, he became homesick for his trap back on Blue Mountain. He went by the commission office, received his pass on the night passenger train and picked up the large check that was waiting for him to take to Bill. The train left Kansas City about midnight and by dark the next night was in Denver. At Denver, he boarded the train on the Moffat Road that would take him to Craig.

At Craig, he found his automobile had been loaned to another friend. In a couple of days, he had it back and left for the long ride to Bill's Ranch at Meeker. He figured while there, he would pay a visit to the T.I. to see his brother Milt.

Two days of leisure ride brought him to Bill's Ranch near Yellow Jacket Pass where Bill asked him if he would not like to come on as Ranch Foreman. Ivan turned down the offer and was paid his wages plus a good reward for taking such good care of the sheep. He spent two days visiting with Milt, after which he drove to Vernal where he visited Merle and his other brothers. Back at Craig, he was filled with homesickness for his Blue Mountain Retreat so he loaded up his horses and rode for the refuge of that lonely place.

When he arrived on Blue Mountain, he thought he might ride by the McNurlan Camp and see if anyone was there. As he closed the pasture gate, he heard a voice from behind say, "Well all be, I see you came back." As he turned around, there stood Guy and Ole Ernest Lange. They were both grinning as if they were the happiest men on earth. Guy told Ivan that after he had left Craig the horse buyer asked him if he could catch him three hundred head of horses to which Guy said he was sure they could. Guy had promised at least seventy-five horses yet that fall for delivery and more if they could catch them. These would be delivered to Wamsutter.

On his way back to Blue Mountain, Guy had stopped at Ernest's Cabin and told him the proposition that the buyer had made. Knowing he would be making a living at horses again, put the excitement back into the old wild horse runner

As they set around smoking after supper, Ivan told of his trip to Kansas City. He told about the large tractors and machinery the farmers now used to farm the land. They wondered how much longer there would be a market for horses. Also, they discussed the large number of horses that they had captured in their life and Ivan said that he had made a record back under the cliff at his trap. Off hand, he figured it was several thousand head that he had caught at that time. The other two had never kept track.

The next morning, the three men headed toward Ivan's trap. Arriving there, they spent two days repairing fences and gates to the valley. There had been few men running horses in the area so it was easy to fill the valley within a few days. The buyer had told Guy that they did not need to be broke. They just needed to be caught and delivered.

The men spent two weeks necking about ninety horses for the long trip to the rail head. They made the trip in five days without any problems. The buyer was there and was pleased to see the fine amount of horses that they had brought. He told them that he had been buying just little amounts from five to ten horses in a group and with this he would have a train load for California.

When the men were paid off, Ivan asked him what the fate of these fine ponies was? The mans replied, "They will feed somebody's Poodle." This made Ivan feel sick inside. They promised the buyer that they would have three hundred head or more for him in the Spring. The men loaded their pack horses with enough supplies to last them until Spring. Also, they took a large supply of oats so their saddle horses would be grain fed for the hard winters months of riding.

They went back to Ivan's trap where they settled in for a long winters work. The winters work was uneventful except for when ole Ernest found a big bay horse that he took "a liken' to." When he had it in the main corral, he roped it. Being a large strong man, he approached the horse, going up the rope hand over hand. As he neared the horses head, he hollered, "Bring me a halter!"

At the same time, he grabbed the horses ears. That old pony sat back and spun away from Ernest, leaving the man holding both ears in his hands. Ivan and Guy were not long in front footing and tying the horse down while Ernest stood there swearing at the ears he was holding. The horse turned out to be a mighty fine animal which Ernest rode for many years.

Spring came and the men were making plans to leave. Ivan had a foreboding about leaving this secure area of his life. He felt that this would be the last time that he would ever work on Blue Mountain. On the night before they were going to leave, they spent a leisure evening in nostalgia visiting around the campfire until late at night and once again the number of horses that they had captured came up in the conversation. Ivan said, "Boys, I will tell you exactly the number of horses that I have caught, because I have always written it down." He went to a spot back under the cliff and struck a match and stood there for a long time counting. When he returned to the fire and sat down, he sat silent for a long time shaking his head. He said, "You know fellows, I have been at it a long time and never realized how many horses I had caught." The other two mustangers pressed him for an answer. He replied, "Fifty-eight-hundred head with saddle scars left on them." Guy replied, "Well kid, I know you caught many that you didn't leave saddle scars on, so we know you have caught over six thousand head in the ten to twelve years that you have been running horses."

The necked horses were all run into the main trap and the men spent all morning opening all the gates that led into the valley. When Ivan opened the last trap gate, he sat for a moment on his horse looking the country over. He knew that he may never see it again.

The trip to Wamsutter took six days. When they got there, the kill buyer paid them for their horses. Ivan vowed to himself that if this was the fate of such good horse flesh, he would no longer be a part of it. With sadness, he started to Craig and a whole new life.

Carey Ranch

Chapter 27

Arriving at Craig, there was much excitement about the Moffat tunnel that had opened February 26, 1928. The people in the Yampa Valley knew at last prosperity was coming. When Ivan went to the bank to deposit his money, there was a message for him telling him his father was in town and needed to see him. Ivan responded and was soon visiting with Hatch. Hatch could lease one-third of the mighty Carey Ranch's hay land with horses and machinery with which to put up the crop, but he did not have the money for the lease. If they could raise the money, they could also lease some of the pastures. He had checked at the bank and knew that Ivan had money saved. Although Ivan knew how his father had treated him in deals in the past, he could not tell his father no. Due to the raising in the Mormon Church, the honor and respect they were taught to God and Father made Ivan feel that it was his duty to go along with Hatch's request.

After paying the lease, Hatch took the remaining money and found a woman and married her. Due to his cruelty, the marriage lasted less than a month. When Ivan inquired about his automobile, he was told Lee had went to Vernal on a visit and while there wrecked the machine and it was ruined. With most of his money in the lease, Ivan was once more back to using horses for his transportation.

The Carey Ranch was owned by two brothers that were in the mining business and lived in Denver. They came to Northwestern Colorado only on holidays. The ranch buildings consisted of five fine houses, two large barns, a cook house and a large bunk house.

The largest house was occupied by the Careys and their household staff when they came to ranch. Also, there were many large sheds in which machinery and livestock were kept. There was a windmill and a water tank set on a high platform which supplied running water for the whole group of ranch buildings. Everything was painted to perfection and this place stood out in stark contrast to the other poorly erected ranches of their neighbors.

This ranch had it's own post office and was known as Carey Ranch, Colorado. Everyday the mail sack had to be taken to the railroad a half mile from the ranch and hung on the mail hook so the baggage man on the train could hook it as the train sped by. He would throw the in coming mail sack out along the track.

Ivan had forebodings about being in partnership with his father, but was mighty happy to at last be started in real ranching again. He figured when the hay and oat crop was sold he would have the money to start in the cattle business and after a few years own his own land.

He decided to go to Denver and talk to the Careys about financing a few head of cattle for him. He was excited about the prospect of getting set up in the cattle business and traveling through the new tunnel. The day he left for Denver he put up the flag to signal the engineer of the train to stop for him at the mail hook. He never told Hatch that he was going to Denver or why, because he did not want him involved in his new plans.

As the engine passed slowly by, he grabbed the ladder that the train crew used and climbed aboard as the engineer opened the throttle. When the train stopped in Hayden, Ivan purchased a ticket and walked to the passenger car where he found a good seat.

As the train traveled over the familiar road that Ivan had traveled many times before, the young man noticed how many new farms and small ranches that now filled the valleys of Northwestern Colorado and wondered if the people would ever stop coming. When the train reached Kremmling, it had to wait for the Mountaineer Express coming east from Grand Junction on the new Dot Zerio line that connected the Denver and Rio Grande line running east to the Moffat Line.

When the Mountaineer passed the waiting train, Ivan was happy to see his cousin Sam Murray in the engineer's seat. (A position he would hold for the next forty years, and in that time he never had a wreck.) The passengers on the train coming from Craig were outside getting a breath of fresh air As Sam's train passed, he saw Ivan and waved his cap while blowing the whistle for some time.

When Ivan's train reached Tabernash, it never changed crews as it had always done in the past. It never even stopped. As it climbed higher, the road was all new and in a few minutes the train was speeding under the Continental Divide at the speed of fifty miles an hour. The passengers quickly closed the windows, but in the six miles of tunnel the train car filled with smoke, making it difficult to breathe. The sky was clear and bright as the train entered the tunnel. Inside with the smoke filling the car, the small kerosene lamp made a futile attempt of giving light.

The passengers who were passing through the tunnel for the first time cheered and made revelry, celebrating there maiden trip through the inside of the mountain. Ivan looked out the window but at the speed they were traveling, he could only see darkness and a blur. He was sure happy to be alive in these modern times even though it was hard to keep up with the fast changing technology. He thought of when he used to go watch the stage pulled by six horses from Price arrive at Vernal. Now the telephone made it possible to talk to a person many miles away. If he got the backing to buy cattle, he would once again own a new automobile. He was brought back to what was happening as the train roared out the East portal. As quickly as the brightness disappeared, it reappeared making it difficult to see for a few minutes.

When the train pulled into the Denver station and Ivan stepped on the platform, he was greeted by his cousin Sam Murray, George Schryer and Conductor Barnes who said they were waiting for him so they could eat supper together. As the men ate supper in the hotel dining room, they talked about the new improvements in the West, notably the Moffat Tunnel. George said it made his work so much easier and with the good times the country was in, he was hauling much longer trains. As the men sat around the table, the warmth and friendship gave Ivan a good feeling he would get the money to buy a herd of stock cows.

The next morning as he sat in the Carey's office, he could not believe what he was hearing as they told him they would like to help him get the money he needed to buy a thousand head of cattle with, but he never had a place to run them. They went on to explain that Hatch never told them or had Ivan's name on the lease he signed. Therefore without Ivan's name on the lease there was no money available. He then explained he had put up all the money for the lease and horse, but they said without his name on the paper he had no legal claim.

Crushed in spirit, Ivan boarded the train back to the ranch. While the train traveled back to the Yampa Valley, Ivan wished he could go back to the security of the horse trap on Blue Mountain but he knew that could never be. This was the way life was so he accepted it. When he stepped from the train at the ranch, he was determined to make the best of it and get ahead in some other way. Ivan never told Hatch where he had been and Hatch never asked.

Ivan worked hard that spring, seeing that the crops were irrigated and producing all they could. His friend Lee Keeling came over every Saturday evening to take him to dance somewhere. Ivan had always went to every dance he could since he was a very small boy. He would rather dance than any thing he knew. One of the hired men asked Ivan if he could borrow his best suit of clothes because there was a girl down on the Elkhead River that was going to be at the dance that night he

Ivan's Buick

wanted to impress. Ivan said, "Sure, go ahead I have my old suit that still looks nice."

When Lee arrived at the ranch, he told Ivan that Iva Lou Ellis from out at Great Divide, was going with Herb Coats the man that looked like Ivan. Herb was the one that got Ivan arrested up in Walden. Ivan thought Iva Lou was a cute little thing. He figured if he could break them up and go with her, he would get even with Herb.

They arrived at the Elkhead school just after dark and the moon was up, making it very bright in the high mountains. When the two men walked across the school house yard, there lay Ivan's new suit on the ground with a very Drunk cowboy inside it throwing whiskey bottles in the air. When Ivan asked him what he was doing, he slurringly said, "That crazy woman has an old man and a bunch of kids and I am going to hit the moon with these bottles and put it out so there will be no love tonight." Ivan laughed as he walked in the smoke filled dance hall.

The piano and the fiddles were well tuned and the musicians were warmed up real good. Ivan danced every dance and had a lot of fun. When the ladies choice came, he noticed Lee go say something to a lady, which Ivan thought was Iva Lou. As the young blonde, cute and petite lady walked toward him, she was not who he thought she was.

When she arrived in front of him, she did not ask him to dance but said, "Are you a cowboy?" Thinking this could be a lot of fun, he never answered, but only pulled up one of his trouser legs to show her he was not wearing cowboy boots. Then she then took him by the hand and said as she led him to the floor, "Good, I'm glad you are not a cowboy because I will never marry one!" That was July 2, 1928.

THE END